People of the book

People
of
the book

Images of the Jew
in
South African
English Fiction
1880 - 1992

Marcia Leveson

WWP WITWATERSRAND UNIVERSITY PRESS

Witwatersrand University Press
1 Jan Smuts Avenue
Johannesburg
2001 South Africa

ISBN 1 86814 263 9

First published 1996

Cover design by Thea Soggot
Typeset by Photoprint, Cape Town
Printed and bound by Clyson Printers (Pty) Ltd, Maitland

Dedicated to the memory
of Philip Segal

CONTENTS

Acknowledgements

This book came about as a result of my interest in South African literature as well as the history of Jewry in South Africa. My research covers texts written by South African authors or authors who have immigrated to South Africa or whose work is set in a South African context. I exclude short stories which have appeared only in journals and have not been reprinted in anthologies. Dates of birth and death are cited, where available, for deceased authors. In quoting from texts I have at all times followed the spelling, setting and punctuation of the original.

I wish to express my very deep gratitude to my family for their encouragement and support through the long gestation period. I thank many colleagues and friends who gave me much invaluable assistance. I particularly mention Professor Joseph Sherman who supervised the thesis on which the book is based. He has been a wise and expert guide. I am very conscious of the very generous assistance Professor Milton Shain has given me, not only because his published and unpublished work has been crucial in constructing a framework for my own research, but also for his many suggestions, answers to queries and his vast knowledge of South African Jewish history. The late Professor Michael Wade showed me important early direction, and Dr Elaine Katz gave me invaluable criticism at the end. I am indebted to Dr Phyllis Lewsen for her meticulous checking of the manuscript, and to Professor Dan Jacobson and Professor Sander L. Gilman for expert advice. I also mention Professor Brian Cheadle, Professor Tim Couzens, Professor Isabel Hofmeyr, Dr Lavinia Braun, Dr Riva Krut, Dr Kathrin Wagner, Phillip Stein, Lionel Abrahams, Jane Starfield, Stella Gavshon, Gillian Jackson, Carlotta Von Maltzen, Barbara Ludman, Marge Clouts, Phyllis Jowell, Stuart

Isaacs QC, Carmel Milner, Sandra Sapire, Irene Friedland, Claudia Braude, Robert Greig, Ruth Nicola and Karen Lazar and the late Brenda Maraney who gave assistance, advice and support. I heartily thank Pat Tucker of Witwatersrand University Press for her excellent editing. I am warmly appreciative of the staff of the Africana, William Cullen, Wartenweiler libraries, and the Landua and Manuscript Collection, all of the University of the Witwatersrand, who have been untiring, knowledgeable and always cheerful. The staff of the Brenthurst Library, the Johannesburg Public Library, the Johannesburg Jewish Board of Deputies Library and the library of the Kaplan Centre, University of Cape Town were most co-operative.

Sections of the book, in an earlier form, have appeared in publications. An overview of the research, entitled 'The Jewish Stereotype in Some South African English Fiction: A Preliminary Investigation', was published in Musiker, R. and Sherman, J. *Waters out of the Well.* Johannesburg: The Library, University of the Witwatersrand, 1988; 'Power and Prejudice: Dan Jacobson's "Jewish" Fiction of the Fifties' was published in *English Studies in Africa* 34(2), 1991; 'The Spoiled Identity – A Study of Antony Sher's *Middlepost*' in *Judaism in the Context of Diverse Civilizations.* ed. M. Sharon, Johannesburg: Maksim Publishers, 1993; 'Mozzel and Brocah! Ikey Moses on the Diamond Fields: The Construction of an anti-Jewish Stereotype', is due to be published in *Proceedings of the South African Jewish Studies Association 14th Annual Conference 1993.*

The financial assistance of the Centre for Science Development towards this research is hereby acknowledged. Opinions expressed in this book, and conclusions arrived at, are those of the author and are not necessarily to be attributed to the Centre for Science Development.

Jews are news

Charles Krauthammer, *Time*, 26 February 1990

Jews play (for both philosemites and antisemites) a critical role in the history of the West, far out of proportion to their actual numbers, occupying the centre of the historical arena, influential, cohesive, resilient, perhaps somewhat mysterious. Neither views the Jewish people as "normal" – with the same mix of rich and poor, famous and obscure, talented and dull, intelligent and stupid as other peoples; they stress, rather the "abnormal", that is, those who make their mark in one way or another on the larger community

– Todd Endleman, *Times Literary Supplement*, 26 June 1987

INTRODUCTION

In 1943, at the height of the Nazi's attempt at genocide, the American Zionist writer and lecturer, Maurice Samuel, asked: 'How shall we begin to account for the mad disparity between the actual proportion of Jewish participation in contemporaneous Western life, and the extent of the world's preoccupation with the Jews?'[1]

Images of Jews feature prominently in literature and the media, on the stage, and in most aspects of human endeavour. In this study I examine the way in which they appear in South African English fiction between 1880 and 1992.

Although it was only in the 1930s that the number of Jews in South Africa peaked at a little over 4 per cent of the white population,[2] they have always constituted a significant minority group. In terms of the social and political dynamics of the country, Jews may now be considered to be part of the white hegemony, but they have never been completely accepted socially either by the Afrikaans- or the English-speaking communities. In spite of considerable assimilation and inter-marriage,[3] historically they have always been considered outsiders. While economic, social, religious or political circumstances determine different ways of regarding Jews, in the cultural imagination of South African writers they figure, second only to the blacks, as potent symbols of the Other. Perhaps this provides some answer to Samuel's question. Humankind is fascinated by difference. Jews themselves are fascinated by their difference.

In surveying approximately 130 primary texts in which the figure of the Jew appears – frequently as a significant vignette – I focus on what I understand to be the author's perception and intention either in constructing an image or merely in referring to a Jew. I take no cognisance of the criteria for defining a Jew in the real world, since in fiction identification depends on the premise that a Jewish character is one whom the author designates specifically as a Jew, sometimes signified merely by the use of a Jewish name.[4]

Authors investigated are various. Most are white, mainly of British stock – colonial writers who visited South Africa, immigrants or their descendants – who carry with them certain presuppositions about Jews inherited from European and, more specifically, British culture. Others are Jews who write in English and are heirs to a multiple tradition: their Jewish background, the British tradition in which they were educated and with which they largely identify, and the norms and discourses of the society in which they live. Further, I include black authors who write in English.[5] While to a certain extent British or American literary traditions inform their fiction, it may also be concerned with issues which are specific to their particular group.

My study focuses on the depiction of individual characters, isolating them from wider textual considerations, relating them to mythological, historical and sociological contexts, and considering the connection between the fictional text and its context. From intra- and extra-textual evidence, I endeavour to establish the encoded attitude towards Jews held by the author. This is dependent on a number of influences but primarily on the mythos – the system of myths, legends, beliefs and stereotypes associated with Jews – that has developed over the last two thousand years. Attitudes are also determined by historical, political and economic circumstances, by actual experiences and perceptions, and by prejudices both negative and positive.

I am guided in my approach by the work of E.D. Hirsch. In his seminal study, *Validity in Interpretation* (1967), he defends the attempted recovery of authorial intention, maintaining that although there may be individual variation in interpretation of a literary work, it is nevertheless produced within a specific retrievable historical and philosophical framework.[6] As a reader myself, I inescapably approach texts with my own set of assumptions and prejudices. These are, however, located within the general parameters and prevailing discourse of those writers whose work I study. I believe that literature reflects social history in a unique way, and that such an approach is an important adjunct to historical research.

Fictional images may derive from other texts – historical, philosophical, biographical or fictional, and these may be influenced by images propagated in the media, by pictorial materials such as cartoons and illustrations, by stage and cinematic productions, by jokes and anecdotes, indeed by the entire social system in which they arise.[7] I show that it is extremely unusual for either Gentile or Jewish South African writers, in their treatment of Jewish characters, to avoid relying on the models of perception and literary paradigms established in Europe or America, deeply embedded in the imagination of the West, and underpinned by texts produced in South Africa at the beginning of the century.

My research reveals that in the work of white, black, and Jewish writers, the image of the Jew appears in a number of fairly rigid stereotypes or a combination of these stereotypes, which are controlled by the attitude held by the author specifically towards Jews. This attitude may be overt or hidden; may be negative or, less frequently, positive; or may be ambivalent. It may be termed *prejudice*, which I use in the common sense of signifying either a favourable or an unfavourable predisposition towards a group or member of a group, usually based on a hastily formed judgement and incomplete premises.

Determined by historical or ideological factors, the bases of prejudice change in content over the course of time and in different circumstances. Possibly because negative prejudice has always been more widespread and potent than positive prejudice, it has been more frequently manifested in fiction. It will be seen that in South African English fiction the negative image of the Jew features strongly. Somewhat less frequently, attempts are made to show the Jew in a positive light. Often he plays a minor role. Almost invariably it is the fact of his Jewishness that is significant.

I demonstrate the occurrence of Jewish stereotypes, with attendant stereotypical situations, in South African fiction. I argue that this treatment of the Jew responds to some of the social, economic and historical conditions that have prevailed within the country and is, as well, significantly related to certain key historical and political events in the history of world Jewry.

– 1 –

BACKGROUND

What is a Jew? Is he an emaciated, hunchbacked, bearded, long nosed villain? Or a greasy, corpulent, cigar smoking capitalist? Is he a subversive bolshevik, a leftist lawyer, a wise and benevolent philosopher, or a Holocaust victim? All these and many others images are so immediately recognisable as indelible aspects of Western thinking about Jews that they can be termed stereotypes.

Stereotypes

A stereotype is a generalised and often exaggerated image of a group of people, constructed from scanty and insufficient evidence, and commonly accompanied by prejudice, either negative or positive.

Social scientists differ in their understanding of the origins of stereotypes. Theorists holding a psychodynamic view believe that hostility, wrongful generalisation and prejudice are natural conditions of the human mind, fulfilling instinctive irrational and self-gratifying purposes, and that tolerance, if it exists, is a learned response. According to this view, unfavourable stereotypes are thought to derive from the operation of two defence mechanisms: the expression of hostility and aggression towards an out-group, and scapegoating.

In his classical study, *The Nature of Prejudice*, Gordon Allport has identified three different processes of scapegoating: that resulting from frustration which generates aggression, which is displaced onto the scapegoat who is blamed for the frustration; that resulting from fear which manifests itself as anxiety, which may then be directed towards the scapegoat; and that resulting from an inability to face the consequences of one's own behaviour. This process involves the displacement of emotion from a logical source to an arbitrary but handy one.[1] During times of social stress, an ethnic, religious or racial group can be made to serve the function of a scapegoat. Jewish communities throughout the ages have been forced to play the role of the scapegoat, and in South Africa, as will be shown, the Jews were frequently blamed for economic problems, especially in the rural areas during the transition towards urbanisation.

The cognitive approach emphasises the innate nature of the process of stereotyping by suggesting that the human capacity for processing information is limited, predisposing individuals to systematic biases which construct and maintain stereotypes. As Rae Sherwood puts it 'the human mind from infancy onwards ... is replete with both good fairies as well as grotesque monsters.'[2] Sander L. Gilman argues that stereotypes arise from the interaction of real life perceptions with the inherited world of myth, and that both these aspects 'intertwine to form fabulous images', which belong neither to the real world nor exclusively to the realm of myth.[3]

The *socio-cultural* view of prejudice and stereotyping distinguishes two approaches. The first regards society as characterised by consensus, in which stereotypes specify the nature of various social groups and support norms by which these groups are expected to behave and according to which they should be treated. Categorisation in terms of stereotypes is a marked feature of colonial societies, which are particularly prone to interpret human differences – ethnic, racial, class or gender – in terms of dominant and subordinate, and of self and Other. The second regards society as comprising groups with different values in competition with one another. This latter is the well-known theory of *in-groups and out-groups*, which proposes that one learns from an early age to internalise and conform to the values and norms of one's in-group, and to seek social approval by opposing the out-group. The creation of stereotypes by which to identify members of the out-group is regarded as a mechanism for dealing with our essential manichean perception of the world as good or bad.[4]

Jewish communities in Gentile society, set apart by the practices of their religion and tradition, have always been considered out-groups, and for many centuries Jews were stigmatised as such by being forced to wear distinctive clothing or badges, and being spatially confined to a ghetto. Coming as immigrants to South Africa, worshipping differently, sometimes dressed in the clothing of the eastern European *shtetl* (village) of their origin, speaking a foreign language or with a foreign accent, the Jews were obvious candidates – second only to the blacks – for the role of the outsider, the Other, in the cultural imagination of white South Africa.

Indeed, from earliest times the Jew was considered an Other. Even after the Emancipation of Jews in Western Europe during the eighteenth century, when secular Jews discarded their stigmatising clothing, entered the Gentile world and participated in the life of the wider community, the idea of the Jew as set apart from the rest of humankind, and belonging to a readily identifiable out-group, was entrenched. Generally Jews were regarded with a specific and distinct form of racial prejudice, a multi-faceted fear and hatred known as anti-Semitism.[5]

Anti-Semitism

Anti-Semitism, the term used for Jew-hatred since the end of the nineteenth century, is sufficiently well documented, and only salient features will be touched on here.

The most compelling of the theories concerning the origin of Western anti-Semitism locates it in the crucifixion myth, where the Jews are seen to play the role of murderers of God.[6] This belief provides the basic impulse behind the superstitious revulsion from Jews and their persistent demonisation in Europe, where, especially during the Middle Ages, they were regarded as the anti-Christ. From the eleventh century onwards a further strong impetus was given to the hatred of Jews by the Crusades. Undertaken in a spirit of religious fanaticism, they unleashed unprecedented virulence and seemed to license the physical persecution which has dominated the history of the Jews down the ages.

From its inception the Christian Church, in its struggle to gain ascendancy over the older religion, needed to discredit, suppress and supersede it, and reacted violently against the very real threat posed by Judaism. Through their teachings, the fanatically anti-Jewish early Church fathers of the third and fourth centuries whipped up in their followers a violent loathing of Jews. They accused the Jews of refusing to recognise the Messiah, and of committing the supreme sin of deicide. For this Jews deserved persecution and also the punishment of permanent exile, but not extermination because their conversion was necessary for the Second Coming. They were the first to project on to the Jews all the libidinous sexual impulses opposed to the Christian ideal of chastity. One of the central tenets of Judaism, the Jews' belief in their 'Chosenness' – that they had been chosen by God as a special people, set apart from other peoples and prepared for a unique destiny – was a direct challenge to the Christian conviction of their own especial status. It seemed to be an assertion of spiritual pride and exclusivity as well as a challenge to Christian dogma, and was therefore a focus for further envy and hatred.

After Christianity had been accepted as the state religion of the Roman Empire in the fourth century, legislation gradually relegated Jews to a pariah state of permanent inferiority. They were barred from agriculture and the pursuit of most professions and transformed, long before the official constitution of ghettos in the sixteenth century, into an impotent urban community. During the Middle Ages they were banned by the powerful European guilds from participating in any commercial ventures other than money-lending (usury), retailing of second-hand goods and peddling. These were the only avenues of contact with the Gentile world, and they were highly visible in these capacities and were resented by the common people as the incarnation of mercantile and monetary values. Some Jews were associated with criminal practices such as 'coin-clipping' and receiving stolen goods, and the image of the Jew as 'bloodsucker' became a potent source of economic as opposed to theological anti-Semitism. Thus the original religious stigma was reinforced by an equally powerful economic stigma and both have persisted to the present day.[7]

What one might term 'political' anti-Semitism developed with the allegation of a Jewish world conspiracy, an idea first proposed in France in 1797. The most widely known version of this theory was the publication in 1903 of *The Protocols of the Elders of Zion*. Drawn from numerous fictional and forged sources, it was compiled by agents working for the Russian secret police, aiming to provoke anti-Semitism in order to divert popular discontent. It purported to reveal a world conspiracy whereby, at a secret meeting, the 'Elders of Zion' aimed to subjugate the Gentiles through financial manipulation. The document was extensively disseminated in translation, and has been used ever since by whatever faction or government felt the need to foment anti-Semitism. In 1921 it was conclusively exposed as a fraud, and shown to have been plagiarised from fictional sources. Yet the influence of the *Protocols* has been enormous and still, at the end of the twentieth century, their authenticity is widely believed. Even when the validity of the text has been doubted, it has in many cases been used cynically for anti-Jewish propaganda. The first Muslim edition, for example, appeared in Cairo in 1951, shortly after the establishment of the State of Israel.[8]

A racial or eugenic form of anti-Semitism became popular at the end of the nineteenth century. In a distortion of Darwin's theory of evolution, it was believed that race was rooted in the 'blood'. All Jews were regarded as intellectually and biologically different from other races, completely unassimilable and liable to taint the vastly superior Nordic race. This belief, which became intertwined with older forms of hostility, reached its apotheosis in Nazi Germany, resulting in the implementation of Hitler's 'Final Solution' – the systematic attempted murder of the entire Jewish 'race'.[9]

Anti-Zionism, especially that version propagated by Muslim fundamentalists, is often regarded as a contemporary manifestation of anti-Semitism. In Muslim theology and literature there is no reference to deicide, and historically in Muslim society Jews were never demonised. Until the middle of the twentieth century they were, like the Christians, treated with some respect as 'Peoples of the Book', but regarded as inferior – as *dhimmis* – because they did not accept the final revelation made by Allah to his Prophet Mohammed.

During the conflict between Jews and Arabs over the establishment of the State of Israel, a brand of Christian anti-Semitism was introduced to Arab countries by the Nazis, and later by the Soviets, which exacerbated what was in the main a battle for the possession of the same land. The *Protocols* and other anti-Semitic materials were very widely circulated in order to explain in terms of a world conspiracy the humiliating defeats of the Arabs at the hands of the Israelis in the wars of 1956 and 1967.[10] On 10 November 1975 the United Nations adopted a resolution stigmatising Israel as 'the racist regime in occupied Palestine ... a threat to world peace and security', and claiming that Zionism was a form of racism. All countries were called on to 'oppose this racist and imperialist ideology'.[11] The resolution was rescinded only on 16 December 1991.[12] Developing countries, in sympathy with the Palestinians, have taken a violently anti-Zionist stance which has at times incorporated into itself European anti-Semitism. However, this does not account for the anti-Zionism expressed by Western intellectuals and politicians, including a considerable number of Jews. Here more complex philosophical and historical issues seem to be subjugated to a view of the Israeli-Arab conflict as primarily a clash between European imperialism and the anti-colonialism of developing countries.[13]

Anti-semitism is clearly a multi-faceted phenomenon, and it has been argued that Jews themselves have contributed to its perseverance by the way in which Jewish society has fiercely protected its own identity. Over the centuries Jews avoided proselytism and tended to live in closed communities. They were seen to follow what appeared to non-Jews to be strange and even barbaric religious rituals including dietary prohibitions and circumcision. Jews spoke Yiddish or Ladino, languages different from those of the countries in which they resided. These differences, particularly the language difference, powerfully served to stigmatise them, and encouraged the perception of the Jews as a strange and foreign race, contributing to the entrenchment of anti-Semitism, and with it the establishment of potent and indelible stereotypes.

One should guard against a tendency to view a stereotype as purely the product of totally unsupported generalisation. Contemporary theorists agree that many contain a core of reality and that in the formation of stereotypes there is often an interaction between irrelevant considerations and what Allport termed 'earned reputation'.[14] In the same way that a stereotypical image may not be completely unfounded, so a scapegoat may not be completely guiltless. Similarly, as R.A. Schermerhorn points out, negative prejudice comes about as a result of circumstances and situations; 'it is not a little demon that emerges in people simply because they are depraved'.[15]

Jews were sometimes, to a greater or lesser extent, guilty of displaying the characteristics or of committing the crimes of which they were accused. For example, in South Africa after the discovery of diamonds in the 1860s in that part of the interior later annexed to the Cape Colony as Griqualand West, the negative image of the Jew was clearly influenced by the perceived criminal association of Jewish fortune-seekers with IDB (illicit diamond buying). Within a short time the image of the fabulously wealthy and powerful Randlord and its cartoon incarnation as 'Hoggenheimer' were taken into the South African version of the mythos.

These images resurfaced during the course of the twentieth century and metamorphosed into the cunning shopkeeper, the wealthy businessman or the kugel – the spoilt, wealthy, materialistic Jewish woman. They also appeared in the work of Jewish writers who have internalised the negative images constructed in Gentile society. Concomitantly, it is unlikely that stereotypes could command such a focal place in literature unless readers were able to identify with them.

While example may at times validate the stereotype, so too may the stereotype dictate the way in which experience is perceived, and stereotypes are frequently instrumental in maintaining and propagating prejudice. When they appear in literature they may be a reflection of the author's prejudice, or of social prejudice generally. They may be used as a method of literary economy, enabling an author to signal the presence of characteristics which are vivid, readily identifiable, and which draw upon existing emotional attitudes in readers. Extra appeal may also be made through humour and exaggeration. But, whether negative or positive, stereotypes are dehumanising. Authors cannot be unaware that the choice of stereotypes has the effect of moulding the reader's attitude towards the character and the group of which the character is a member. When a stereotyped character is identified as a Jew, for example, the reader's attitude is inevitably directed beyond it to Jews generally. Perpetuated in popular consciousness through folklore or literature, stereotypes quickly become fixed, and strongly reinforce perceptions.

The Evil Jew

The evil Jew is by far the most ubiquitous Jewish archetype in the Western imagination. This figure dates back to the biblical persecutors of Jesus, especially Judas, the betrayer. Jews first arrived in England with the Norman Conquest and by the Middle Ages an image was fixed, and invariably comprised an enlarged and hooked, even monstrous, nose, an unpleasant odour, and frequently a speech impediment. In art the Jew was often shown with horns and a tail, in grotesque and often lecherous poses. He appeared or was described in mystery and passion plays, sermons and folk legends as a terrifying red-haired, long-nosed devil.

Important myths coalesced around this malevolent figure, which invited at the same time, both ridicule and derision. There was the false accusation that the Jews desecrated the Christian host wafers and practised ritual murder, killing Christian children as a means of collecting blood for the making of Passover matzos and in mockery of the passion of Jesus. The alleged murder by Jews in 1255 of the boy, Hugh of Lincoln, a charge which circulated for many generations in ballad form, demonstrates the active fostering of legend by literature, and the 'blood libel' has been invoked as late as the twentieth century. Since the Middle Ages was a period of intense religious fanaticism, these and like accusations led to such violent anti-Jewish feeling that the Jews were expelled from England in 1290.[16]

It was only after this time that religious plays were performed to the general public, outside the confines of the Church and in the vernacular. These performances, reinforced by legends, superstitions, sermons and literary representations, produced a particularly hardy stereotype of the Jew as a devil incarnate, dedicated at all costs to the destruction of Christianity. Significantly, the image was constructed in the popular imagination in circumstances where there was no real presence against which to measure it. This illustrates the way in which a stereotype may be shaped not so much as a result of perception but, in the absence of the group stereotyped, through texts, superstitions and myths which contain what Gilman terms the 'fantasy life' of a culture.[17]

A further impetus to the demonisation of the Jew was given by the false belief propagated in Europe that the Jews, as revenge on Christians, had brought about the Black Death of 1347-1360 by poisoning wells. In reprisal, tens of thousands of Jews throughout Europe were killed. The notion of the Jew as poisoner was further strengthened by the high profile of Jewish doctors in medieval and Renaissance Europe, some of whom were also accused of poisoning their patients.[18] The myth was preserved in the popular imagination by the vivid portrait of the Machiavellian Barabas, the poisoner, in Christopher Marlowe's *The Famous Tragedy of the Rich Jew of Malta* (1590). In all these cases, examples of the operation of the scapegoating device can be noted. References to these libellous accusations recur through the ages and resurface, as will be shown, in South African fiction.

By the end of the sixteenth century the two images of the Jew as mutilator and usurer were commonplace. Shakespeare's unforgettable Shylock, in *The Merchant of Venice* (1605), vividly combines them, and was to become one of the most compelling stereotypes of all time. Despite several attempts to perform Shylock in a sympathetic light, a negative image gained additional potency from striking portrayals on the British stage during the eighteenth and nineteenth centuries. Throughout Europe the image of the evil Jew took root as part of the collective unconscious. Nurtured by the pervasive and convincing interaction of legend and literature, it possessed a clear-cut iconography which had a close association with evil-doing and money. The image acquired sinister and exotic features which were again largely a construct of the imagination and based only partly on real life factors.

After 1664 Jews were once again legally allowed to settle in England. Arriving from Holland and Portugal and later from the ghettos of Europe, they were viewed as foreigners – doubly outsiders. While the establishment of the English branch of the house of Rothschild at the beginning of the nineteenth century greatly enhanced the financial prestige of Jews, it also provided a focus for envy. Relationships between the wealthier and longer established Jewish families and the English aristocracy may well have been cordial, with a relative frequency of intermarriage and conversion to Christianity, but it was only gradually and with much difficulty that the civil disabilities of Jews were lifted. England was the last country in Europe in which Jews were enfranchised.

Anti-Jewish feeling remained powerful at a popular level, and literary portrayals of Jews continued to be constructed within a context and way of thinking which, in a recent study, Bryan Cheyette has named a ready-made 'racialized discourse'.[19] The idea of the Jew as a foreigner, an exotic, belonging to a race apart, fired the

European imagination. Attracting the attribution of lechery applied to the Jews in former ages, the exotic assumes the characteristics of sexual Otherness. The predatory Jew becomes one motif in anti-Semitic thinking.

On the English stage and in the music halls of the eighteenth and nineteenth centuries, as well as in literature there are many examples of minor Jewish villains, usually connected with magic or petty criminality. Illustrated newspapers and magazines were fond of making Jews their targets, and a description of a Jewish seller of old clothes in 'Hollywell Street' in *Punch*, 2, January – June 1842, typically sneers: 'Do you vant a coat? ... a vaistcoat? ... a cloak, better as new?' ... There stands IKEY LEVY, glancing mildly from his doorway as a jackal from his tomb!' [20]

These papers frequently made a popular target of Benjamin Disraeli, a converted Jew who became Prime Minister, satirically linking his politics with his Jewish origins. In fiction the most striking image was that of the Jewish fence, Fagin, in Dickens's *Oliver Twist* (1837-1839), who vividly recalls medieval images, having red hair and a penchant for blasphemy and poison.

During the nineteenth century anti-Semitism in England lost the visceral, demonic character of its earlier expressions. It became, rather, a diffuse and polite manifestation, a social, snobbish dislike, which Colin Holmes describes as an 'attitudinal hostility'.[21] Latent anti-Semitism, however, was exacerbated after the mass emigrations from eastern Europe of the 1880s, which produced a five-fold increase in the number of Jews in the country – still an insignificant 0,38 per cent of the population – and a clustering of foreign looking and speaking Jews forming a distinct community in the East End of London.[22] Despite accelerating intermarriage, particularly of the older established Sephardic Jews, often with the lesser nobility, the immigrants from eastern Europe were generally viewed with hostility and some revulsion as an unassimilable 'race', materialist, unduly attached to family ties and tainted with shady practices. The notoriety of the Rand gold mining magnates encouraged a belief that 'financial' Jews were behind the Anglo-Boer War of 1899-1902, and many Edwardian pot-boilers refer to Jewish conspiracy theories.[23]

The colonial authors in South Africa, who were mostly immigrants from Britain or of British stock, inherited preconceptions about Jews derived from Victorian attitudes and general mythology, from the popular literary and dramatic images, and often also from contact with actual Jews in Victorian English society.

The Wandering Jew

The second potent image is the figure of the Wandering Jew, which has its origins in the myth of Cartaphilus, who having mocked Jesus at the Crucifixion, was condemned to eternal wandering. The figure appears in Wendover's *Flores Historiarum* (1228) as a Jewish shoe-maker, Joseph Cartaphilus. The legend circulated in popular ballad form.

Renamed Ahasuerus, the Wandering Jew resurfaces in folk literature in Germany at the beginning of the seventeenth century, and later in English legend and literature where it evolves from the prototype, sometimes even shedding the aspect of Jewishness. During the late eighteenth and nineteenth century it popularly appeared in different guises, such as the monk, magician or hypnotist, notably in M.G. (Monk) Lewis's *The Monk* (1796) and George du Maurier's *Trilby* (1894). Resonating with a sense of Romantic mystery and alienation, it is used by Romantic writers. Some tended to identify themselves with this awesome and even tragic character who seemed, like them, to be set apart from mankind, doomed to perpetual suffering, and marked out for a special destiny. The Wandering Jew is a shifting image, taking on different colouring in different periods, sometimes horrifying, at other times quite sympathetically presented, reflecting varying ideological responses to the Jew.[24] In South African fiction this figure appears most frequently in the guise of the *smous* (pedlar).[25]

The Good Jew

The image of the saintly Jew, which appears infrequently in literature, derives not from perception or from mythology but from the author's conscience, in an effort to provide a counter myth to Shylock. The attempt to show the Jew in a favourable light, either as an expression of solidarity with Jews or in a positive effort to counteract anti-Semitism, is a product of the liberal tradition which grew out of concepts developed during the Enlightenment of the eighteenth century.

The rational philosophy which developed at this time undermined blind confidence in the theological basis of truth, substituting a reliance on the facts of science to be discovered by man's innate intelligence. One of the results of this shift was that it weakened the theological underpinnings of anti-Semitism. The liberal ideal of toleration, and the belief that every person deserved political, intellectual, economic, and religious freedom, led liberal thinkers to accept the concept of universal brotherhood, and the belief that all men, regardless of their religious convictions, should enjoy full civic and national rights. Before the French Revolution such views certainly did not encompass the Jews, and it was only later and gradually, during the course of the nineteenth century, after a long and difficult struggle, that Jewish political and social emancipation was achieved.

Writers working within this liberal tradition often display a philo-Semitic attitude. Not to be confused with a general tolerance, philo-Semitism manifests itself as a sentimental prejudice in favour of Jews, holds them up for reverence as descendants of the patriarchs, or reveres them for specific favourable personal or 'racial' qualities.[26] Philo-Semitism may be connected with other ideologies. In South African fiction, for example, it may be used as part of a conscious attitude of opposition to racialism in any form.

One of the first positive images of the Jew in English fiction appears in an eighteenth century English novel, Tobias Smollett's *The Adventures of Ferdinand, Count Fathom* (1753), where a Jew, Joshua Manasseh, lends money without interest, and is clearly constructed as an anti-Shylock. In Germany, Gotthold Ephraim Lessing drew a sympathetic Jew in his play, *Nathan der Weise (1779)*, which was the model for the Englishman, Richard Cumberland's play, *The Jew* (1794). Cumberland's character, Sheva, although a money-lender, is also a philanthropist, performing good deeds by stealth. The lack of popularity of this play – and of all the attempts to create the figure of the Jew-saint – strongly suggests that this image has never been a dynamic or convincing one. Since it did not appeal to the impregnable hostilities engendered by mythology and the basic human need to hate, deride and mock the Other, the attempt to soften the presentation of the Jew by appealing to conscience, morality, and sentimentality produced images which lacked the vitality and potency of the caricature.[27]

Throughout the nineteenth century, parallel to the negative images, figures of benevolent Jews appeared on the stage and in fiction – usually as a defence of the Jew or a response to accusations of anti-Semitism. The kindly Mr Riah, in Dickens's *Our Mutual Friend* (1864-1865), was a direct response to a reader's objection to the villainous Fagin. Daniel Deronda, paragon of all virtues, Mirah, the good and beautiful Jewess, and Mordecai, the visionary, in George Eliot's *Daniel Deronda* (1876) are mouthpieces expressing Eliot's philo-Semitism. Maria Edgeworth's pro-Semitic novel, *Harrington* (1817), was written under pressure to atone for the negative Jewish characters in her earlier novel, *The Absentee* (1812). As will be seen, the few instances of good Jews in South African fiction are similarly sentimental and propagandistic.

Following Walter Scott's beautiful and saintly Rebecca in *Ivanhoe* (1819), a portrait which captivated British readers, writers generally treated Jewish women more favourably than Jewish men. Oliver Cohen-Steiner suggests that this favourable attitude was encouraged by Chateaubriand, the nineteenth century French novelist and essayist, who cleared Jewish women from complicity in the death of Jesus, and emphasised their role as nurturers and comforters. Possibly, too, Jewish women were immune from the stigma of involvement in finance. Nevertheless, constructions of Jewish women almost always display an ambivalence: while they are usually granted moral qualities coeval with their beauty, they are simultaneously shown as sexually seductive – mostly with exotic Sephardic (eastern) features – and even threatening to Christian men. Often their Jewishness is neutralised by their being married to a Christian or being found to have non-Jewish ancestry.[28]

Perceptions of actual Jews are grafted on to the images created by the literary and dramatic portrayals from medieval times onwards, and blended with myths and stereotypes assembled over the centuries. Since each new text must be understood as embodying references to its predecessors, these images contribute to an ever expanding mythos. The three main stereotypes – the evil Jew, the Wandering Jew and the good Jew – with attendant stereotypical situations – reappear in South African fiction.

The Jews in South Africa

Among the European settlers at the Cape during the seventeenth century there had been a small number of Jews in the service of the Dutch East India Company. These, however, were all converts to Christianity, since the Company required its servants to belong to the Hervormde Kerk. Therefore, any real Jewish presence in the country can be identified only during the period of the Batavian Republic (1803-1806) and subsequent British rule (1806-1910), when Jews were allowed to practise their religion openly.

The earliest professing Jews came from Germany or Britain, quite a few arriving with the 1820 settlers – British families who settled in the eastern Cape – so that by 1858 there were sixty Jewish families in the Cape Colony. The first permanent congregation of Cape Town was formed in 1841 and the slowly growing community lived in comparative harmony with the surrounding population.[29] Being a small minority, relatively well off and acculturated, and identifying with the British way of life, they were subject to the forces of integration and assimilation. By the time of the granting of Responsible Government to the Cape Colony in 1872 they were generally tolerated, not being regarded as a specific out-group, but as a sub-group of the dominant white caste. In 1860 Lady Duff Gordon observed:

> These Colonial Jews ... have the features of their race, but many of the peculiarities are gone. Mr L who is very handsome and gentlemanly, eats ham ... he is, he says, a thorough Jew in faith, and evidently in charitable works, but he wants to say his prayers in English ... he and his wife ... have not forgotten their old persecutions, and are civil to the coloured people, and speak of them in quite a different tone from the other English colonists.[30]

Although this view of the typical 'Englishman of the Mosaic Persuasion' appears to be positive, stressing the Jew's charitable work and his special relationship with another out-group – the 'coloured people' – there is a significant reference to appearance, which will become an almost standard marker in South African fiction in which Jews appear.

Throughout the nineteenth century, Jewish pioneers, mainly from Germany or the East End of London, gradually settled in the interior, predominantly as traders. Many young Jewish men were drawn to the country by the discovery of diamonds in 1867 in the vicinity of what would later be known as Kimberley, and gold in the Transvaal during the 1880s. Jews associated with the diamond rush were the first to capture the imagination of writers, and were almost invariably regarded in a criminal light as associated with IDB.

After the pogroms in Russia following the assassination of Czar Alexander II in 1881, and until about 1910, approximately 40 000 Jews emigrated to South Africa from eastern Europe.[31] The emigration of Jews – part of general westward migration – was accelerated by their effort to escape punitive legislation, economic dislocation and conscription.[32] The influx radically altered the demographic composition of the South African Jewish community, since most of the newcomers were Yiddish speakers from the area in Lithuania, Poland or Russia known as 'the Jewish Pale of Settlement'. Of these, some continued to wear the long sidelocks and distinctive clothing of the strictly observant Jews of the shtetl. Many were impoverished and unkempt. A few were skilled and semi-skilled artisans – watchmakers, shoemakers, bakers and barbers – but most were traders and small shopkeepers.

The new arrivals, unlike the assimilated Anglo-German community, were regarded by the urban Gentile population as fundamentally alien – part of the 'dirty proletariat from the Polish Russian border'.[33] In the Cape they eked out a precarious existence, often hawking old clothes or trading as small shopkeepers. More frequently they travelled as smouse, peddling being a relatively easy occupation for a *greener* (newcomer). The figure of the smous would become an important Jewish stereotype.

Feelings against Jews intensified after the third major wave of Jewish immigration in the 1890s which brought the most impoverished eastern Europeans yet to arrive, and coincided with an economic recession in the Cape Colony from 1902 to 1910. A contemporary Englishman's description of the immigrant Jew about to embark for South Africa from Southampton is revealing:

> I saw him from the quay. He might have been a somewhat younger edition of Charles Dickens's Fagin ... His

nose was hooked most semitically. His unkempt beard
was red. His bowler hat with generations' dust upon it
was dented in. His frock coat was undesirably greasy ...
He was bound for South Africa.[34]

Again, intact through the centuries, is the marker of appearance.
Further stereotyping is evident in a newspaper report of 1896 which
described a typical Jewish immigrant as 'the apparition of a slovenly,
unkempt and generally unwashed edition ... of the wandering Jew'.[35]

Notwithstanding its hostile reception, the Jewish population in
South Africa grew rapidly. In 1880 there were about 4 000 Jews in
the country; in 1891 Jews numbered 10 000; and by 1899 there were
about 24 000 Jews in a total white population estimated at 850 000.
More than half the Jews had emigrated directly from eastern Europe,
approximately 7 000 from England, and at least 3 000 from Germany,
of whom many had lived for some time in England.[36] Most settled
within a three mile radius of Market Square in the slums of
Ferreirasdorp and lower Commissioner Street. By 1904 Jews constituted 12 per cent of the white population of Johannesburg which was
disparagingly known as 'Jewburg' or 'Jewhannesburg'.[37] They were
pejoratively known by Gentiles and even by the more acculturated
Anglo-German Jews as 'Peruvians' – generally believed to be an
acronym for Polish and Russian Union, a Jewish club established in
Kimberley during the diamond rush.[38] Often the press unequivocally
branded these immigrants as 'scum'.[39]

The researches of Charles van Onselen first focused attention on
the Jews' heavy involvement in the liquor trade.[40] After the sale of
liquor to blacks was prohibited in 1897, their activities continued
illicitly. The general population, as well as the majority of the Jewish
community, regarded this as a disgrace, constituting a blatant exploitation of the black mineworkers, and Jews were lambasted in the
press and in popular cartoons. Van Onselen has shown that some
Jews were involved in other shady activities such as gambling and
prostitution, which strongly supported the criminal image of the Jew
already established on the diamond fields.[41] Other popular occupations for Jewish immigrants were to own or work in a shop –
usually a concession store – near the mines, or to run a *kaffireater*
(eating house for blacks near the gold mines). During the following

decades hotel-keeping became a common occupation, especially in country districts, but trading of one sort or another remained the primary occupation for immigrant Jews.

In the Cape during the 1890s there was considerable public and governmental agitation to control the immigration of aliens. In 1902 this culminated in the gazetting of the Immigration Restriction Act, a precedent followed in other parts of the country, now under British rule. Although primarily aimed at controlling the influx of Asiatics, it also excluded anyone who could not sign his or her name in European characters.[42] Since Yiddish, the language of the Eastern European Jews, was written not in European but in Hebrew characters, the Act posed a direct threat to Jewish immigration. In 1906, under pressure from the Cape Jewish Board of Deputies, the Cape Government, reluctantly followed by those of Natal and the Transvaal, relaxed the language restrictions, accepting Yiddish for the purposes of the Act as a European language.[43] A growing feeling of hostility towards the Jews, however, was expressed from the Christian pulpits – both Dutch Reform and Anglican – and in newspapers. Mainly xenophobic, this was also, as from earliest times, a religious hatred, vividly reviving the notion of the Jews as murderers of Jesus.

Towards the end of the nineteenth century, general rural poverty had produced increasing numbers of *bywoners* (tenant-farmers) who, owning no land themselves, were unable to make a living as unskilled farm labourers because such work was done by blacks. Furthermore, many farmers, suffering from the distress of the Anglo-Boer War, from drought and cattle disease, went bankrupt and were forced to sell their land. Some land was indeed bought up by Jews who were considered exploiters of the less fortunate. Many of the uprooted Afrikaners tried to find employment in the towns, where they came into direct competition with the upwardly mobile Jews, who were mostly already urbanised and busily carving out a niche for themselves.[44] In the Cape, especially, the Jews were perceived as having contributed to the hardships of the Afrikaners through *verneukery* (swindling) and sharp, even unscrupulous business practice. They became a convenient scapegoat for the generalised ills of society.

The image of the Peruvian was particularly strong on the Rand and in Cape Town where the Jews settled mainly in District Six, among the coloured and Indian groups.[45] They were frequently pejoratively associated with those considered racial outsiders – regarded as 'the equivalent of Chinamen and Coolies'[46] – and disdained as unhygienic, diseased and consequently depraved.

Within the established Jewish community itself, the eastern European immigrants were often viewed with embarrassment as being likely to undermine the precarious social position of the longer settled Jews. But this was counterbalanced by the many immigrant Jews who earned reputations for probity, industry, and upward mobility. Jewish prosperity, however, was ambivalently regarded by the general population, in the same way that the success of the Rothschilds in England during the previous century had evoked admiration tempered by strong envy. In the north, some Jews who had made money on the diamond fields went on to invest in the gold mines or the Johannesburg stock exchange. The powerful and highly visible magnates – not all of them Jewish – had an immense impact on the popular imagination. Thus at around the turn of the twentieth century, the image of the Jew in South Africa was a multiple one.

Following the lead that had been set in Britain, where the high profile of Jews in European banking and finance made them readily available targets for attack, an influential Cape Town weekly, the *Owl*, started a fashion of scurrilous caricatures directed against the Jews. These were based either on the Randlord – the sinister and powerful financier thought by many to be controlling South African society and even fomenting the Anglo-Boer War – or the image of the avaricious Jew – the filthy immigrant who deprived the locally born colonial of employment, and exploited the local population. The *Owl*'s cartoonist, Heinrich Egersdörfer, was particularly vicious in his creation of a 'Goldbug' – a bloated, cigar-smoking magnate, with stereotypical and exaggerated Semitic features. In 1903, D.C. Boonzaaier, cartoonist for the Cape Town daily, the *South African News*, drew his version, 'Hoggenheimer', named after a British musical comedy character then appearing on the Cape Town stage. Leering from the pages of several Cape newspapers on which Boonzaaier worked, 'Hoggenheimer' became a household word, and contributed greatly to the way in which the Jew would be regarded for many years to come.[47]

'Hoggenheimer' may be a corruption of 'Hohenheimer' (Home on High). This was the name of an opulent residence belonging to the largest mining house, the Corner House, and was first built and occupied by Lionel Phillips in 1893. It is no accident that the syllable 'hog' in the name 'Hoggenheimer' is synonymous with 'pig' or 'swine'. This has a double significance. In the first instance it connotes grossness, corpulence, dirt and vulgarity, but also, since pork is well known to be forbidden by the Jewish dietary laws, it implies all that is loathsome, unclean and taboo. Indeed, the insulting connection of Jews with pigs is of very long standing. Originating in the thirteenth century in Germany, a libel concerning the 'Judensau' depicted Jews suckling from a sow or eating its faeces. It gained widespread popularity and was propagated in illustrations in books and broadsheets and in carvings on churches and town halls.[48]

The Yiddish language was used by the vast majority of the eastern European immigrants, as opposed to English, which was becoming more commonly heard among the acculturated middle class and the second generation, and Hebrew, spoken by some Zionists. In European literature generally the ascription of Yiddish expressions or accent has been one of the cardinal stigmata of the Jew, and, since Yiddish was a strong cultural component of the Jewish experience in the country, it is not surprising that it becomes one of the integral aspects of the negative stereotype in South African fiction. Paradoxically, the Jewish community had, since the diamond field days, been generally identified with the British. Although a number of Jews fought with the Afrikaners during the Anglo-Boer War, animus against all Jews was intensified among the Afrikaners by the displaced aggression against the English who had recently defeated them.

When the hostility towards the influx of foreign Jews had been linked to the controversies surrounding the importation of indentured Indian and Chinese labourers, a new Immigration Act was passed allowing for the exclusion of people 'unsuited on economic grounds or habits of life'.[49] By catching many prospective Jewish immigrants in the net of its vague provisions, this Act had the effect of restricting Jewish immigration. Feelings ran high against Jews during the First World War when they were accused of shirking war duty, of disloyalty, war profiteering and parasitism. In 1915 two Johannesburg newspapers, the *Rand Daily Mail* and the *Sunday Times*, accused Jews of 'not responding to the call to arms in proportion to [their] ratio in the general population'.[50]

Parallel to this perception of the Jew as the exploitative capitalist was a widespread belief that the Jewish immigrants from eastern Europe were Russian 'bolsheviks'. It was often supposed that the Jewish smous was actively spreading 'bolshevism' and fomenting political agitation among the rural black population to whom he had easy access.[51] Anti-bolshevik hysteria was widespread after the First World War, and fastened on the Jews who were once again convenient scapegoats. This view was not without some foundation. Many Jewish immigrants to South Africa had been exposed to a long tradition of Jewish involvement in socialist ideologies and anti-Czarist politics in pre- and post-revolutionary Russia and eastern Europe. As a result some, but not all, brought with them to South Africa a tradition of enthusiastic support for oppressed people.

During the first decades of the twentieth century a number of Jews assisted Mohandas Gandhi, then a practising lawyer in South Africa, in his campaigns on behalf of the Indian community. The post-1917 immigration included a number of individuals who had been active members of the *Yiddisher Arbeter Bund*, the powerful anti-Zionist socialist workers' movement of eastern European Jewry in Poland and Lithuania. They joined a number of predominantly Yiddish speaking organisations such as *Po'alei Zion* (Workers of Zion), and the *Yiddisher Arbeter Klub* (Jewish Workers' Club) which had an affinity with the Communist Party. Jews were also prominent in the Yiddish-speaking Branch of the International Socialist League, and many individual Jews were prominent in the radical wing of the Labour movement, in trade union work as well as in the South African Communist Party formed in 1921, and from the late 1930s onward the Zionist Socialist Party.[52]

Despite Jewish left-wing involvement, and despite the evidence adduced by Professor MacCrone, based on contemporary socio-psychological research, which tends to confirm the popular belief that Jews were more liberally inclined than Gentiles on racial questions,[53] by and large the Jewish community in South Africa was predominantly conservative.[54] Nevertheless, the perception, especially among the Afrikaners, has been that the Jewish community has leftist leanings. The Jew was regarded as a *kaffirboetie* (kaffir lover), which was merely a version of the bolshevik, since no differentiation was made between the Jew's alleged radical or liberal tendencies. The pre-war Peruvian image, which in some instances fused with the hugely popular Hoggenheimer image, now acquired a third, bolshevik, dimension. Although this composite construct was contradictory, in one form or another it evoked strong emotion. Allegations were made that 'Bolshevist Russian Jews' were behind the miners' strike, known as the Rand Revolt, of 1922. A number of attacks appeared in the English press, where the Jew was portrayed as 'the low down alien ... with his lining full of worthless roubles, his head full of anarchist ideas, and his pocket full of bullets'.[55]

The xenophobic responses of the local population were fuelled throughout the early part of the century, and well into the years of the Second World War, by the presence of a number of highly visible *meshulokhim*, religious Jews raising funds for religious institutions. Because of their peripatetic behaviour they can be regarded as typical Wandering Jews who kept the image of the shtetl Jew – the outsider – constantly before the public. Most Jews in the country were staunch Zionists, strengthening the belief that they were clannish, and reinforcing the view that they had divided political loyalties. Thus, almost any pretext was found for the disparagement of Jews, demonstrating the operation of the scapegoating device which, as has been suggested, often derives from frustration and anxiety.

Anti-Jewish feeling was further complicated by a strongly racial component which echoed popular eugenicist views and regarded the Jews as of a different stock from the Dutch or British settlers. The fear of interbreeding, already strongly apparent in attitudes towards blacks, was applied to Jews as well. In 1925 The League of Gentiles was formed. Its aim to boycott Jewish traders may, in part, have been encouraged by the considerable jealousy the general population felt about the upward mobility and success of many of the Jewish immigrants, but there were also sinister elements of racial discourse in its statements. The *Rand Daily Mail* reported a secret meeting in which it was alleged that 'Jews amounting to 6 per cent of the population control 94 per cent of the food supply'. The League called for the Government to intervene to 'protect the gentile, particularly to protect our womenfolk', invoking the spectre of the lascivious demon Jew, bent on rape and even murder.[56] This image, which had already entered South African fiction in the novels of Stephen Black and William Westrup, persisted in attenuated form for many years.

By 1930 when Jewish immigration reached a peak, Jews constituted 35,3 per cent of the total number of immigrants. Further, the Jewish community's increasing involvement in commerce – about 66 per cent of the 80 000 Jews in the country were engaged in commercial occupations – and its predominantly urban location, supported the growing image of the 'commercial Jew'.[57] Thus the image of the Jewish shopkeeper or merchant, itself a variation on that of the stereotypical usurer, was powerfully endorsed. The alleged sharp business practices of some Jews were highlighted by the report published in 1932 of the Carnegie Commission, which had been engaged in investigating the problem of 'poor whitism'.[58] It would seem, therefore, that negative perceptions of the Jew, certainly in the press and generally in the public view, were widespread.

In 1930, during the period when South Africa, like the rest of the world was suffering a severe economic depression, the Nationalist-Labour Government, following a precedent set in America, introduced an Immigration Quota Act. By restricting countries from which immigration was freely allowed, and by specifying that only fifty immigrants from each eastern European country, chosen from persons likely to become assimilated with the local inhabitants, would be permitted to enter the country, the Act drastically reduced the flow of Jewish immigrants. Although the word 'Jew' was not mentioned in the Act, it drew wide public support, being clearly directed against the Jews from eastern Europe – a fact which Dr D.F. Malan, leader of the *Gesuiwerde* (Purified) National Party admitted in 1937.[59] The passing of the Act demonstrated the almost universal assumption held by the majority of white society that the Jews were insufficiently 'Nordic' or 'western', and not fully acceptable to the main white groups.

With Hitler's rise to power in 1933, the influence of German National Socialism was strongly felt in South Africa. General economic frustration, coupled with anti-British feeling, predisposed many Afrikaners, not only those of German origin, to Nazi propaganda imported from Germany and South West Africa. Existing anti-Jewish feeling was fired into virulent anti-Semitism. An indigenous mode of Nazism flourished, and a number of influential anti-Semitic organisations were established – the Nazi Party had already been formed in 1932. Within months various Nazi-type 'shirt' organisations were launched, the most powerful of which was the Greyshirt movement, (South African Christian Socialist Movement) (1933), led by Louis Weichardt. Boasting a paramilitary wing, and imbued with violent ideas of racist anti-Semitism, the Greyshirts put enormous pressure on the Government and created an atmosphere of hysterical opposition to the Jews. In Johannesburg and Cape Town posters which bore swastikas and proclaimed 'Kaffirs and Jews indecently assault white girls',[60] significantly linked the two groups as racial Others threatening the white race.

In 1934 the Greyshirts published a document, supposedly discovered in a Port Elizabeth synagogue and allegedly based on the *Protocols*. Although this was exposed in court as a forgery, the Greyshirts were not deterred. They claimed that 'the Jew made the Boer War', incited the 'kaffirs' against white civilisation, constituted an '[a]nti-Christ in our midst', and 'adopted the vilest practices imaginable for the degradation of Christians ...' 'Having grabbed the finances,' they continued, 'most of our women are already doing their bidding.'[61] An offshoot of the Greyshirt movement, the Gentile Protection League, put out propaganda which even alluded to the 'blood libel' canard.[62] In 1939 Dr Malan spoke publicly of 'the Jewish problem which hangs like a dark cloud over South Africa'. 'Behind organized South African Jewry stands the organized Jewry of the world,' he said.[63]

The rhetoric of these anti-Jewish outbursts, with references to the *Protocols*, the blood libel canard, the myth of the lascivious Jew, the bogey of the Other, the stereotypes of the bolshevik, anti-Christ, imperialist and Hoggenheimer, abundantly demonstrates that during this period in South African history all the components of religious, superstitious, economic and racist anti-Semitism were being invoked. Feelings against the Jew, rooted in prejudice with its attendant fears and resentments, were unashamedly orchestrated by politicians, and not only by Afrikaners. English-speaking parliamentarians such as Sir Patrick Duncan, Interior Minister during the early 1920s in Smuts's South African Party Government, and Richard Stuttaford, Interior Minister under Hertzog in 1939, were equally responsible for creating the threatening climate.[64] The fact that both language groups were implicated in hostility towards Jews may, in a large measure, account for the virulence and widespread nature of the anti-Semitism of this period.

Taking advantage of a loophole in the Immigration Quota Act by which Germany was not one of the prohibited countries, 5 534

German Jews, escaping Nazi persecution, arrived in South Africa during the period between the rise of Hitler and the outbreak of the War. The result was that xenophobic, anti-Semitic agitation from the fascist organisations increased markedly. The Gesuiwerde National Party supported the Greyshirts on the Jewish issue, and within the party a violently anti-Semitic group, the *Nuwe Orde* (New Order), founded by Oswald Pirow, energetically propagated menacing anti-Jewish activity, especially in country districts, and even among blacks.[65] Dr Malan advocated the halting of German-Jewish immigration but was pre-empted by the Hertzog-Smuts Fusion government which, in 1937, passed the Aliens Act. In stipulating principles of 'desirability' and 'assimilability' in all new immigrants, it effectively ended Jewish immigration. The number of Jews in the white community levelled out at approximately 4 per cent.[66]

Jews were labelled 'Asiatics', and were thus clearly demarcated not only as religious outsiders but also as members of the despised black out-group. Here the tacit categorical link between the Jew and the black operates vividly in a South African context. Pandering to anti-Jewish sentiment, the Act also contained a clause which regulated the right to assume a new surname or alter an existing one. This was a way of ensuring that the Jewish name as a label of outsiderhood would remain indelible.[67] An Anti-Alien Amendment Bill introduced in 1939 by Eric Louw, member of the Gesuiwerde National Party, but not passed, proposed to introduce a test for Jewish parentage which demonstrated a flagrantly Nazi type of anti-Semitism.[68]

Literary manifestation of the high feelings of this period are found only later and in retrospect, the anti-Semitic novels of Oliver Walker and A.A. Murray being written in 1949 and 1959 respectively. Jewish literary response takes the form – also retrospective – of the family-saga or nostalgia novels of Dan Jacobson and Rose Zwi. In contemporary Yiddish fiction, however, the problems of the direct manifestations of anti-Semitism were dealt with more immediately and more fully.[69]

In 1937 the Witwatersrand Council of Churches passed a number of resolutions condemning anti-Semitic propaganda and, in the same year the South African Society of Jews and Christians was formed in an effort to promote good relations between Christians and Jews.[70]

Afrikaner opposition to South Africa entering the Second World War rendered the Afrikaner nationalist movements even more receptive to Nazi influence. The *Ossewa Brandwag* (Sentinels of the Ox-wagon), formed in 1939, was the most powerful paramilitary expression of this process. Rabidly anti-Semitic, it once again tapped the huge reservoirs of national frustration and hostility among the Afrikaners, which led to the outbreak of many anti-Jewish incidents. Gradually, however, when Germany was seen to be losing the war, when the realities of the Holocaust became known and the extent of Jewish suffering shocked the world, cracks appeared in the edifice of anti-Semitism and the anti-Semitic movements lost power. All the same, hostilities between Jewish youths and Greyshirts continued to take place sporadically throughout the war years. Even after the war a series of violent clashes took place on the steps of the Johannesburg City Hall between Jewish ex-servicemen and anti-Semites.[71]

With the victory of the National Party in 1948, the Afrikaners, having gained political ascendancy, no longer felt as threatened by Jewish economic competition. As more Afrikaners gradually entered the urban middle class and the commercial and professional world, and became well known as intellectuals, artists, and entrepreneurs, the Jews were perceived to be less menacing. Cordial relations developed between the Government and the new State of Israel, established in 1948, and the goodwill in a fair measure extended to the Jews of South Africa. Afrikaners felt more confident that the problems posed by Jewish immigration to South Africa had been solved, and they drew a parallel between the situation of the beleaguered Israelis and their own position in relation to the blacks. They respected the Jewish homeland, and the concept of the 'Chosen People' operated positively, since the Afrikaners believed themselves similarly to be the Chosen People in South Africa.

After the middle of the twentieth century, images of Jews in the fiction of Gentiles became conspicuously more benign than before. Nevertheless, the anti-Jewish stereotype of the flashy and dishonest businessman persisted in the media and in fiction. Anti-Jewish propaganda material continued to circulate at a popular level and sporadic anti-Semitic incidents, such as the defacing of synagogues in Johannesburg, took place.[72]

The National Party's policy of support for Israel continued under successive prime ministers, even when Israel's criticism of South

Africa's racial policies and support for black Africa and for sanctions against South Africa put the government under strain. South African Jews generously sent funds to Israel, and frequently went on *aliyah* (emigrated to Israel), moves which were considered by some to demonstrate once again their dual loyalty. After the Six-Day War in 1967 and the Yom Kippur War of 1973, enthusiasm and admiration for Israel increased among white South Africans. A new concept of the Israeli Jew as a powerful and courageous warrior rivalled the older stereotypes of the money-loving plutocrat, the bolshevik, and the filthy Yiddish-speaking Peruvian.

The latter image had already been substantially eroded following the upward mobility of the second and third generations. At the same time, the concept of the Jew as victim, suffering under Nazi oppression, was also challenged. Since Israel was favourably viewed as a bulwark against Soviet communist influence, the South African Government initiated a policy of pragmatic co-operation with Israel which extended to dealing in arms, a move which was to antagonise those with left-wing sentiments.[73]

As the Government's implementation of the policies of apartheid hardened, it took exception to the presence of South African Jews in visible roles in such left-wing organisations as the African Resistance Movement, the Communist Party, the Congress of Democrats, and the Liberal and Progressive Parties. Some Jews were detained under the 90-day clause of the General Law Amendment Act of 1963, and they were prominent both as defendants in political trials and as counsel for the defence of those tried in terms of the Suppression of Communism Act. Although the vast majority of Jews did not participate in radical politics, the number who did attracted public attention, like the highly visible diamond dealers or the Randlords before them. The Jewish leftist – a later version of the bolshevik or kaffirboetie stereotypes – would become one of the most popular of all late twentieth century images. In Hugh Lewin's autobiographical *Bandiet: Seven Years in a South African Prison* (1974), a passage describes an interchange between a warder and a political prisoner:

> I heard the talking down the passage, then could recognise Nel's voice, raised angrily against Rowley

Arenstein, just down the row – and Rowley's patient, persistent replies. 'Jood,' said Nel, 'Jew – you're a communist because you're a Jew – you're a Jew so you must be a communist.' (p.215)

In strikingly similar terms, Denis Goldberg, a member of banned left-wing organisations, spoke of his prison experience:

> As a Jew in prison you saw it all ... a sergeant greets in the morning, to each political prisoner, 'good morning Jew, good morning Jew, good morning Jew,' whether they were Jewish or not. He gets to me. I say I don't like this and I won't have it ... So the next morning he comes down the passage and says, 'good morning communist, good morning communist, good morning communist.' If you're a Jew you must be a communist, and if you're a communist you must be a Jew. If you're opposed to apartheid you must be both, whether you are or not.[74]

This recent version of the bolshevik stereotype appears in the writing of Nadine Gordimer, Caroline Slaughter, Alison Stewart, Laurence Lerner, Modikwe Dikobe, Mongane Wally Serote, Bryce Courtenay and others.

While the United Nations resolution linking Israel ideologically with the racist South African regime brought Jews and the Afrikaner establishment closer together, tension between Jews and Muslims increased, especially after the Israeli advance into Lebanon in 1982. Throughout the 1980s there were clashes on university campuses between Jewish students and Muslim students who supported the Palestinians.

The dominant issue in South African politics had become the relationship between blacks and whites, and the Jews were finally fully accepted as members of the white group. While it is no longer socially or even politically acceptable to express anti-Semitic sentiments in public, anti-Semitism has by no means disappeared in white circles.[75] The *Afrikaner Weerstandsbeweging* (AWB), the militant, neo-Nazi organisation formed in 1981, once again advocated that

Jews be deprived of political rights, and the *Blanke Bevrydings-beweging*, founded in 1987, also propagated Nazi and anti-Jewish ideology.[76]

By 1979, continuing the upward mobility trend apparent since the turn of the century, 45,6 per cent of Jews in South Africa were employed in professional or administrative capacities and only 32,7 per cent in commerce.[77] This trend is reflected in fiction. While the Jewish shopkeeper still appears, by the 1980s images are largely those of professionals. At the beginning of the 1990s the percentage of Jews in the white population of the country had declined from a high of 4,75 per cent in 1936 to approximately 3 per cent, following increasing emigration from South Africa after the Sharpeville massacre of 1960 and the Soweto uprising of 1976. This drop in numbers has been offset by the immigration of a large number of Israelis to South Africa.[78] There has been a significant increase in the membership of ultra-orthodox movements, so that in Johannesburg, and to a lesser extent the other main cities, it is now common, as it was a hundred years ago, to see Jews wearing side-locks and distinctive clothing. The impact of these Jews has not yet entered the mainstream of South African fiction.

It is against this background that the appearance of the Jew in South African fiction will be surveyed.

A local mythos emerges comprising a distinctive set of indigenous stereotypes with certain recurring attributes: stigmatising physical and language characteristics, usually as a correlative for moral qualities; ascribed legendary characteristics derived from the European models; specific South African contributions.

Although, as 3 or 4 per cent of the white population, the number of Jews in the country is very small, the number of Jewish characters in South African fiction is relatively large. Since the image of the Jew is used to signify the villain, the outsider, sometimes the do-gooder, and to lend local colour, it frequently appears in the form of a vignette, or is flattened to a caricature, which appeals to crude basic emotions by operating through compression and simplification, and with very little scope for detailed characterisation. Gentile authors make virtually no attempt to characterise Jews, who frequently appear as concepts rather than characters. This is probably because, although there is a fair amount of social integration, most Gentiles are not very familiar with Jews, except at a superficial level, or because, as has happened over the centuries, the exotic elements of the Jewish stereotypes have had so powerful an effect on the imagination of authors that they take precedence over subtleties of characterisation. The early portraits of Jews appear to set up basic models for the stereotypes which appear in different forms throughout the twentieth century.

— 2 —

IDB AND 'OTHERS'

The first significant images of Jews in South African fiction are associated with the discovery of diamonds. A strongly negative stereotype was established, which would resonate throughout the following century.

During the first half of the nineteenth century images of Jews did not enter South African colonial fiction. The acculturated Anglo-German Jewish community of the southern and eastern Cape, constituting a mere 0,23 per cent of the white population, represented no numerical or economic threat. Consequently group relationships were largely peaceful and hardly noteworthy.[1] However, with the discovery of diamonds in the late 1860s, and the large scale exploitation of the gems in the 1870s and 1880s, Jews were heavily represented among the speculators converging on the fields, and their numbers increased proportionately.[2] A strong Jewish community was established in Kimberley, centre of the diamond trade. Besides fortune hunters, the diggings attracted writers and journalists. Stories and poems began appearing frequently in local and overseas newspapers and, arising out of the mining experience, seventy novels were published, at first in England, and after 1893 in South Africa itself.[3]

It is notable that the colonial text consistently reflects the dominant model of colonial relationships, which Abdul JanMahomed has categorised as a 'manichean opposition between self and Other'. JanMahomed has demonstrated that a fascination with the ideas of the Other – what he calls the 'fetishization of the Other' – is a characteristic of the colonial text. He argues, however, that there is little 'truth-value' in representations of the Other in this writing, which are tantamount to romance.[4] David Spurr disagrees. He argues that '[t]he question that matters ... is, finally, not how one literary form differs from another, but how writing works, in whatever form, to produce knowledge about other cultures.'[5] Most colonial writers quite seriously believed that they were writing history, and incorporated into their work as much historical fact and local colour as they could.[6] No doubt there was exaggeration and distortion for propagandistic or sensational effect, but if critically handled these texts may well become valuable source material for the study of contemporary perceptions.

In the literature of the diamond fields, the most common fictional model, which portrays an opposition between white colonisers and the physically threatening Other, the colonised black, is sometimes replaced by a different model, which reflects not a physical but an economic opposition. This often takes the form of a tussle between the law on the one hand and the wily criminal on the other. Here the figure of the Other is frequently that of the Jew, who is almost invariably linked with the trade, illicit or otherwise, in diamonds or gold.[7]

It was not coincidental that Jews were among the first to participate in the mineral revolution. The essentially impermanent social condition of the Jew in Europe over the centuries, which left him constantly poised to flee from discrimination, persecution and conscription, meant that for him the accumulation of capital assets became a necessity. Thus the suitably portable trade in diamonds attracted many young Jewish men. Several Jews who emigrated to South Africa in the 1860s and 1870s, had already been engaged in the diamond trade in England or Germany. The Lilienfeld brothers, for example, German Jewish immigrants who had become prosperous merchants in Hopetown, bought some of the important early stones in 1867 and resold them to a London firm. Within a few years German Jews became prominent among the diamond buyers, and Jews were represented among the diggers and *kopje wallopers* (petty diamond buyers) as well.[8]

Fluctuations in the diamond industry and the consequent unsettled economic circumstances in the Cape, produced a climate in which immigrants, particularly fortune-hunters, were not welcomed. Rather, they were viewed by the local population with suspicion and hostility, and were often cast in the role of scapegoats. Although many Jews failed at the diamond diggings, there were sufficient successes among them to draw negative attention. The historian, J.A. Froude, invoking the familiar negative stereotype, wrote that he had observed among the diggers 'a hundred or so keen-eyed Jewish merchants ... gathering like eagles over their prey'.[9]

Perceptions are largely based not on the average individual but on the flashy, exaggerated figure who catches the attention and fires the imagination. Thus the image of the Jew was a construct based not upon observation of the many law-abiding bourgeois, pious or acculturated Jews, but upon contempt for and envy of the conspicuous eccentrics. Indeed, the spectacular success of the flamboyant Barney Barnato, who arrived on the fields in 1873 from Whitechapel in London, and whose colourful career was widely followed and reported, did much to foster the growth of a powerful mythology.[10] In the emerging stereotype of the Jew, all the Jews come to South Africa as outsiders, either directly from Germany, or from Germany or Poland by way of Whitechapel. This construct would seem to derive from amalgamation of the strong Barnato image with that of the German diamond buyer. Further, and most centrally, these fictional Jews are all involved in criminal activities, particularly illicit diamond buying, IDB.

When it was estimated that up to 50 per cent of all transactions were illegal, the Diamond Act was passed by the Cape Parliament in 1882, providing for very harsh penalties for IDB. However, 'the trade', as it was called, was regarded as a type of sport, and if practised by Gentiles, as a 'gentleman's crime'. IDB and all its ramifications proved to be a trope which fascinated writers, giving rise to a number of stereotypes which persisted in South African colonial fiction. Notable are the gentleman pioneer, the barmaid, the shifty or savage black, and the villain. The most sinister of the stereotypes is that of the outsider, the Other, who is of a different race or comes from a different country and speaks a broken or accented language.[11]

Since each individual social group has a specific set of images arising from its history, culture, and prejudice which encodes its perception of the Other, it will select at any given time a model that best reflects its current presuppositions about the Other. In the fiction arising from the mining experience, the Other sometimes appears as the corrupt Jewish Illicit Diamond Buyer (IDB), since, together with the black, the Jew eminently fulfils in the South African psyche the conditions of Otherness. In fact, the substitution of Jew for black as model for the Other has earlier precedents. Sander Gilman has made the startling claim that the concept of colour is itself not intrinsic and is merely a function of Otherness. He argues that the association of blackness with Jews is part of Christian tradition where medieval iconography always juxtaposed the black image of the synagogue with the white image of the Church.[12]

Gilman has also suggested that during the nineteenth century the categories of 'black' and 'Jew' again became interchangeable. While the black native was established in European mythology as the embodiment of colonial anxieties, he was, by his very nature, at a distance from society. The Jew, however, was feared as a more immediate threat because he was daily present in society, and ever increasingly demanding access to bourgeois life.[13] The clash between the heroic Gentile – usually the detective investigating IDB – and the evil Jew – sometimes assisted by a black or Asian – becomes a key construct in diamond field writing.

The primary marker of the Jew in this emerging stereotype, as it has been since Jews first appeared in medieval drama, is a distinctive appearance. Over the centuries, through exaggeration and distortion, 'Jewish' features have crystallised into a prominent nose, dark skin, low forehead, shifty, beady or piercing eyes, full lips, greasy hair – by this time usually dark and no longer red – small, often weak stature, and a cunning or sly expression. It is notable that in the coding of 'Jewishness' many of the features highlighted are similar to those attributed in colonial fiction to the black. Significantly these physical characteristics, which reappear throughout the nineteenth and twentieth centuries, are used to represent moral as well as physical degeneration, and are usually introduced by the epithet 'ugly'. They were very popular in scurrilous cartoons depicting Jews in the British *Punch* and later the *Cape Punch*, the *South African News*, and especially the *Owl* and *De* (later *Die*) *Burger*, and would be used obsessively by colonial writers in the construction of Jewish types.

One of the first fictional works to depict the Jewish IDB was a novel, *IDB or the Adventures of Solomon Davis*, published in 1887 by an Englishman, W.T. Eady. The chief character is a Jewish card-sharper from the East End of London who travels to Kimberley to make a fortune on the diamond diggings. The author describes Solomon, stressing that 'the repulsive fullness of his lips, and the sinister curves at the corner of his mouth, betray[ed] greediness and cunning of no common intensity'.

He continues: 'Solomon's eyebrows very nearly met over his prominent nose, and this ... added, in a disagreeable manner, to the sly expression of face imparted by his mouth ... [and] his eyes, whose glance was constantly shifting ...' (pp.7-8). As well as the prominent nose and shifty eyes, the reference to 'greediness and cunning', and the epithets 'repulsive', 'sinister' and 'disagreeable', signal that Solomon is set up to play the stereotypical Jewish villain. Notably, features attributed to Solomon – 'fullness of ... lips' and shifty eyes – are fixtures of the black stereotype. Solomon's criminal potentialities would seem to be inbred since gratuitous reference is made to his parents who keep a drinking parlour where they rob any Christians who might happen to stray inside (p.2). This is possibly an oblique and very attenuated reference to the myth of ritual murder. The author casts aspersions on all the Jews in the novel. He refers to a group of London Jews who

> aired their black suits and stove-pipe hats in synagogue on the day of atonement, where they howled away the transgressions of the previous twelve months in company with a crowd of temporarily mournful hypocrites like themselves, and then straightway went out of there with their monstrous noses elevated to catch scent of the first swindle that might be floating around. (p.3)

Here Jewry's most sacred day, the Day of Atonement – spelt in the text without capitals as an indication of contempt – is mocked and is conflated with Jewish ugliness and criminality. It is no accident that in one sentence the 'monstrous' Jewish noses and the reference to a 'swindle' are juxtaposed. This is an early and typical example of what will become commonplace in subsequent South African fiction, the linking, for pejorative and anti-Semitic effect, of the discourse of Jewish religion or Jewish custom with that of criminality. The choice of the word 'howl', with its barbaric and animalistic overtones, is, as well, the first appearance in South African fiction of the identification of the Jew with the animal or sub-human, a variation of a long-established colonial trope in which animal imagery is used to designate the sinister Other.

Solomon emigrates to the diamond fields where he becomes a bold, cunning and unscrupulous diamond-dealer and an IDB. Two aristocratic Gentiles – Bunton and Cormack – also involved in IDB, represent its gentlemanly and sporting aspect. The author shows them as mere petty criminals whose actions are prompted by nothing more than a gambling drive, and they are ultimately destroyed by the Jew.

Solomon is also a poisoner who escapes hanging thanks to the lying testimony of two Jews – 'Thomas Jones' and 'George James' (whose real names are Moss and Raphael). The allusion to poisoning may be yet another link with myth, this time the superstitious accusation that the Jews had caused the Black Death by poisoning the wells. The last chapter is entitled 'Mozzle and Brocah' (good luck and blessing), which is the traditional formula Jewish diamond dealers use to clinch a deal. Here the narrator uses the phrase sarcastically in order to celebrate Solomon's escape from deserved prosecution, and thereby to reinforce a negative image of Jewish diamond brokerage.

Having made a fortune, Solomon takes the unlikely Gentile name of 'Montague Vaughan'. The narrator suggests 'Mr and Mrs Solomon Davis would never have made their way in London Society' (p.343). Thus he concludes that through dishonesty and cunning, IDB, blackmail and murder, the Jews have clawed out a spurious social niche for themselves. He claims:

> They are aspiring to further promotion; and the lady talks to her confidential friends of the possibility of her being presented at an early Drawing-room; while the husband, over his prime Cubans and midnight hock-and-seltzer, occasionally lets fall a whisper as to his being elected at one of the leading West End Clubs. (p.344)

This text suggests, as do so many others of this time, that the Jew is an inveterate social climber, and an assimilationist who is earnestly trying to conceal evidence of his Jewishness. The Jews named 'Thomas

James' and 'George Jones', already noted, have attempted to follow the same pattern. In the colonial fiction of this time, Jews are frequently shown as making a fortune, concealing their origins, changing their names and buying a house in Park Lane. Michael Ragussis has identified this as a 'trope of conversion of the Jew'[14] which does seem to be constructed from real perceptions, strongly, though not entirely, based on the figure of Barney Barnato. Although he changed his name – originally Barnett Isaacs – Barnato did not do so in order to conceal his Jewishness. The domestic spectre of the Jewish Other is particularly threatening since it insidiously seeks to hide behind the mask of a Gentile name.

In J.R. Couper's novel, *Mixed Humanity* (1892), the Jew, Ikey Mosetenstine, is 'absolutely the biggest I.D.B. on the Fields' (pp.26-27), displays all the qualities of 'cunning and shrewdness' (p.71), and is 'small in size, ill-formed and ugly' (p.113). He is contrasted with Captain Searight, the Gentile Irishman who although also villainous, is a 'fine, handsome, athletic-looking fellow, with good features' (p.71) who is 'of fair complexion and the proud possessor of a fine blonde moustache' (p.2).

Far more fully developed is a fictional Jew of comically demonic proportions – Julius Hermann, alias Hermann Van Werther. He is centrally important in Stephen Black's *The Golden Calf: A Story of the Diamond Fields*, a novel published in 1925, based on his play *I.D.B.* of 1912. Hermann is 'dark and bearded, neatly dressed and feline, obscure and magnetic ...' (p.43). The narrator relishes the description of his eyes '[which] burned over the black beard covering all his face' (p.45). His looming presence recalls something of Hoggenheimer. Besides his involvement in IDB, Hermann is also a bigamist, seducer and blackmailer. As his 'magnetic' appearance suggests, he is that potent figure, the exotic Jew, who is simultaneously repellent and fascinating.

He is clearly a descendant of Svengali, who has passed into the popular imagination as the epitome of the sinister and mysterious bogeyman. Svengali, a Jewish hypnotist who features in George du Maurier's novel, *Trilby* (1894), uses his powers to transform a beautiful Gentile girl into an incomparable singer and to cast a sexual spell over her. The sexually compelling villain was a principal player in nineteenth century melodramatic bodice-rippers, and was shipped to South Africa in the baggage of colonial writers. Although the Jewish origins of Svengali have largely been ignored as the figure has assumed mythic stature in the twentieth century, they are the source of his effectiveness as a symbol, for they invoke not one but three earlier Jewish prototypes with either sinister or mysterious connotations – the medieval demon, the licentious exotic and the Wandering Jew.

In Black's novel, the presence of stereotyping is all too obvious. Not only is the Jew evil, magnetic, darkly bearded, and involved in financial scandals, but his principal victim is a beautiful Gentile girl. Although an unmarried mother and an IDB herself, she is named Lily White, crudely symbolising purity and innocence, and significantly contrasted with the evil and 'black' Jew. In the same way that the black has been regarded as sexually threatening, so has licentiousness often featured as an aspect of the Jewish stereotype, since the sexuality of the Other is always particularly menacing.[15] The concept of the Jew preying on the innocent Gentile girl became established in the South African mythos, and surfaced in newspaper reports during the time of anti-Alien agitation at the beginning of the twentieth century.

Only at the end of the novel, when Hermann swells monstrously in evil and rapacity, is his concealed Jewishness revealed. Just before he shoots himself, he intones: 'This is a day of humiliation for me, of lamentation ... Julius Hermann's Yom Kippur, the day on which the fools triumph over him ...' (p.317). This is the first time his Jewishness has been acknowledged by the narrator. It serves as a climactic uncovering of 'Jewish guilt'. Suspicions held by the other characters and by the reader are finally satisfied, and a situation of complicity between narrator and reader is created, which acts as a powerful reinforcement of the negative image. It is a further instance of the coupling of the Jewish religion with Jewish criminality.

Anti-Jewish stereotypes appear in a collection of interlinking stories published in 1899, entitled *Knaves of Diamonds: Being Tales of Mine and Veld*, by G.[C.] Griffith (1859-1906). One of these stories, 'The Diamond Dog', describes a Jew from Whitechapel with the German name Augustus Löwenfeldt, who is a licensed diamond broker, stock and share dealer, IDB and, like Dickens's Fagin, a fence. Here the Cockney and the German Jew are conflated as they are so often in colonial fiction, and the physical description once again boldly incorporates several typical markers of the stereotype. The narrator relishes the description of how Löwenfeldt's 'prominent eyes kept wandering restlessly about the little room'. Gleefully he recounts how 'his fleshy, pendant under lip trembled every now and then with the movement of his heavy jaw, and his fat, lavishly-jewelled fingers kept alternately drumming on the dirty table and wandering aimlessly through his black and rather greasy locks' (p.2). It seems as if in order to construct a figure of a Jew, the author has consulted a ready-made list of the negative markers. Notably, these markers recur with only minor variations throughout the twentieth century in South African fiction, and have become a stock from which writers, lacking any significant knowledge of Jews, and frequently lacking much literary ability, are able to draw. In so doing they simultaneously contribute to and perpetuate the anti-Jewish prejudice from which the stereotype arose.

The juxtaposition of icons of flashy jewellery, connoting wealth and ostentation, with dirt or tawdriness, here metonymically representing criminality, is featured in another story in this collection, 'The King's Rose Diamond'. In this story, a Jew, Mickey Mosenstein, 'made his *debut* as a dealer in cheap jewellery and shop-made outfits ... and [was] now looked upon as one of the smartest and most successful "operators" on the Diamond Fields' (p.60). He unscrupulously cheats and manipulates his gullible relative, Joshua Mosenstein, known as Jossey Mo, who gets his own back by turning the tables through blackmail, after Mickey has become rich Michael Mosenstein Esq. of London. Contrasted with these Jewish IDBs – low-class and ugly social climbers – is once again the figure of the gentlemanly IDB. In several of these stories he is a Gentile, a Yankee named Seth Salter, who is sympathetically drawn, and although involved in the same underground trade is constructed as a hero. In 'A Run to Freetown', the narrator describes how Salter successfully bluffs the inspector, Lipinski and:

> suddenly pulled his left hand out of his trousers pocket, and held it out to the inspector with the palm full of rough diamonds ... Like lightning, a revolver jumped out of [Lipinski's] coat pocket. Seth Salter burst into a loud laugh ...

> "Waal, boss, I did think you had a better eye for klips than that ... can't you see they're all schlenters (counterfeits)? There's no law agin carrying *them* round, I reckon." (p.34)
>
> The glasses were filled again and the Yankee clinked his against the inspector's with as much cordiality as if they had been the best of friends. (p.38)

Salter, the Gentile, even uses the Yiddish word, 'schlenters', so associated was IDB with Jews. The inspector readily forgives Salter – as does the author – seemingly because he is a Gentile.

After 1886, with the discovery of huge gold deposits on the Witwatersrand, many company owners became interested in investing in gold, and moved to the Rand. The minority who made fortunes or increased their existing fortunes were conspicuous, especially in the overseas press. The figure of the millionaire capitalist – the Randlord, or in its South African guise, the cartoon figure of Hoggenheimer – became a new and very potent version of the negative Jewish stereotype, and entered the popular consciousness by way of journalism, the stage and the music-hall. There were few equivalent literary portrayals, a far greater literary impact had been made on writers by the diggers and IDB operators, who were more visible on the streets of Kimberley, a small town, than the Johannesburg magnates who operated behind the closed doors of the large corporations and the stock exchange.

Both the Svengali and the Hoggenheimer figures reappear metamorphosed in the character of Rudolf Feinbaum, a villainous Johannesburg businessman, also an illicit gold buyer, who preys on young Gentile girls. This more domesticated version of the earlier types can be found in *The Debt* (1912), a novel by William Westrup (1881-1949). Feinbaum makes one of his typists the object of his sexual advances and practises on her his rather comical hypnotic powers:

> Feinbaum had absolutely no serious intentions as regarded Ethel ... [H]e derived quite a lot of entertainment from experimenting upon her emotions ... [H]e could bend her to his slightest wish, and he loved to prove his power ... It

frequently seemed to her that Feinbaum could read her
inmost thoughts with uncanny correctness, and she was
afraid of him. (pp.107-108)

He corners Ethel in his office. 'He was watching her as a cat might
watch a helpless mouse – a sneering smile on his lips ...' (p.134) This
leads to a scene of ludicrous melodrama:

Feinbaum rose with a snarl of anger and rushed at her.
She tried to leap out of his way ... He seized her savagely
and dragged her across the room. Then he thrust her on
the couch and stood over her ... He laughed ...
devilishly – and bent over her. She felt his hot breath on
her face ... [and] fell back with a gasp of agony, helpless
in his iron grip, and half fainting. (p.151)

The *frisson* is all the stronger because Feinbaum is a Jew. Other
characters regard him not as a Svengali type but as a version of
Hoggenheimer:

"Mr Feinbaum? Good gracious, why he's an utter *pig*.
Look when he came to dinner last week. Tilted his chair
back, stuck a hand in the armhole of his waistcoat, with
all the fingers spread out, and – picked his teeth! ... I
think he is a loathsome toad." (p.67)

This caricatured figure of the vulgar and disgusting Jewish
businessman has its attendant animal iconography of pig and toad –
metaphors which persist throughout the century in the work of anti-
Semitic authors. The discourse used here employs imagery both of
animals and of devilishness which simultaneously suggest the sub-
human and the demonic aspects of the Jewish stereotype.

Evident in the passages quoted thus far is the way in which the
authors are unable or unwilling, in their depiction of the Jewish
bogeyman, to move beyond stereotypical caricature. This is because
the proper function of popular literature is to entertain and to pander
to basic emotions. The vividness of the negative stereotype, drawing
on ready-made anti-Semitic hostility, is immediately recognisable to

readers, and is emotionally extremely effective. Consequently, popular fiction is noteworthy in its ability to perpetuate and reinforce stereotypes.

The Jewish woman as an important figure appears for the first time in Westrup's next novel, *The Toll* (1914). Julia Leverton is constructed both in terms of the stereotype of the beautiful Jewess popular in nineteenth century fiction, and with some allusion to the sexually seductive Jewish woman, a variant of the sexually threatening Jewish male. This new type would recur, and later modulate into the figure of the kugel. The character's Jewishness is signalled immediately:

> Julia Leverton ... was Jewish, and already her figure was more than plump. She had a bright colour, and was rather given to the use of powder. It was merely a habit for her skin was far too good to require any artificial effects. Her eyes were large and almost black, and she had a glorious mane of black hair. When she smiled she showed teeth beautifully white and even, if a little large for modern ideas of beauty ... Except for a vague suggestion of coarseness, her face was almost beautiful ... But she was but a couple of inches over five feet in height, and the plumpness of her figure tended to make her look even less ... she was a delightful companion ... and perfectly satisfied with herself and the world in general. Also she was fond of jewellery, and had a *penchant* for rather startling colours in her dress ... She herself was essentially materialistic. (pp.6-7)

Despite the presence of positive epithets, there are several qualifying phrases and references to ostentation and materialism which point to the author's attitude. The novel is set in Johannesburg during the time of the conspicuous prosperity of the Rand magnates, hence images of the Jew as vulgar money-maker and money-lender recur. Julia Leverton advises a young friend about her fiancé, comparing him unfavourably with her own husband:

> "More fool he to work for other people! Look at Hermann. He's his own master and we don't starve. Of

course he works, and works very hard indeed; but it is for himself. You'll hear people laugh and sneer about the Jews, Molly, but they are not such fools as to let other people make money by using their brains ... Hermann will find his feet in a week, and will be making money as fast as ever." (p.11)

The Jewish woman praises her Jewish husband, but the heavy and repeated stress on the making of money seems to suggest the author's grudging admiration for the industriousness of the Jews, heavily tinged with envy. This is coupled with a snobbish distaste for their flashiness, social climbing and upwardly mobile propensities, apparent in the following discussion between the young woman, Molly, and her fiancé:

"... Why on earth did we say we would go to dinner with those people?"
"Goodness knows. But they've been quite sweet to me all the way out. And coming up in the train they arranged everything for me."
"They're Jews," he commented.
"I suppose so. Why?"
"Oh, nothing much. Only I hate Jews, dear. Of course, there are good and bad among them, just as there are among other people, but the only ones I've ever encountered have been pretty bad. Perhaps I hate them because they seem to make money so easily. Envy, you know."
"I'm sure you'll like the Levertons, Hugh. It never occurred to me to think they were Jews. I don't think I have ever met any before."
"You'll meet plenty of them up here. Leverton seemed quite a good sort, except that he wore a diamond ring, and ordered dinner at the Carlton. But what a mob he had to meet him!" (p.34)

Although only the prejudiced Hugh openly expresses the popular negative image of the Jew – ' "... the only [Jews] I've ever encountered have been pretty bad" ' – Molly's comment, ' "it never occurred to me that they were Jews" ', betrays her consciousness of the stereotype against which these supposedly 'different' Jews are measured. There is even a glancing reference to a diamond, which continues the persistent linkage of the Jew with the diamond trade. The social climbing Jew is mocked, and the passage ends with a flourish and a sneer at the Jew's appearance. A character refers to ' "[t]hat beery-looking fat man who drove them off in his car" '. ' "Mrs. Leverton … is *already* flashy *and* fat," he concluded triumphantly' (p.35). However, other aspects – the fact that the prejudiced Hugh is lightly satirised, and the continued way the narrative tends to undercut extremes of anti-Semitic feeling in the text – resembles the practice of those writers who create ambivalent images.[16]

As in Europe from at least the seventeenth century, the second marker of the Jew in early South African fiction is the ascribed use of a Yiddish accent or Yiddish expressions. Since language is both a means of communication and a bearer of a nation's culture and history, the importance of language as a measure of control and power cannot be overestimated.[17] In the depiction of a Jewish character, the ascription of a language which is for a Gentile reader or audience either incomprehensible or else a kind of pidgin, has come to be another major marker of the Jew's condition of Otherness. As a device denoting a subordinate and inferior culture, it indicates the user's lack of control of the tools of the dominant culture. As such, it signals the user's disempowerment and evokes in audience or reader both contempt and hilarity.

In the earliest literary representations of Jews, this pidgin took the form of a gibberish purporting to be Hebrew. It was proffered as a secret and sub-human language, connoting what was perceived to be the corrupt and ludicrous beliefs and practices of the Jews. When the Jew became secularised during the eighteenth century, and he came to be viewed less as a medieval demon and more frequently as a usurer, the distinguishing linguistic identifier shifted from Hebrew to Yiddish as the negative label of the Other.

Yiddish was regarded negatively throughout Europe. Besides being the language of despised Jews, it was perceived as a corrupt form of German, adulterated by Hebrew, and was associated with the jargon of thieves – even non-Jewish thieves – assuming in the common mind an aspect of criminality. Thus, in a literary context, merely to suggest that a character has a Yiddish accent is to allude to this aspect of language marking, and to signal the innate duplicity and degeneracy of the discourse of the Jew, and his condition of inferiority, marginality, and ridiculousness.[18]

Whatever their origins and with few exceptions, the Jews in these early South African texts are stigmatised by the way they speak: they use Yiddish expressions or speak broken English with a Yiddish accent.

In J.R. Couper's novel, *Mixed Humanity* (1892), the Gentile, Searight, becomes involved in shady business with a Jewish IDB, Fagenstine, who chants:

> 'Ve vant to talk a leetle beeshiness … You vant my advice?
> Vell now you zell him for yourself. Vait now I yust tell you
> vat I does for a good turn for you. I know a bloke vat buys
> shtones. I tink he might give you twenty pundt for dat
> von.' (pp.66-67).

This represents what the author imagines a Yiddish accent to be and has very little consistency or basis in reality. Another of Griffith's stories – 'The Diamond Dog' – features once again Augustus Löwenfeldt, who speaks a totally unrealistic mixture of Cockney and Yiddish. He half-whispers:

> 'Itsh no good, Loo … the old plants will all be played
> out now that this infernal new law ish passed. The
> gonivahs (thefts) will be harder to get than ever, and
> look at the rishk – fifteen years on that blathted
> breakwater just for being found with a few klips on you!'
> (p.3)

Here the Yiddish accent is represented only through a lisp, most importantly in the word 'blathted'. In fact there is no 'th' sound either in German or in Yiddish. This is a remnant of the speech defect attributed to the Jew in newspaper cartoons and on the English stage during the nineteenth century.

In his study of the Jew in drama, M.J. Landa identifies Dickens, in his fondness for grotesque detail, as being responsible for first labelling the Jew by a lisp. He suggests that the lisp comes about because of the difference in the pronunciation of Hebrew by Sephardic and Ashkenazi Jews:

> I have noticed in one or two over-eager students a tendency to lisp in their anxiety to reproduce with meticulous fidelity the 's' which has henceforth to be a 't' ... Something similar in the days of the increase of the Ashkenazi Jews in England with the simultaneous decline of the Sephardim, which was accompanied by rivalry and a certain amount of bitterness, may have led to a lisp by way of mimicry ... Perhaps some enterprising Jewish comedian of the day, accentuating the peculiarity, stumbled on a novelty which secured a laugh and set a fashion. And Dickens ... taking his knowledge of Jews from the stage, adopted it as a literary style which subsequently became naturalized and stabilized.[19]

As Landa hints, perhaps the lisp has even earlier precedents. According to John Gross, the role of Shylock was played at Covent Garden in 1817 by a Jewish actor, a Mr Sherenbeck of Rochester, who used a lisp which had already become a regular feature of Jewish dialect on the stage.[20] The lisp or Yiddish accent, as a useful marker of the negative stereotype, persists throughout the twentieth century.[21]

The Exception – A Favourable View

Although in the fiction of this period the Jew appears most often as evil or despicable, there are a few exceptions which prefigure the ambivalent or positive images prevalent in fiction from the 1920s onwards. In Colin Fraser's *Saartje* (n.d.),[22] a Gentile character who sells diamonds is quoted:

> Yes, he believed the buyer was a Jew – they mostly were. He was quite satisfied with the price given. He had had

no trouble with Jews at any time ... [H]e agreed that a good deal of rot was talked about these Jewish buyers. He was well aware that at Lichtenburg at all events, the digger was an improvident fellow and when he found himself hard up, in spite of good 'finds,' he blamed the Jew. On the diggings, at any rate, they had done good service, and deserved every penny they made. They were the sutlers of the digger's army, and very good sutlers too. Before they went there, the life of the digger was hard ... Now for a few shillings, the digger could obtain a meal either in the middle of the day or at night ... yet the cry arose every now and then – "the digger does the work, and the Jew makes the money." (pp.71-72)

This is one of very few examples of a tentatively favourable view of the Jew, but the lack of characterisation and the banality of the observations underscore the theory that the characteristic stereotype is formed not by the tame and acceptable, but by the eccentric and outrageous figures. Noticeable, however, is the shadow of the popular negative perception and anti-Semitic discourse in references to 'trouble' and 'blame', and the quoted saying – 'the digger does the work, and the Jew makes the money'.

Early examples of negative images in the work of writers of Jewish descent

Isaac Israels (1860-1907), born in London, who travelled in New Zealand and South Africa, was a theatre impresario who adopted the name, 'William Luscombe Searelle'. Israels was probably of Jewish origin, but it would seem that he was keen to obscure this fact. He wrote a fictional account of the early Transvaal, *Tales of the Transvaal*, published in 1896. One of the characters is Ikey Schlenterpollock, a swindling Jew with a Yiddish accent. The name is Yiddish for 'dishonest Pole'. Described as being six foot tall, he may be based on Ikey Sonnenberg, a tall Jew well known in the Transvaal at this time. Schlenterpollock verneuks a Boer out of a farm and sells him a fake gold watch.[23] This linkage of swindling and a gold watch would be taken up by other writers in the following century, notably Olive Schreiner and Francis Brett Young.

Julia Frankau, an English woman of Jewish descent, wrote a novel, *Pigs in Clover* (1903), under the pseudonym Frank Danby. One of the chief characters is Karl Althaus who had made money on the gold and diamond fields. The narrator claims that he 'swindled natives, bamboozled Dutchmen' (p.106). While Karl is benevolent and not always unsympathetic – the stereotypical deprived background in Whitechapel is sketched – the author has recourse to a number of negative stereotypes. Karl's mother is a 'fat and perspiring widow' (p.99) with 'coarse hands' (p.100). She is duped by a shabby and contemptible Polish Jew who, besides being an 'insatiable *schnorrer* (advantage taker)', 'wheedl[es] and whin[es]' and is 'greasy' (p.100).

The narrator provides a lengthy analysis of Karl's attitude towards Jews and Judaism which is a jumble of contradictions. Karl admires Jews: 'Give me a Jew rather than a Christian any day in the week; he's got more guts in him ... I'd like to keep every custom and habit and ceremony he's got ...' (p.97), he says, but he deplores Judaism. He tells a Christian woman: 'Ah! you've got a religion, we've only got a tradition, an obstinacy, and even that our priests tell us of in Hebrew ... a dead tongue, dead as the religion they don't preach' (p.96). Karl dismisses Judaism as '[a]n empty thing of ceremonies, without the great Sacrifice, or the lesson of Love, without the Cross, and without the Crown, and no Christ to intervene for sinners ...' (p.96). His confidant exclaims: 'Why!, you are not a Jew at all' (p.97). This is another depiction of the assimilationist Jew, and may represent Frankau's own attitude towards Judaism, as may be inferred from the assumption of a Gentile-sounding pseudonym.

Possibly the most interesting of the early texts are those written by Louis Cohen (1854-1945),[24] in which the negative stereotype features strongly. Cohen, who was half Jewish, was born in Liverpool, emigrated to Kimberley from London with his cousin, Barney Barnato, and started out with him as a small-time diamond buyer. A prolific writer and journalist, he was enormously popular in his time. During the 1870s he contributed sketches to the *Dutoitspan Herald* under the pen-name 'Majude', the term for a Jew used by blacks, which attests his consciousness of his Jewish heritage. These sketches were reprinted as a collection, *Gay Young Creatures*, in 1880.[25]

In 1913 he published a scurrilous volume of sketches, *Shloma Levy and other Vagaries*. The sketches in this volume were reprints of articles that had appeared in the London financial paper, *The Rialto*. In the familiar colonial mixture of Cockney and Yiddish, Shloma Levy writes from the diamond fields:

> My dear Becky, – By my health and yours, I curse my luck for bringin' me into this medina (country), and von't I say my prayers vhen I turn my back on it! Upon my word, there is some grand Yiddisher shwells here who talk nonsense and put on a lot of guiver, but, by the sponge the Rabbi cleans himself with, you may believe me, they are the greatest shlenterers I ever see. Ven they make a few shtiebers (coins) they vant to be goyim (Gentiles) and run after the shiksas (young Gentile women) in the drinkin' places ... You remember fat Shloma Levy – curse him! – who came with me to this medina? By yours and mine, if he ain't turned out a regular bad 'un, and after me a-holdin' his son Solomon at his brismelah (circumcision), too, and being thanked as a mark of respec' by Mr. Moses, who mohelled (circumcised) him. Vell, ven I ran away from Ventworth Street with Mutchey Levy's goods, I vanted to do business with the posh here, but I had no mozzle (luck), and Shloma kidded me to go in for gonivas, vich I tried at once, though I vas a greener at the graft and knew as much of dimints as the Rov does of ruaching (probably – fornicating). So I commenced the dimint trade vith twenty pound, a ring of wurst (sausage), an afkowman (contraband) ... and fifty shlenter quids – to say nothing of the chasan's (cantor's) bettin' book, vich I gonophed (stole) from him ven the old rosher (important person) vas a-starin' the first day of Pasach (Passover) at the ladies in the gallery as if he could eat them, and vich I keep for mozzle and barocha (blessing). Vell, s'elp me, the first night I opened for bizness in my place, ... a black man vith a stupid face bought me a dimint the colour of the wart on the Shocket's (ritual slaughterer)

nose ... I bought it a bargain, payin' the nigger vith the shlenter quids. I vished him good luck ven he took his hook, and after a-prayin' and a-eatin' a basin of fremsil (lentil) soup, vich you couldn't get better in your mother's house, I vent to Shloma Levy's and sold him the dimint for forty pounds, the momzir (bastard or fool) payin' me in bank-notes. (pp.15-16)

The conflation of three separate discourses in Shloma Levy's speech is striking. The traditional or ceremonial is elided with that of criminality, especially IDB. As well, words of a Hebrew origin, not native to Yiddish but part of religious discourse, are used in a debased sense. 'Ruaching', for example, which derives from 'ruach' meaning 'spirit', is here transformed into a disparagement. Slang for 'fornicating', it suggests that the rabbi knows nothing of spirituality. Similarly, the word 'afikoman' refers to the piece of matzah hidden during the Passover Seder. The slang usage with its slippage towards a suggestion of criminal contraband is purposeful. Praying, eating and trickery are deliberately juxtaposed for satiric impact.

There are, as well, other satirical references – the chasan 'a-starin' at the ladies as if he could eat them' reflects a deliberate irreverence, as does the mention of the sponge the Rabbi uses for washing himself and the wart on the Schocket's nose. There is a seemingly fortuitous allusion to circumcision, which is a deliberate derogation of a practice known to evoke an anti-Semitic response in many Gentiles. Satiric allusion is made to the 'trope of conversion of the Jew' – possibly better regarded as a 'trope of assimilation' – in a further reference to Jews who 'vant to be goyim and run after the shiksas'.

In this collection of stories, all the markers of the anti-Jewish stereotype are guyed, those of appearance being supplied by the many satirical illustrations, in the manner of *Punch*, of Jews of ugly appearance, with long, hooked noses. The style and racy dialogue of these sketches is reminiscent of theatrical burlesque, and it is no coincidence that Cohen himself once unsuccessfully tried to run a theatre in Kimberley. It would seem that the construction of the Jewish stereotype in South African English fiction owes as much to the example of the Jew on the British stage as to contemporary British fiction. Although he appears to be writing comedy, in so doing Cohen belittles and degrades sacred aspects of Judaism, and refers to all the well worn clichés of the diamond fields. Since Cohen was himself half Jewish, he would seem to evince a fair measure of self-mockery.

The three writers, Searelle, Danby, and Cohen, were themselves those very assimilationist Jews who feature prominently in the fiction of the Gentile writers. It has already been noted that, particularly among English Jews, there has always been a strong movement towards assimilation. The need to dissociate from what was regarded as the stigma of Judaism is an aspect of a Jewish identity problem, documented during the twentieth century as 'Jewish self-hatred'. This phrase, which should not be confused with Jewish self-criticism, was popularised by Theodor Lessing, a Jewish convert to Protestantism, in an attempt to isolate certain qualities which he perceived in himself. 'Jewish self-hatred' – or Jewish anti-Semitism – continues to be reflected in South African fiction up to the present day.[26]

— 3 —

AMBIVALENT IMAGES

As early as the first half of the nineteenth century Jewish smouses were to be found travelling by foot or on mule carts, trading among the *trek boere* (nomadic farmers) and the local people, both black and white, in the Cape Colony.[1] Some of these smouse later set up trading stores and even became prosperous.[2] In the aftermath of the Nazi-inspired anti-Semitism of the 1930s and 1940s, South African Jewish historiography, seeking to stress the Jewish contribution to the South African economy, has propagated a glorified mythology of the good relationship between the Jewish smous, or country storekeeper, and the mainly Afrikaans farming community. A number of contributors to Saron and Hotz's important study, *The Jews in South Africa*, often basing their evidence on oral sources, point out that Jews were respected by the pious Afrikaners as the 'People of the Book'. The farmers in isolated districts, they argue, appreciated the usefulness of the smous, whose wanderings put him in touch with the rest of the colony and beyond.[3] The linguistic affinity between Afrikaans and Yiddish also made relationships easy.[4]

However, more recent research by Gideon Shimoni, Riva Krut and Milton Shain shows that the Afrikaners had varying perceptions of these pioneer traders, and were often ambivalent or even hostile towards them. In his latest study, Shain has amply demonstrated that long before the outbreak of Nazi-type organised anti-Semitism, there was considerable anti-Jewish feeling circulating in the country. He refers to a number of sources such as newspaper articles and confidential reports of government inspectors of the 1880s and later, that indicate that the Jewish smous and shopkeeper were increasingly widely perceived as being dishonest, cunning and exploitative. Hostility extended to many of the Jews involved in the ostrich feather industry in the Oudtshoorn district.

Shain suggests that in times of stress and anxiety, Jews in the hinterland became symbols of foreign intervention and change. They were readily available as scapegoats and became potent images of the feared and hated Other. Hence arose the stereotype of the 'blood-sucking' *Boereverneuker* (swindler of farmers), living by his wits, and at all costs bent on making money out of the gullible Gentile.[5] Shain quotes the typical view of a nineteenth century Englishman, Martin J. Boon, who complained: '... under the sneaking "ferneuking" Jew, German and Hollander [the Dutch] are in the hands of Shylocks, and ... in having their pound of flesh, they lose their farms and ... the Hebrews are their masters.[6]

In the *Cape Punch* of 1888, the Jewish smous is satirised: 'A Jew or "Boereverneaker" may always be known to a farmer by the shape of his nose, by the many rings on his fingers, and by the tongue being too large for his mouth. Avoid such. The Bible says they are a stiff-necked and perverse generation ...'[7] While all these are the perceptions of Englishmen, similar sentiments can be found expressed in contemporary Afrikaans newspapers and reports.[8] The allusion to Shylock and the stereotypical reference to physical features cast doubt on the notion that the Jews were universally regarded with pious admiration as the 'People of the Book'.

The smous, the itinerant trader with a pack on his back, wandering across the landscape of a country foreign to him, is obviously an avatar of the Wandering Jew, an ambivalent Jewish stereotype. Indeed, the fiction of this time is frequently ambivalent concerning Jews. When Jews appear in fiction, either two Jewish characters – one bad and one good – are juxtaposed or the writer may construct a Jewish character, ostensibly good, in which remnants of the evil prototype and negative attitude can be uncovered; or one Jewish figure may exhibit both bad and good characteristics simultaneously.[9]

Gentile Writers

W.C. Scully

W.C. Scully (1855-1943), an Irishman who emigrated to South Africa as a child in 1867, was an unlucky prospector in the early days of the diamond diggings at Kimberley and the gold finds at Barberton in the eastern Transvaal. He was then employed in the colonial service in several Karoo towns, and on the northern border near Bushmanland. He wrote a number of novels and short stories with a South African setting. Contemporary critics likened Scully to his exact contemporary, Olive Schreiner, drawing attention to the fact that both believed themselves to be realists who recorded the colonial situation as they experienced it.

Scully's novel of the Bushmanland desert, *Between Sun and Sand*, was written in 1894 and published in 1898, during the peak period of Jewish emigration from eastern Europe. The text provides an example of the typically South African tension between the colonial writer-as-novelist and writer-as-historian. The main characters are two brothers – Nathan and Max Steinmetz – shopkeepers in an Afrikaner community, born in Whitechapel of German-Jewish parentage. Nathan, the elder, who had previously been a smous, deals illegally in ostrich feathers, and becomes involved in an intrigue concerning diamonds. As has been suggested, by the mid-1890s Jewish involvement in all these occupations carried negative connotations. In casting Nathan as the villain, Scully's text makes crudely exuberant use of all the already well-established negative markers of Jews, from occupation to physical appearance:

> Nathan was ... a low-sized, knock-kneed man of fair complexion which burnt to a fiery red on the least exposure. His features were of the lowest Hebrew type – his lips were full and shapeless, his nose large and prominent, ... money was the only god worth worshipping ... [He] sneered at every impulse or aspiration that did not have gain for its object. (pp.119-120)

Nathan is a full-blown anti-Jewish stereotype, large-nosed, ugly and avaricious, no different from the Jewish villains who people the pulp fiction centred on the diamond fields. His complexion is atypically portrayed as 'fair', but this is necessary to ensure that his subsequent painful death from sunstroke and thirst in the desert is plausible. The phrase, 'the lowest Hebrew *type*' (emphasis added), betrays the author's unabashed acceptance and uncritical use of stereotyping.

A bold and unusual choice for a colonial writer, the hero of this tale is a 'Hottentot' who is befriended by a young Jew, Max, brother of the villainous Nathan. As in some diamond field fiction, the supposed despicability of Jews is underscored by this connection with a black man. Scully's ambivalent treatment of the Jew is apparent in the portrait of Max. At a first glance this might appear to be flattering, but stereotypical suggestions of avarice and decadence are encoded in the text:

> Max had a face, which, had Raphael seen it through the bars of the Ghetto gate at Rome, would have made him take pains to secure the young Jew as a model. It was one of those faces which one only – and that but very rarely – sees in the youth of Israel. Its shape was a pure oval. The skin was a clear olive, and the eyes were large, dark, and melting. His jet-black hair clustered over a broad, low forehead, and his full, red lips were arched like the bow of the Sun-God. As yet the stress of trade had not awakened the ancestral greed which would one day dominate his blood and modify his physiognomy. Small in stature and of perfect symmetry, he did not give one the idea of possessing either strength or activity; in fact he looked like a languorous human exotic who had strayed from the canvas of some 'Old Master' whose brush was dedicated to physical beauty. (pp.28-29)

The physical stigmata are all present, coupled with the overt attention to exoticism, which harks back to popular earlier images. Max's hypnotic good looks, far from being a favourable characteristic, can thus be read as connoting latent power and even evil. Scully's description of 'the ancestral greed which would ... modify his physiognomy' strongly suggests that – following the example of anti-Semitic novelists

– he makes the correlation between appearance and morals. Later, the narrator again pointedly links his interest in money to his Jewishness: 'Max was rapidly developing from a boy into a man, and many of the little traits specially characteristic of modern Israel began to show themselves in him' (p.111). As he ages he 'develops a keenness and aptitude for business' (p.227). This is left merely as a hint of disapprobation.

The most telling touch, however, that betrays Scully's anti-Jewish feeling is the fact that Max's Jewishness is never acceptable to the author, to the other characters, or even to Max himself. Although Max is finally rewarded with the hand of a Christian girl, she is of suspect ancestry, possibly even Jewish herself – 'her features had a strongly Jewish cast' (pp.239-240) – suggesting the ultimate alienation of the Jew, fit only to mate with his own kind. Old Schalk, uncle of the prospective bride, is outraged at the idea of his niece marrying a Jew:

"You promised to marry *him* – a Jew – one of those who denied the Lord Jesus and crucified Him?"

"I am sure Max did not do that; for one thing, he was not born at the time."

"Don't tell me! If he did not do it himself his forefathers did and the Lord laid a curse on the Jews." (p.57)

"Another thing I should like to know," said Old Schalk; "that is, why they eat children in the synagogue?"

It was strange to hear the echo of one of the lying cries of the Judenhetze in this remote corner of the African Desert ...

"Yes; they are a wicked lot in their religion," continued Old Schalk. "Fancy a religion that forbids one to eat pork and teaches you to eat children – not their own children, oh no, but Christian children that they steal in the streets of the towns, and then fatten up for the Passover!"

"But uncle, I don't think they do so any more," said Susannah ... "It was long ago that they used to do that."

"What does a girl like you know about such things? Did we not read about it in the book which Uncle Sarel lent to us, and didn't Jan Roster say it was quite true, and that they caught the Jews doing it in Russia the other day?" (p.63)

Directed both against the gullible Susannah and her bigoted uncle, the irony would superficially seem to attest to Scully's rejection of the excesses of Judenhetze (Jew-hatred), as the narrator condemns the ritual murder myth as 'lying'. However, closer examination of the text suggests that the author, as a typical Victorian colonial, at least in part accepts and endorses all these accusations which remain potent subtextually. Although Susannah feebly protests that the practice of murdering children may well have occurred in the past, neither the characters nor the narrator are made to suggest in any convincing manner that the accusations are anything other than outdated. This allows Old Schalk to end the discussion by asserting that the story was heard 'the other day'.

Given the intensely anti-Jewish feeling prevalent at the time the novel was written and published, some specific authorial refutation would have been required to counter its inherently anti-Jewish impact. On the contrary, however, Schalk's reiterations – the phrase 'eat children' and its echo in the word 'children' occurs four times in the quoted text – serve to reinforce in Scully's readers many of the popular negative preconceptions about Jews. Further evidence of Scully's attitude is found in the way in which the author causes Max to react to these imputations with deep shame, and to seek to escape from them in an urgent desire to be baptised:

> Max had not the slightest objection ... He had left his people when but a child, and had thus never acquired that pride of race which so distinguishes the average Jew, and which often causes him to cleave passionately to the observances of that religion which still keeps Israel a separate people, even after all faith in dogma may have perished ... Max had come into contact with no Jews except Nathan and others of his class. These had earned the young man's unmitigated contempt. As to Christianity – he looked upon its profession as a mere matter of convenience. (p.229)

The contempt Max felt for Nathan 'and others of his class' would seem to be primarily a class contempt, which the narrator projects on to the evil Jewish character. Max's disdain for the religion of his birth is similar to that of the assimilationist Jews of diamond field fiction. Like them, he desires to escape the class to which the label of the Jew assigns them. But, significantly, Max escapes the author's outright condemnation, since he has been separated from 'his people' when a child, has distanced himself from his 'race' and has not acquired what the narrator contemptuously refers to as a 'pride of race'. Thus, although Scully usually invokes the discourse of race in order to categorise the Jew, here he blurs racial characteristics with those of class.

Further, the text suggests the Jewish character's profound cynicism regarding religion, by which the author nullifies any spiritual advantages that might be gained through baptism. In spite of baptism, as Nathan had earlier expressed it, the Jew remains a Jew: ' "What has God got to do with it? A Jew is a Jew, God or no God, and a Christian is of no use except to make money out of" ' (p.121).

Nathan is clearly a villain, and his Jewishness sets him up perfectly to play the role – he has revealed his 'Jewish' avarice, the mainspring of his actions, by stealing the 'Hottentot''s diamonds. His eyes are 'small and colourless, but exceedingly bright and glittering' (p.120), prefiguring his lust for diamonds.

While Max is protective of and sympathetic towards the 'Hottentot', and is the first instance in South African fiction of the caring Jew, the kaffirboetie, he is, as has been suggested, by no means free of the taint of 'Jewish' evil.

The Jewishness of both brothers is destroyed: for the one by death, for the other by conversion to Christianity. Although conversion is the culturally established means by which the Jew is allowed to enter the Christian community, Scully implies that Jewish characteristics can never be fully mitigated by conversion.

In *The Harrow (South Africa 1900-1902): A Novel*, published in 1921 but written between 1904 and 1907, Scully once again sets himself up as historiographer. Scurrilous and flagrantly pro-Boer, the novel was planned as an exposé of alleged injustices in the country before and after the Anglo-Boer War. He constructs an imaginary town in the Cape, 'Jagersdorp', which is a paradise until taken over by powerful Jews in the

1870s. Once more his feelings about 'Jewish' evil are exposed. When war breaks out, the local Jews, either involved in commerce or agents of the British – particularly Aaronson, Hisch, Anton Schnekenbohrer and Julius Rosenbaum – passionately side with the British. They stir up trouble between the loyalist (pro-British) Boers and the British. Jewish spies for the loyalist side are 'hawk-nosed men with Yiddish accents' (p.22). These *agents provocateurs* are 'mainly ... Jews of the lowest class – bookmakers whose occupation was for the time being gone, itinerant hawkers and peddlers whose itinerary the war had interrupted. In fact, all the local parasitic dross of Israel that battens wherever gold abounds ... ' (p.22).[10] Animus against the Jews here is partly racial – hence the sneers about appearance and accent – but also mainly on account of their jingoistic propensities and opposition to the Boers.

Olive Schreiner

Scully's more famous contemporary, Olive Schreiner (1855-1920), is celebrated as a feminist and liberal, and is identified with support for the cause of the weak and exploited. Yet, as a woman of her times, her ideas on the Jew were confused. She shows evidence, in both her fiction and her non-fiction, of indulging in stereotypical thinking. An important character in her last novel, *From Man to Man*, published posthumously in 1926 but written between 1873 and 1884, is designated merely as 'the Jew'.[11] This anonymity suggests a type rather than a fully rounded character, and signals the presence of a mythos. 'The Jew' is the chief agent of the downfall of Bertie, the pretty but weak sister of the central character, Rebekah. As an itinerant money-lender and diamond speculator, 'the Jew' demonstrates the specific South African configuration of the negative stereotype. True to type, his sensuous love of riches is the keynote of his character:

> the Jew ... lit the candle and took from under his pillow the parcel of stones. Carefully he opened it and, examining the stones, selected the one which Bertie had touched that evening. He held it in the palm of his hand, looking at it by the candle light. Softly he touched it with the forefinger of the other hand, caressing its soft, soapy

surface as a mother might the hair of a child with which she was to part. (p.334)

Closely recalling Fagin,[12] the genealogy of Schreiner's Jew is similar both to that of Scully's characters and those of the fiction of IDB. The German origin and sojourn in London are typical. Schreiner's character, however, merely visits and trades in the Cape Colony; his base is in London. He projects a stronger sense of mystery and alienation than do Scully's characters, and like the Jewish IDBs in diamond field fiction, functions more strongly as a representation of the Other. The portrait owes something to the actual presence of single Jewish men travelling to and from the fields as diamond buyers. While he is an incarnation of the Wandering Jew, his portrait contains many of the markers of the negative stereotype:

> He was a small man of about fifty, with slightly bent shoulders and thin, small limbs. His face was of a dull oriental pallor, and his piercing dark eyes and marked nose proclaimed him at once a Jew ... He spoke with a strong foreign accent. (p.328) "All ze drawers, ze wardrobes are your sings in; ven you vant zomezing you vill open zem! ... I vill tell ze woman zat she bring your supper soon ..." [he tells Bertie] ... He put on a short black jacket, greasy and shiny ... (pp.350-351)

The 'piercing' eyes and orientalism are aspects of the exotic, and the nose, accent and dark complexion are of the standard evil type; he even wears Fagin's 'greasy' jacket. Having lured Bertie to London, he sets her up as his mistress and keeps her prisoner in his opulent mansion.

Schreiner's portrayal of the Svengali situation – a relationship between a manipulative besotted Jew and a beautiful powerless Gentile woman – predates the publication of Du Maurier's *Trilby* by more than ten years, suggesting that both she and Du Maurier draw on mythological sources. In Schreiner's text the myth-base is complex. It is another example of the figure of the wealthy Jewish diamond dealer who, having made good on the fields, buys a house in Park Lane. When he suspects, incorrectly, that a relationship has developed between Bertie and his half-Jewish cousin, 'the Jew' casts her into the streets to become that archetypal Victorian fallen woman, the prostitute.[13] The description of 'the Jew''s house with its chandeliers and velvet curtains, has overtones not only of Victorian melodrama, but of fairy tale – 'the Jew' playing the 'Beast' to Bertie's 'Beauty'.

Schreiner's portrait of 'the Jew' – like that of many Wandering Jews – is not entirely negative. Discussing the plot in a letter to Karl Pearson, she implied that the villainy of the Jew was by no means her main focus.[14] In fact Bertie, seeking escape from scandal, is not unwilling to leave South Africa with 'the Jew'. Further, Schreiner adds certain touches to her portrait in order to suggest that, despite his covetousness and final ruthlessness, 'the Jew' is somewhat tender-hearted, and his background has been one of deprivation:

> Far away, across the mist of fifty years, he saw again a little garret room under the eaves in a North German city, where a small dark-eyed boy and girl played together when their parents had gone out to their work and had locked them in … and then it was later and a boy of seventeen and a girl of sixteen whose parents had died in Germany were living alone in London in an East End garret … the boy raised his cry "Old clothes! Old clothes!" and raised his eyes anxiously to the grim rows of houses to see if from door or window came an answering beck or nod … (pp.331-332)

Again Schreiner alludes to fairy-tale, since a prototype for this passage may be found in some of the tales of Hans Andersen or the brothers Grimm. Here, the fairy-tale aspect is fused with images from the cartoons of *Punch* in which the Jew was so frequently portrayed as the old clothes man. The multiplicity of sources, illustrated by 'the Jew''s inconsistent behaviour and phoney accent, results in a totally unrealistic portrait.

A further ambiguity can be traced in Schreiner's construction of a second Jewish character, Isaac, the shuffling, long-nosed servant of 'the Jew', who has compassion for Bertie and, when she has been cast into the street by his angry and jealous master, offers her all his savings. But since this truly unselfish character is a simpleton, it would seem that Schreiner suggests that unselfishness can only flourish and avarice be neutralised when 'Jewish' intelligence is damaged.

Other texts also demonstrate Schreiner's ambivalent attitude. During the 1870s she wrote a novel, *Undine*, partially based on the circumstances of her life, published only in 1929. Jews, particularly smouse, are for the most part shown unfavourably. Using the derogatory animal reference, she describes them as 'little snivelling weasel-like creatures who come out third class and, as soon as they land, supply themselves with a wagon and a couple of mules and become "smouses", hawking false jewellery and damaged clothing among the Dutch farmers and growing rich on it'(p.152).

In order to symbolise contemporary capitalists, she refers in an essay in *Thoughts on South Africa* (1923), posthumously published but written between 1890 and 1892, to the dishonest smous who sells a glittering but defective clock:

> *Remember the Jew smous's clock!* There may be Jew smouses going up and down in this civilization of ours; and they deal in other things besides clocks. They will traffic with you for your land, your freedom, your independence, your very souls – for they hold that '*every man has his price!*' – and they will give you in exchange that which will not wear – a gilt-lined robe, which, soon as you wear it, will eat the flesh of freedom from off your bones ...[15]

However, in the same text the better class of Jewish immigrant is portrayed ambivalently. They are

> gentleman Jews, with their polite foreign manners and their fascinating foreign English, who will make you swear round is square and sell you to the devil before your face, and you shall never know it, who will squeeze you to a pulp to get your last shilling today, and to-morrow, when your wife is starving and no Christian will help her will give her ten. (pp.152-153)

This should be read together with a strange passage from a letter written in October 1898: 'The people at this boarding house seem nice and pleasant, especially a little Jew man and his young Jew wife. It's funny I always like Jews! I seem always to see their best side, under an often repulsive surface'.[16] Here Schreiner seems aware of her contradictory attitudes. She has internalised the stereotypical view of Jewish appearance, and takes for granted a Jewish propensity towards avarice; and yet the Yiddish or German accent is referred to as 'fascinating', and she emphasises Jewish generosity.

She displays her ambivalence once again in further passage from *Thoughts on South Africa*. Attempting to rebut the arguments of those who alleged that Jews possessed the quality of instinctive greed, she wrote that if the Jew were released from the constraints of a limited occupational choice, 'though his descendants would undoubtedly inherit his nose they would probably show no inherent tendency to lend money at sixty percent'.[17] Her intention may be to counter anti-Semitism, but her tone is ambivalent, and she again alludes to two of the shibboleths of anti-Semitic discourse – the Jewish nose and usury.

Some years later, although her liberal sentiments dictated what would appear to be a strong defence of the Jew, this endemic ambivalence is still obvious. 'A Letter On the Jew' was written in 1906 in response to anti-Alien agitation.[18] It purports to be an impassioned championship of Jews – Schreiner writes of 'the great Jewish race' – and takes a high moral tone against anti-Jewish discrimination:

> Since first I gave any thought to impersonal matters it has always been to me a subject of astonishment and pain – and yet most of astonishment – to observe the manner in which the so-called civilised nations of Europe have regarded, and in some cases still do regard, the members of the great Jewish race ... And I am yet more astonished when I am told that the Jew should be kept out because he has nothing today to offer the world but unholy financial methods, and that he is incapable of any other aim than making wealth for himself. (pp.6-8)

Yet this very 'crime' of typing the Jew as an 'unholy' financier, to which she objects, is integral to her own fictional and non-fictional treatment of Jews. The 'financial' Jew is a stereotype which she unwittingly propagates. In her Letter she writes: 'For ages the Jew ... was driven to finance and dealing in money as the one path open to him ... Today the Jew excels in finance' (p.8). Her fictional construction of 'the Jew' in *From Man to Man* is itself based on this very premise.

Later in the Letter she even alludes to physical aspects, mentioning that the Russian Jewish immigrant to South Africa appears 'broken, crushed and dwarfed' (p.10). 'I felt,' she wrote, 'that these people needed but a little space, a little chance, to develop into some far higher form' (p.10). This is revealing of an elitist and ingrained belief that the Jews are a 'lesser form' of human being, an attitude which was fast becoming prevalent in the eugenicist type of anti-Semitism developing in Europe. There is further evidence of stereotyping in the reference to so-called good Jews and 'Jewish' virtues – idealism, belief in social and political reform and association with culture – which will become commonplace in the work of philo-Semitic writers.

Edgar Rosenberg warns us that in considering ambivalent images of Jews the reader should be on guard against believing that every manifestation of good feeling towards Jews should be treated with scepticism.[19] But while Schreiner's attitude, both in her novel and her prose, may show evidence of an attempt to transcend a negative image of the Jew, it is undeniably patronising and marked by stereotypical thinking.

Pauline Smith

Pauline Smith (1883-1959) in her collection of stories, *The Little Karoo* (1925), and her novel, *The Beadle* (1926), treats as vignettes the smous, the shopkeeper and the merchant who also acts as auctioneer. Smith was the daughter of an English doctor practising in the Oudtshoorn district and, as a child she accompanied her father on his calls to outlying districts in the course of his work among the Afrikaners. She left South Africa for England at the age of thirteen, but in 1905 and 1913-1914 made two important journeys back to the Cape, and kept a diary of her impressions. She used her childhood recollections and her diary extensively as source material for her fiction. Of her own creative processes she wrote: 'In my work I could set down nothing which I did not "see", or, often painfully, feel and know to be true'.[20] Thus, although fictionalised, her constructions of the Little Karoo and its inhabitants, mainly the Afrikaner farmers and the poor white *bywoners*, owe much to memory and perception.

In *The Beadle* there is a brief reference to a young Jew, Elijah, who with his grandmother, is an immigrant, escaping the pogroms of Russia:

> It was to Zandtbaai – a little port which lay half-way between Cape Town and Port Elizabeth – that their wanderings had first brought the old Jewess and her grandson in South Africa, and from there, by way of Princestown, the young man had tramped one summer down the Aangenaam valley with a pack of patent medicines for men and beasts on his back. In the valley he had done good business and, coming again some months later in a dilapidated buggy drawn by two ancient mules, he had brought with him a little box of cheap jewellery, some rolls of coloured print, reels of cotton, tapes, buttons, gaily coloured handkerchiefs, as well as those patent medicines upon which his fortune was founded. (pp.13-14)

Smith's fictional account of a typical Jewish smous is written in a tone of sympathetic admiration. The dogged 'tramping' beside the 'dilapidated buggy' and 'ancient mules' stress Elijah's struggle and diligence in seeking to make a living for himself and caring for his grandmother. In this light his upward mobility is a positive attribute:

> his business had steadily increased and finally, hiring a bit of ground from Mijnheer van der Merwe at Harmonie, he had built for himself and his grandmother the little 'winkel' in which they now lived. Here they sold prints and calicoes, bags of coffee beans, rice, sugar, salt, spades and buckets, cooking pots, kettles, gridirons, combs and mouth-organs, sweets, snuff, and many patent medicines ... At the end of the previous

month of July young Shokolowsky had bought part of the bankrupt stock of a Platkops store-keeper, and the little shop at Harmonie was now overflowing with such an assortment of goods as had never before been seen in the Aangenaam valley. With these the young man expected to do much trade at the coming Sacrament, but already their fame had spread abroad ... (*The Beadle*, pp.14-15)

It is instructive to compare this with a non-fictional description of a smous. In 1904 'A Farmer Pure and Simple' wrote to the editor of the *Cape Times* complaining that

[smouses] obtain at the start of their career a small credit from certain merchants, mostly without any reference, upon which they stalk the country with a bundle on their back, soliciting custom in a very humble way from the poorer farmer on their beats, and as they never pay for food or shelter, and sell inferior articles at enhanced prices, the very fair profit they make is clear gain which is immediately invested in a donkey ... Up to this stage there is not much harm done, but now the man becomes dangerous. He soon sets up a permanent shop at or near some of the farms he has been frequenting in a humble capacity and now begins the steady plotting and planning for the expropriation of his poorer Dutch neighbours and customers ... His prey at first consists of the poor Bijwoner who owns a few sheep, ostriches or cattle, from which a very precarious income is derived. This man is inveigled into buying and purchasing far above his intimate income by the insidious and ingratiating manner the Jew knows so well how to adopt.[21]

The difference in tone between Smith's description and that of the pseudonymous 'Farmer' is encapsulated in a comparison between Smith's word 'tramp' and the hostile 'Farmer''s choice of the predatory 'stalk'. Smith idealises and sentimentalises the smous's enterprise. According to the 'Farmer', it should more correctly be regarded as a 'dangerous' example of Jewish cunning, avarice, and exploitation of the 'poor Bijwoner'.

In a story from *The Little Karoo*, 'Anna's Marriage', Smith describes a Jewish trader:

> Philip brought one day to Brandtwacht a strange young man who was a Jew. Philip said the Jew was his friend, and that Anna must take him over the house and show him the furniture ... She did not know it ... but Philip was now a bankrupt and the Jew had come to make a list of all the things that must be sold to pay his debts ... on the way to Piet Grobelaar's he met again the strange young man who was a Jew. As they stood talking together in the road brother Ludovic rode by on his horse, and the Jew, who seemed angry about something with Philip, called Ludovic to stop ... And the Jew asked him if he were going to old Piet Grobelaar's for the Brandtwacht sale ... Ludovic asked the Jew to stop the sale until he could fetch our brothers from their farms and together they would see what could be done to save the Brandtwacht lands. The Jew promised ...
> (pp.60-61)

This Jew is an extension of Elijah Shokolowsy in a later and more prosperous manifestation, when he has accumulated some capital and makes a living by buying up bankrupt stock and reselling it at a profit.

A comparison of the fictional account with the entries in Smith's diary from which it was quarried, reveals a striking resemblance between the fiction and the reported anecdote. The relevant passage from the diary attempts to duplicate speech patterns:

> And then there came the Jew man that was to have the sale and talk with Rex at the gate – and while they stand there my brother Gert ride past on his horse ... And Rex and the Jew they talked harder than ever, and the Jew got angry and call out to my brother who was already past them – And at first my brother Gert would not

turn, but afterwards he turn and ride back to them and the Jew ask him if he had heard about the sale ... And my brother Gert ask the Jew to stop the sale till he can see his other brothers ... and Stephan rode back to Rex and the Jew to tell them there will be some arrangement made by all the brothers and the sale must be stopped ... but Stephan he come to some arrangement with the Jew by himself, and he did not deal fair by my other brothers, he did buy most of the lands by himself ... and Stephan and Rex and the Jew went down to the toll house and stopped the sale ... (29 August 1913)[22]

Although the diary entry purports to be the transliteration of direct speech, it is a fiction itself, operating at one remove from direct reportage. The extent of the modification through Smith's selective recollection cannot be measured. The story, however, has emerged from the crucible of her imagination, and the changes made in this final stage result from a blend of the author's aesthetic considerations with her perceptions, attitudes and intentions. An immediately noticeable change in the fictional text is the repetition of the epithet, 'strange' applied to the Jew, which introduces an important exotic element not present in the diary version. Smith grafts on to the original text her own perception of the Jew as an alien, and reflects traditional thinking. She also projects what she understands as the Afrikaner people's perceptions of Jews, a subject which greatly interested her, as she remarks in her diary:

one notices very frequently among the [Afrikaners], the upper classes among these are so hopelessly suspicious of the English, more so of them, in a way, than they are of the Jews, and I can only think it is a result of the old grudge against the English for doing them out of their country. It is against the English *as a nation* that this suspicion works. The Jews are not a nation to them in the same way. A nation must possess a country, and the Jew without a country of his own is still so evidently labouring under the curse of the Almighty that he is not to be feared in quite the same way as the English. And then the Jew's cunning appeals too to the Boer, who is 'slim' in much the same way as the Jew himself, but not so successfully ... The Jew stands for them not on an equality, like the English, and so to be feared and hated, but is somewhere vaguely between the lowest of poor christian whites and those coloured races who ought still to be slaves ... I ought not to have run on like this ... but this subject always interests me, and it is only on paper that I can ever straighten out my thoughts about it. (25 April 1914)[23]

The Jew as outsider is illustrated and developed in Smith's fiction. As in all legends of the Wandering Jew – and Elijah Shokolowsky has been treated as an avatar of the Wandering Jew – there is a degree of sympathy. The Afrikaner attitudes that Smith reports show no respect for the Jews as 'People of the Book', but clearly judge them as 'labouring under the curse of the Almighty'. Although considered damned and of a lower caste than any white person, they are not feared.

Smith does not discuss the sort of fear of competition and exploitation expressed by 'A Farmer Pure and Simple'. What she does record is her understanding of the way in which the Afrikaner equates Jews not with the English but with the 'coloured races'. Thus, in Smith's understanding, the rural Jews, like those on the diamond fields, were similarly perceived as racial Others.

In returning to the comparison of the passage from 'Anna's Marriage' with the relevant passage from the diary, it appears that in both texts the Jew is 'angry', although it is not clear why he is angry. In the fictional text, the anger is more clearly directed against the prodigal and bankrupt Philip. The practice of Jews of buying up mortgages was widespread and generally deprecated – there were numerous references in the press to the way in which the Jewish smous and shopkeeper 'ruined' farmers in this way.[24] When it comes to a fictional representation of the Jew, however, Smith removes any suggestion of his connivance with the dubious brother, Stephan, and the Jew appears to act entirely fairly.

Smith has subtly altered her source material. As in the previous passage on Elijah, her imaginative mediation is sympathetic towards the Jew. By removing the shadow of culpability from the Jew, she has thrown the blame more unambiguously on the feckless Philip, thereby heightening the tragic outcome of the story. Philip's young wife dies of a broken heart as a result of his profligacy. This may suggest that while Smith was by no means unaware of the sharp practices of some Jews, as some entries in the diary make clear,[25] her attitude towards Jews is more balanced than that of the Afrikaner people who supply the material for her diary. The very subtle differences between the diary entries and the fictional depiction of Jews point to the sympathetic operation of her widely acknowledged compassionate imagination, her 'sense of pity', and tragic vision, which encompass the situation of the Jew and which are apparent in the entire thrust of her work.[26]

An old Jewish woman, grandmother of Elijah, appears in both the novel *The Beadle* and the short story 'The Miller', from *The Little Karoo*. She runs a small store in a Karoo village near Oudtshoorn:

> old Esther Shokolowsky, called simply, by reason of her faith, the Jew-woman, was a tragic and mysterious being who to the end of her days remained a stranger ... She was a small bent woman ... and in her faded grey eyes the only vital expression ever seen was one of terror. Terrible things had happened to her in her own country ... and from the memory of her sufferings even in old age she found no escape.
>
> It was to Zandtbaai – a little port which lay half-way between Cape Town and Port Elizabeth that their wanderings had first brought the old Jewess and her grandson in South Africa ... (*The Beadle* pp.13-14)

The Jew-woman is based on recollections of two Jewish storekeepers who lived in the Longkloof, recorded in Smith's diary of 1914:

> The Jewish woman herself came in looking a different creature. Last time her loneliness and misery made us feel quite wretched, for no woman *can* be so lonely and outcast as a Jewish woman is on a farm out here, I think, visited by no one and counting no one her neighbour

in any sense of the word. Since then a second Miss
Fleisman, not quite so awfully plain as the first, has
arrived, and the mother looks mentally and physically
very much stronger and more cheerful ... (20 April
1914)[27]

After tea Kathy and I went to the shop. It is kept by a
very talkative Jewish woman, her son, and an assistant.
Kathy cannot stand the woman and is so severe that she
'dries her up'. (21 April at Mill River)[28]

It is apparent that in constructing the fictional character the mysterious and tragic elements are heightened, partly in order to invoke
sympathy and also as a means of stressing the exotic. In addition,
her loneliness is emphasised and sentimentalised, in order to convey
the compassion which is Smith's main intention. This will be an
important aspect of the construction of the Jew-woman in her story
'The Miller', where the complexities are reflected through the
consciousness of the miller:

for the old Jewess herself Andries had a pity that was
not unmixed with fear. Terrible things had happened
to the Jew-woman in her own country before she had
escaped from it with her grandson Elijah. It was the
memory of these things that made her creep about her
house like a frightened animal. In no other human
being had Andries ever seen such fear as one saw
sometimes in the Jew-woman's eyes ... (pp.35-36)

Like the prototypes in the diary, the figure of the Jew-woman is
presented in an ambivalent way. The miller may pity her, but he
fears her as well. Although no foreign accent is ascribed to her and
none of the expected physical attributes of the traditional anti-Jewish
stereotype appear, she nevertheless represents the mysterious, fear-
invoking Other. On the other hand, the kindly respect accorded her
by Mevrouw, the farmer's wife stands in striking contrast to the
diary report of Kathy's reaction to the talkative Jewish woman. Once
again, it is apparent that in her imaginative constructs, Smith
habitually softened and sentimentalised the image of the Jew.

Andries ... remembered how, for the first Thanksgiving after she came to Harmonie, the Jew-woman,
old and bent and thin, cringing like a hunted animal,
with her thin grey hair tied up in a handkerchief, had
come to Mevrouw van der Merwe with a cake on a
blue-and-white plate ... the Jew-woman had said to
Mevrouw:
    'If it is not right for Mevrouw to take this cake that I
have made, to sell it at the Thanksgiving for the Lord,
let Mevrouw give it to her grandchildren, for it is a good
cake that I have made for a thank-offering for my
grandson and me.'
    And Mevrouw had answered: 'Is not your Lord also
my Lord?' (p.35)
    ... though [the Jew-woman] baked a cake for the
table, and came every year to look over the wall, [she]
remained always, by her faith, an outcast from the
gathering. (p.38)

Only the cake is accepted, not the Jew-woman herself, who remains
an outsider, an 'outcast' from the Afrikaans community. The way she
looks 'over the wall' symbolises her exclusion. However, this places
her in a strategically favourable position from which she is able to
assist and comfort the dying miller:

the miller turned, wild-eyed and suffering, to the old
Jewess for help. He tried to ask her to call Mintje to him,
but he could not speak. Nor could he hear what it was
that the Jew-woman, looking at him so strangely, said.
For some reason which he could not understand she
took him by the hand and began leading him away from
the wall, through the grove, towards her store ... [she]
drew him down on to a low mound ... and leaving him
there, ran, unbuttoning her apron as she went, down to
the stream. She dipped her apron into the clear running
water and brought it back to press, icy cold, against his
throat and chest. She took off her shawl and made a
pillow for his head. (pp.38-39)

Intuitively, she understands his longing to make amends to his wife. In order to summon the wife, she dares to penetrate the Church service, alien and hostile to her. The tragic and compassionate tone of this extract functions as part of the emotional matrix of the text. The Jew-woman's activities such as the washing of the miller's face – recalling in its cadences the biblical washing of feet – have quasi-religious overtones, and provide for her an aura of sanctity. Thus she figures emblematically as an image of saintliness and compassion, and can in part, be regarded with Isaac in Olive Schreiner's *From Man to Man*, and perhaps with Scully's Max Steinmetz, as one of the first examples in South African fiction of the good Jew. As will be shown, the compassionate aspects of this stereotype are frequently and paradoxically a function of the Jew's very condition of Otherness.

Smith's ambivalent sketches of Jews demonstrate the simultaneous presence of three prototypes: the negative image which evokes fear; the figure of the Wandering Jew – mysterious and partially sympathetic; and the compassionate and saintly Jew.

Although in Afrikaans fiction generally, some ambivalent or sympathetic figures of Jews appear, Afrikaans authors contemporary with Smith were much more negative towards Jews. In his discussion of the Afrikaans *plaasroman* (farm novel), J.M. Coetzee suggests that 'xenophobia or moralism or both triumph over analysis of forces'. The Afrikaans authors, he argues, viewed the crisis on the *platteland* (rural areas) more explicitly as a 'conflict between the peasant and capitalist modes of production'. Common in the work of D.F. Malherbe, Abraham H. Jonker, Jochem Van Bruggen, and C.M. Van den Heever, is the figure of a scheming, villainous Jew, coming to the country in order to look for viable farming operations in which to invest. Set in opposition to the townsman is found the figure of a peasant farmer who has to mortgage his land.[29]

Stephen Black

Stephen Black, whose depiction of the evil Jewish IDB has been examined in the previous chapter, was obviously keenly interested in the Jews, since he has left a number of vivid portraits in his work. In his novel *The Dorp* (1920), which is set in 1915 during the First World War, he chronicles the life of a fictional town, Unionstad, peopled with

Afrikaners, Englishmen, an Indian family, and a Jew and his relatives. The plot concerns political rivalry between the Afrikaners and the English – the 'Nats' and the 'Saps' (South African Party); and the denouement, the marriage between an Englishman and an Afrikaans girl, tends to recommend harmony between different groups. The tone of the novel is genial and light-hearted, and the treatment of the Jewish smous, Abraham Schlimowitz – in vivid contrast to the evil Julius Hermann in his novel *The Golden Calf* (1925) – is relatively good-natured, albeit ambivalent. Schlimowitz is described in what seems a favourable light:

> He was a stoutish individual of medium height, with a vigorous frame and a short, thick beard. Keen eyes bulged somewhat from his full brows, which only made them appear more humorous; his nose was pendulous but full, his voice throaty, virile and resonant ... Indelibly stamped all over [him] was the mark of the Slavic Jew ... with an accent that made the unpretentious Taal as guttural as Yiddish, it was like the inevitable completion of a phrase in music. (p.66)

Although Schlimowitz also possesses the qualities of 'buoyancy', 'vitality', 'humour' and 'humanity' (pp.72, 253), hints of the stereotype appear in the allusions to distinctive physical features and a Yiddish accent. The ambivalence can be noted in the use of qualifying phrases: the 'keen' eyes 'bulge', the nose is 'pendulous' but 'full', the voice is 'virile and resonant' but is also 'throaty' and 'guttural'. The Jew may appear to show many favourable characteristics, but the text strongly suggests a contrary reading:

> Schlimowitz was not either a hard-hearted or a cruel man. He was true to type – utterly unlike the popular concept of a Hebrew Shylock. Centuries of race oppression had, of course, endowed him with ruthless cunning in commerce, which to him was life ... (p.190)

In Black's construction of a Jew, the figure of Shylock, coupled with similar stereotypical markers – hard-heartedness, cruelty, cunning and commercial ability – is so fixed in the author's mind that his attempt to neutralise these at a stroke with the one word 'not' fails to destroy the effect. Black repeats the very phrases used by Schreiner in her ambivalent references to the Jews in her non-fictional writing. The give-away phrase 'of course', referring to how oppression has endowed Schlimowitz with 'ruthless cunning', is used without irony, and is a further pointer to Black's attitude. 'Cunning' is a central component in the character and behaviour of this smous, whose upward mobility is also stressed. The narrator describes how he

> had made his periodical visits to Unionstad on a bicycle ... On this comfortless contraption, the poor Jew covered many hot and weary miles ... in the first stage when Schlimowitz landed from Odessa, he thought, as a Russian Jew, that it was a good thing to be pitied. Often, therefore, he played the "*schnorrer*" in business, asking for bargains almost as charity. But soon his quick intelligence discovered that it was better to be envied than pitied. The bicycle became a horse; the horse would soon become one of a pair drawing a Cape cart ... petrol was still so abominably dear ... *oy, yoy, yoy*! (pp.67-68)

This passage is very similar in detail to Pauline Smith's description of Elijah Shokolowsky, although the narrator's heavy-handed attempt at irony – the reference to '*shnorrer*' and the self-pitying '*oy, yoy, yoy*!' – conveys an unmistakable sense of authorial distance from the Jew, and displays the language marking which is a feature of the negative image, aspects which Smith significantly avoids.

Further, the name, 'Schlimowitz', is a play on the Afrikaans word 'slim', meaning clever, which idiomatically connotes cunning. Black was obviously fascinated by the smous. In his play *Helena's Hope, Ltd.* (1910) Black created the figure of the wily smous, Abraham Goldenstein, who buys up farming land from an innocent Afrikaans girl, knowing that it is gold-bearing. At the end, the smous becomes a wealthy Parktown financier. The name, 'Goldenstein' is clearly, like 'Schlimowitz', stereotypical. Billed as 'A Mirror of Rand Life', the play was intended to be fully representative of the relationship between Jews and Afrikaners, and to demonstrate the ruthlessness of the Jew. Another play, *Backveld Boer* (1928), also features an upwardly mobile smous who becomes a Rand attorney.

The name, 'Schlimowitz', becomes more significant as the plot unfolds. While appearing to conspire with Van Ryn, an Afrikaner 'Nat', to buy up a store belonging to an Indian trader and evict him from the town, Schlimowitz cunningly plots to take over the store himself, to control a monopoly on the trading in the district, and simultaneously to out-manoeuvre both the Afrikaner and the Indian. Schlimowitz pretends to share Van Ryn's xenophobic attitudes. Van Ryn fulminates:

> "These accursed coolies are going to ruin our land ... we must stop them! If the British Empire wants to reward them for fighting the Germans, let it give them votes and money in their own country, India!"
> "Hoor, hoor, Oom," cried the Jew. (p.74)

In reality, the Jew is not interested in politics, and cares nothing for the plight of the Indian, despite the similarity in their social and political situations. He is relentlessly self-absorbed, and Black underscores the typical perception that the Jew's primary concern is 'business':

> Schlimowitz ... longed to tell these men what he felt – that he had no country, no party, and no club; that he had not the slightest desire to fight anyone – that in short, all he wanted was to do business. (p.70)

As the machinations of Schlimowitz are recounted, the tone, while still jocular, becomes more cynical:

> Ever since his daughter had warned him against the Jews in general, and Schlimowitz in particular, Van Ryn had been waiting to come to a clearer understanding with his anti-Indian ally ... Schlimowitz was undoubtedly buying far more produce on the farms than in the past. Boers on whose properties Van Ryn held mortgage bonds were even selling a considerable percentage to the Jew. (p.102)

> He did not neglect to cultivate the acquaintance even
> of his prospective victim Mahomet ... Both dealers
> made a profit – it was only the unhappy owners of South
> Africa – to-day the Boers, tomorrow the British, the day
> after the Kafirs – who gained nothing. They were the
> eternal sponges, always to be squeezed dry by these
> superior traders from the east ... (p.105)

In showing Afrikaner resentment of foreigners – Jews and
Asiatics – the passage alludes to the anti-Alien agitation of the
period, resulting in the passing of the Immigration Act of 1913,
which aimed at stemming the influx both of foreign Jews and of
Indians. Nevertheless, Van Ryn is very ambivalent towards
Schlimowitz. He becomes aware of his double-dealing:

> Curiously enough Van Ryn even now did not dislike
> Schlimowitz. The genial rascality of the Jew failed to
> irritate or antagonize him; there was fundamentally
> nothing antipathetic about the man. Ah ... if he had been
> an Englishman it would have been different ... he could
> not meet Oakley without feeling 'the hair rise on his back'
> ... while this *vernuiker* of a Jew could come along and play
> dirty tricks with impunity. He could not account for it
> except that the English were so confoundedly *hoogmoedig*
> (haughty). They came into other people's countries,
> *verdom* (damn), and tried to be *baas* (boss), ride the high
> horse ... no that he could not stand! ... One could talk to
> the Jew; he always had a soft answer to turn away wrath,
> though without doubt he was a *schelm* (rascal) ... Van
> Ryn had noticed that even the few combative, argumen-
> tative, cocksure Hebrews whom he met were English
> Jews. (pp.251-252)

Anti-Jewish discourse – signalled by references to '*vernuiker*' and
'*schelm*' – is balanced by anti-English epithets, and the use of
Afrikaans distances the speaker from both Englishmen and Jews.
This is reminiscent of the passage from Smith's diary which revealed
Smith's perception of the way in which the rural Afrikaners feared

the English more than the Jews. Notable here is an interesting sidelight on the Afrikaners' perception of the 'genial rascality' of the eastern European Jew as opposed to the 'combative, argumentative, cocksure' English or Anglo-German Jews.

As in the novels of Scully and Schreiner, a second Jew is introduced, and though all Jews are presented ambivalently, the two Jews roughly represent either predominantly good or predominantly bad qualities. In *The Dorp* Schlimowitz's brother-in-law is merely a lesser version of Schlimowitz himself. He too is shrewd and cunning, 'excellent at buying bankrupt or salvaged stock.' (p.253) '[W]ith the genius of his race [he] could so smell money and values that to him the finest tea or the meanest Boer meal, considered in terms of cash, was as familiar as old furniture or salvaged typewriters' (p.255). However, the brother-in-law lacks the older Jew's vitality, being 'slighter, darker, paler' (p.253). He is a second-generation, more assimilated Jew, who was born on the Rand, and 'neither fasts at Passover nor refrains from eating bacon' (p.253). The correlation between his Jewishness and his shrewdness in business reinforces the impression that, despite the relative geniality of Black's construction of the Jewish characters, there is more than a suggestion of the avaricious 'commercial' Jew. The error in portraying Jewish custom – Passover is not a time of fasting – shows that Black's understanding of Jews and Judaism is based on very slender knowledge.

A Jewish Writer

Sarah Gertrude Millin

Born in Lithuania, Sarah Gertrude Millin (neé Liebson, 1888-1968) was brought as an infant to South Africa when her parents settled on the Vaal River diamond diggings near Kimberley. She grew up among coloured children and experienced at first hand their consciousness of exclusion from white society, which paralleled her own sense, as a Jew, of exclusion from Gentile society. In 1924 she published a novel, *God's Stepchildren*, which has become notorious as an apparently racist denigration of the coloured people. In 1980, in a highly influential article, J.M. Coetzee argued that Millin's ideas were underpinned by concepts of racial taint and inferiority, and popularised by German

National Socialist race theories originated by Gobineau in the nineteenth century.[30]

Recently Lavinia Braun has attempted to demonstrate the fallacy of this argument by pointing out that Millin's treatment of the coloured person, far from being condemnatory, is based on what Marie Pienaar has described as 'a profound knowledge of the subject, an understanding on [sic] – in the final analysis – a deep-felt compassion for the victims of conflict caused by racial differences.'[31] Braun argues that Coetzee fails to discriminate between Millin's dramatisation of the consciousness of stigma and the ascription of stigma, because he fails to appreciate the way in which Millin's consciousness of her own 'stepchild-like status as a Jewess in South Africa' leads her to a sympathetic identification with the pain and shame experienced by other members of minority groups. Braun points out that the concept of the 'stepchild' was first used by Heine to characterise the Jews of the nineteenth century in their relationship to their German heritage. Heine was read in the household of Millin's parents, and his ideas profoundly affected her.[32]

Further, Braun argues, her unpublished writing proves that far from being a racist, Millin believed herself to be of the ranks of those 'negrophiles' who are '[s]eeking to escape from their ranks of the inequal ... of the pitiable into the ranks of the pitying, escaping from their own plight as sort of untouchables ...' Millin had written: 'I should imagine the high percentage of Jewish negrophiles of our day has to do with (1) their understanding of racial separateness (2) their desire to escape it themselves'.[33] Hence Millin's own desire to escape, to 'exorcise something in [her]self', what she later called 'the not-quite element',[34] which would seem to determine her understanding and portrayal of the same consciousness in many of her characters.

While the author herself was profoundly, even naively, unconscious of the ambiguity of her own writing, it would seem that neither Coetzee nor Braun appreciates the ambivalence in Millin's treatment of both the coloured person and the Jew, the latter particularly evident in her unpublished writings.

A few years after *God's Stepchildren*, Millin again tackled the subject of minority groups in her novel, *The Coming of the Lord* (1928). Retrospectively she analysed the theme of the novel: 'The minority peoples I considered in *The Coming of the Lord* were – the

Jews apart – the Indians; the Germans, suspect after the Great War; the natives. Their problem formed my theme.'³⁵ The plot is drawn from an historical incident, the encampment of a group of black religious zealots, the Israelites, at Bulhoek in the Cape Province in order to celebrate the Passover year in 1920-1921, and the government's violent destruction of the camp.

For the most part, however, the novel concentrates on the Jews. 'My theme arose from Jews,' she wrote. 'What, I asked myself, as so many are doing to-day, was this thing one called the Jewish Problem? Why were Jews more resented and rejected than other peoples plainly their inferiors?'³⁶ By referring to what would become known as the psychodynamic theory of prejudice which holds that 'hostility, wrongful generalisation and prejudice are natural conditions of the human mind' she reasons:

> The Jewish Problem, I decided, was a minority problem. A minority problem – any minority problem ... was a problem not of the minority but of the majority ... The majority ... persecuted the minority ... because the natural tendency of the animal or human being was towards both cruelty and cowardice, and to inflict pain without incurring danger ideally satisfied this tendency. The Jews had for several thousand years been a helpless minority wherever they appeared. They formed thus admirable subjects for the exercise of a safe brutality. They had no doubt their faults, like all human beings, and one might find many reasons for their persecution [but] ... [t]he fundamental reason ... was bad human nature.³⁷

The novel is, as she intends, an exploration of the minutiae of inter-group relations, an analysis of the problems of prejudice and marginality, and the consciousness of stigma and alienation.

The use of parallelisms underscores the author's treatment of the problems of different groups. A central character is Isaac Nathan. Known throughout as 'Old Nathan', he is an elderly, immigrant Jewish shopkeeper. Dr. Diethelm is an elderly German doctor. Both are outsiders in the community in which they live. Each ultimately loses a son, and their loneliness draws them together. Old Nathan feels himself set apart from the rest of the community, which views him with kindly tolerance: 'He had no part ... in the social life of Gibeon ... [He says:] "... I am here popular like the idiot of the village".' (p.4).

The chief focus, however, falls on Saul, Old Nathan's son. He has studied medicine in England and thus represents the upwardly mobile second generation. Millin focuses on Saul's interaction with the wider community from which his father feels excluded, exemplified in his friendship with a black doctor, his romantic involvement and putative affair with a Gentile woman, wife of the local attorney, and his dealings with the attorney himself. The troubled relations of Saul and his father are shown as a conflict between the older and younger generation, and between the traditional and the more modern Jewish response to Gentile society. This is an early treatment of a problem which would become an area of fuller examination as the century proceeded.

In the character of Saul, Millin has depicted a Jew struggling with the difficulties of being a Jew in the South Africa of the 1920s, when religious and social anti-Semitism was exacerbated by the charge that the Jews had not pulled their weight during the First World War. Saul had felt compelled to join up:

> "I must go," said Saul.
> "Why?" asked Old Nathan.
> "Because they say that Jews –" ...
> They were both convinced, he and Saul, that Saul would be killed in the War. (pp.12-13)

Saul survives the war, but ultimately loses his life in another situation in which his conscience has become involved. He feels drawn to another outsider, a black man:

> [Saul] was lonely, and once ... he strolled into Dr. Tetyana's waiting-room, and sat down, as man to man, to talk to the Kaffir.
> It was the first time any doctor in Gibeon had done such a thing. And Tetyana, indeed, would have preferred it if it had not been a Jew, for a Jew had not the same

standing as another European ... Still, a white skin was a white skin, and a painful exhilaration mounted in Tetyana when Saul walked into his room. (p.108)[38]

Although the black man judges the Jew lower on the social scale than other 'Europeans', he himself feels racially inferior to *any* white man and tries compulsively to impress him. Because of his own deeply ingrained sense of stigma, Saul empathises with the black man's social embarrassment:

> Saul, understanding what moved Tetyana to this persistent self-explanation, was so sympathetic with him that the Kaffir's heart overflowed. He offered to do this and that for him, he offered finally to take him to the camp of the Levites on the Heights of Gibeon. (p.109)

Through a sense of obligation, Saul accompanies Tetyana on a dangerous mission to the camp of the Levites, and remains out of a sense of duty when the government troops attack. He meets his death from a stray bullet. In constructing Saul as a type of martyr, who sacrifices himself in the cause of the black-white friendships, Millin uses the typical image of the kaffirboetie. However, her portrait of Saul's relationships with members of other groups, and his tortured sense of his own identity as a Jew, is more complex than previous fictional treatments.

> ... Saul Nathan was two men. One of him lived among the people in the big world, and had their interests and their conventions, and even their thoughts and traditions and standards and prejudices. And the other lived in a little ghetto, and suffered and enjoyed with his own, and looked out on the big world, and himself in it, with shame and amusement and satisfaction and sorrow and contempt. That really doubled his life. (pp.96-97)

Here is a powerful evocation of the sense of outsiderhood and self-division which Millin claimed as a characteristic of her own thinking. Although Saul is an assimilated Jew – he was not taught to read

Hebrew and has studied overseas – he feels rejected by the Gentiles of Gibeon, and his most earnest wish is to escape from 'the undesirable society of his fellow-Jews' (p.99). He is 'filled with resentment that he belonged to a race that so hampered simplicity of progress' (p.101). For him 'progress' means the ability to move into the Gentile world, and Saul is therefore an avatar of the Jew of diamond field fiction, bent on assimilation.

Invoking what would become the socio-cultural view of prejudice, in which stereotypes are used to define barriers and prescribe behavioural patterns, 'Old Nathan' warns his son how difficult it is for a Jew to cross the established barriers between the social groups, however much he may wish to do so:

> "Every anti-Semite has his favourite Jew ... of whom he says: "This one is different from the rest. I will take him to myself." Sometimes that gives the Jew pleasure. He is happy not to look or seem like his brothers, because it is not what a person can call a fashionable thing to look like a Jew ... It is besides, an achievement, a triumph, for a Jew to be accepted as an equal by those who have hitherto despised him, even when, in his secret heart he despises them ... You don't know Hebrew ... so get me an English Bible from the shop ..." ... Old Nathan ... found a passage in Esther. " 'Think not'," he read, " 'that thou shalt escape in the King's house, more than all the other Jews ...' "
> "A Jew stays a Jew, Saul." (pp.97-98)

Elsewhere Millin dramatised Gentile animosity towards Jews. The unsuccessful Gentile attorney, Duerden, regards the successful Jewish attorney as 'a small, ugly Jew called Bramson, with thick lips and bandy legs'. He muses: ' "what I always came back to was why a Jew called Abrahamson should take the name of Bramson ..." ' (p.36). The narrator comments: 'He meant (though he did not know what he meant) that a Jew should not attempt to take a protective colouring and so lose his natural handicap ...' (p.36). Here Millin makes reference to the Gentile irritation with the assimilationist tendencies of Jews, and in the phrase – '[o]ne had only to spurn such

a man, and he came to heel, cringing' (p.42) – she has glancingly
alluded to that discourse in which anti-Semitic writers use images of
animals to derogate Jews.

Perhaps all the characters articulate aspects of Millin's own
thinking. That she felt ambivalent about aspects of her own Jewishness is borne out by her frequent references to the consistent self-
division, the 'not-quite element'. In spite of the empathetic treatment
of the problems of Jewish characters, some of her unpublished work
betrays negative reactions to Jews. In the draft of a speech which she
delivered during the First World War, Millin suggests that social
manoeuvring is a function of Jewish self-rejection:

> The Jew is by nature a climber ... and very often the
> only way a Jew can mark [h]is ascent – can distinguish
> himself from the others – is to deny his Judaism. And
> this, I believe largely accounts for the fact that so many
> Jews who rise in the world try to cast from them their
> Jewishness & assimilate. It is simply one way of self-
> assertion.[39]

Echoing the phraseology used during the Gentile outcry against the
Jewish 'scum' entering the country at this time, she goes on to
deprecate the first-generation Jewish immigrant to South Africa as
'the down-trodden, under-sized, undeveloped fugitive from the
ghetto'. She asserts that when the upwardly mobile second generation
thrive and improve their appearance, they become estranged from
their 'oriental' parents and may exchange religion for socialism:

> They look differently, they speak differently, most of all
> they think and feel differently ... [T]hey are far far more
> like their gentile neighbours than they are like their own
> progenitor ... The result is, often ... [a]n estrangement
> not only from family life but from Jewish life.[40]

It might be significant that Millin wrote this at the peak period of
anti-Semitism in South Africa. It is possible that she has refracted
in her writing those very prejudices in her society which she has
internalised. The character of Saul Nathan, therefore, is a working

out of this thesis which she was thinking about at least ten years before she wrote *The Coming of the Lord.*

Later, in an unpublished article, 'The Right to be Ugly' (1933), written on her return from a visit to Palestine in response to a request from a Zionist women's newspaper, she seemed to revel in stereotypical thinking. Ostensibly praising the Zionist endeavour, she speculated:

> The ... beauty of ... Palestine is that the Jews don't have to think about their Jewishness because it does not leap up and hit them on their Semitic noses ... They possess something no Jews in other parts of the world have known for two thousand years – the right, at last, the blessed, blessed right to be ugly in a Jewish way.[41]

In an attempt to define what she means by 'ugly', she resorts to xenophobic terminology:

> Of course, the Jew is rather ugly: Not uglier than the Southern European, but uglier, without question, than the typical Briton ... a Jew must often ask himself: to what extent does his foreign ugliness affront his host? ... For that it does affront his host he cannot doubt ... And yet it is only lately he has begun to appreciate to the full how quite repulsive he must be to strangers. It needed the Germans to smash in his Semitic nose to make the Jew see himself adequately mirrored.[42]

Millin attempts to explain that she meant to endow the word, 'ugly', with a sense of foreignness, difference and set-apartness, which was an integral aspect of her thinking about marginalised people. Nevertheless she reveals a high degree of internalisation of the stereotypes engendered by anti-Semites, as well as a vague understanding of the very process of that internalisation. She writes:

> ... The Jewish face is not liked by the other nations.
> It isn't even much liked by the Jewish nation. One can't, after all, hear for thousands of years that one's

appearance is not what is [*sic*] should be without developing a self- consciousness about it ... In short, the Jew is
tortured by the knowledge that he does not belong ...
The Jew *is* a peculiar person ... He simply cannot get on
with his life ... because he is so distracted with thinking
about his Jewishness ...[43]

Millin was surprised that the editor of the newspaper was 'shocked
and hurt' and refused to publish the article. She seems to have been
unconscious of how easily her words might have given offence. In
the same way that Coetzee, nearly fifty years later, identified a strain
of racism in Millin's treatment of coloured people, so did the editor
of the Zionist women's newspaper respond negatively to what was
perceived as a blatant example of the anti-Jewish thinking of a Jewish
writer. Possibly, in writing for a Jewish paper, Millin felt a sense of
freedom in exploring for her own in-group the perceptions and
prejudices which she herself has internalised. In 1941, in her
autobiographical work, *The Night is Long*, she defensively explained
that in her article she had merely intended to show

> how Jews, alone among peoples, had, until now, lived in
> the world, always suspect, under critical eyes, under
> hostility, under injustice, on probation, on sufferance, in
> torture, in pain, ugly to others, thus ugly to themselves –
> never unbuttoned, easy, free-breathing, at home. To-day
> they were at home. They had their National Home. They
> were all ugly in the same way, they had the right to be
> ugly, therefore they were not ugly.[44]

The muddle is never resolved; the insistence on 'ugliness' is never
retracted. Despite a personal racial pride, a strong sense of the
consciousness of stigma is apparent in both Millin's published and
unpublished work, and in that self-division she believes to be the result
of her 'step-childlike' status as a Jewish woman in South Africa. She
does not fully analyse her own attitudes, and while deprecating some
prejudices, she replicates others. She works within the parameters of
established stereotypes – probing, examining, protesting against,
satirising some of them; but in endorsing others, reveals that, as a

Jewish writer, she has become infected by those attitudes to Jews found in the early twentieth century South African *zeitgeist*. The muddle was to pursue her all her life. Despite her life-long abhorrence of anti-Semitism and the liberalism of her early attitudes, she was to become, in her later years, an enthusiastic supporter of the Nationalist Government's policy of apartheid.[45]

— 4 —

ANTI-SEMITISM AND ITS EFFECTS

In the middle years of the twentieth century, the South African Jewish sense of identity was problematic. This was a volatile period, spanning the Second World War, the Holocaust, the birth of the State of Israel and the entrenchment of apartheid during the 1950s and 1960s. The memory of the legislated pre-War restriction on Jewish immigration from eastern Europe and Germany exacerbated the horror and grief felt by South African Jews at the Holocaust tragedy.

The active expression of anti-Semitism when Greyshirt activity loomed ominously is vividly expressed in the recollections of an expatriate South African, 'Margaret', member of a London Jewish Women's History Group:

> I was going to have my tonsils out … [in] 1945 or 46 … After visiting hours were over, one nun started saying things to us Jews like "you deserved what the Germans did to you in the war", and generally taunting us. She also said something about circumcision … I think it was Easter time and they re-enacted some aspect of the betrayal of Christ with me as Judas. (pp.44-45)

The mixture of fear and self-confidence experienced by 'Margaret''s father is captured in the following extract:

> The day I was born in 1941 … was the day [my father] signed a deal to buy Lenon's Building in Adderley Street

... he told me why he considered the buying of this property to be so important ... It was the year Jews and other 'undesirables' were being transported to concentration and slave-labour camps all over Nazi-occupied Europe ... My father said that if Weichardt (the Greyshirt leader) ever came into his office to humiliate him as a Jew, he'd shoot him and then himself, and he wanted to have something to leave to his wife and children ... In the mid-sixties, this building, that the family could hardly afford to buy, was sold for a large sum of money ... When I was two, my parents bought a large house ... in Rondebosch ... Shortly after we moved in, some young boys were discovered breaking windows ... they confessed it was because we were Jews ... Dad, having rapidly changed his attitude from one of being prepared to draw blood, if necessary, took on the role of the merciful Jewish sage ... he asked ... that the boys worked in the weekends to earn enough to pay for the breakages and ... donate the money to their school's War Fund. (pp.42-43)[1]

The Nationalist Government's support for the new Jewish State partly alleviated some of the vicious anti-Semitic excesses of the 1930s and 1940s and gave South African Jews a sense of relative security. A great many South African Jews identified with Israel and were stirred to a deep sense of pride which increasingly strengthened the strong Zionist commitment of the community. Within South Africa itself, the rapid upward mobility of many Jews was demonstrable in their widely felt presence in the financial, professional, entrepreneurial, social, and cultural life of the country, especially in the larger cities.

The community was a hybrid one. The eastern European Jews tended to become acculturated and absorbed into the longer established, English-speaking section. Although there were some Jews who remained in country districts and who so identified with Afrikaner culture that they were known as *Boerejode* (Afrikaner Jews), these were comparatively few. More often, fear of the rise of Afrikaner nationalism drove the Jewish community as a whole to identify with

British culture and its more liberal political affiliations. At the same time, remembering the persecutions suffered in Europe, Jews felt grateful to a land that had offered physical security and material prosperity, and on the whole avoided overt political dissent.

Joshua N. Lazerson has described the Jewish community of this period as an 'insular' one, with Jews keeping largely to themselves,[2] although following the twentieth century trend of social assimilation of out-groups, social mixing with the Gentile white group did become more frequent. A residue of anti-Semitism still remained – mostly clandestine, but sometimes overt. Ostracism in some social clubs, anti-Semitic electioneering propaganda, and the occasional desecration of synagogues persisted.[3]

The ambiguous effects of anti-Semitism on individuals and communities has been closely examined by Michael A. Meyer, who suggests that the devaluation of Jews in the eyes of non-Jews may produce disparate effects.[4] On the one hand it may result in a renewed affirmation of Jewish identity. In South Africa at mid-century this is noted in the establishment of Jewish sports and recreational clubs and institutions and, after 1948, of Jewish day schools. The purpose of all these was both to foster unique Jewish values and as safeguards against anti-Semitism and exclusion.

Following the world-wide revival of interest in ethnicity after the 1960s, the erosion of the concept of Empire and the consolidation of new national states, South African Jews showed a growing interest in writing about the immigrant experience and in the collection of Jewish memorabilia and oral history which would lead among other things to the establishment in the 1980s of centres such as the Isaac and Jessie Kaplan Centre for Jewish Studies and Research at the University of Cape Town. An opposite response was manifested in the case of some Jews who disidentified with Judaism, assimilated, and, internalising the hostile anti-Semitic beliefs, were even subject to the phenomenon known as Jewish self-hatred. Albert Memmi reminds us that '[e]very oppressed person rejects himself to ward off the rejection of others.'[5]

The fictional responses of Gentiles and Jews to the anti-Semitism of the mid century were very different.

The Sympathetic Approach

Peter Abrahams

The first non-Jewish author consistently to employ a positive image of the Jew is the coloured writer, Peter Abrahams, born in Vrededorp, Johannesburg in 1919. In his sketches 'Jewish Sister' and 'Brother Jew', and the story, 'Hatred' from *Dark Testament* (1942), written during the Second World War, as well as the novel, *The Path of Thunder* (1948), published shortly after the war, Abrahams shows a marked philo-Semitic attitude. He uses his understanding of the oppressed condition of Jews throughout the world as a paradigm for exposing and exploring the stigmatised position of the coloured people of South Africa. This is an example of the sympathetic identification of one out-group with another. In 'Jewish Sister' a Jewish woman is described by the narrator in very positive terms:

> ... [S]he was very beautiful. She was slender and straight. She always wore an old dress. She was with child, too. Unlike most European women, she did not try to hide it. She walked barefooted; her toes embracing the dry leaves and making them crackle. I also walked barefooted most of the time ... She had dark brown hair. Long dark brown hair. She always let it loose, and the thick strands reached down to her waist. That had a lot to do with my feeling for my Jewish sister.(pp.28-29)

As a distinct contrast to the fat and hunched Jews of popular anti-Semitic categorisation, this Jewish woman is slender and straight. Unlike the bejewelled and overdressed stereotype, she wears an 'old dress' and is 'barefooted'. The narrator values this simplicity as a strong link between them. Barefootedness is symbolic of their shared dispossession. This sketch belongs to a section of the volume demarcated by the subtitle 'I Remember ...' – a signal to the reader to recognise the personal, autobiographical content. Significantly, the emotion that the narrator feels for his 'Jewish Sister' is primarily sexual. This is made explicit, not only when he evokes her luxurious hair and sexual fertility – she is 'with child' –

but more explicitly at the opening of the story, where she greets the coloured man:

> "I hope you won't be very disappointed if I'm not quite what you expected all Europeans to be!"
> A slow smile, deep and kind, and full of something strange, crept over her face. Her eyes were bright ... After she had spoken she grabbed me and kissed me on the mouth. A fierce hard kiss. Warm and clammily moist. It stirred something inside me. "I've wanted to do this very badly for a long time!" (p.27)

The notion of sexual relationships between black or coloured people and Jews has entered the mythos of the Jew in South Africa. It would seem to be based on actual events. In an interview for a collection of pieces on Sophiatown, Phillip Stein has placed on record that he knew of several white women who cohabited with blacks. Stein recalls:

> One told one's mother that you were going to visit someone in Pretoria and disappeared to Sophiatown and stayed in the room for two days over a weekend – and the most surprising young women you would never expect to have the guts to do this were capable of doing this. They came from middle-class homes of every kind in Johannesburg and it is very hard to guess at the motivation of the women concerned – I imagine, inevitably, it was a mixture of sex and idealism.[6]

Sexual liaisons between young Jewish women and black men should not be confused with the irregular unions between single and often isolated Jewish men and coloured or black women, which took place during the last century and early part of the present century. Early immigration brought far more Jewish men to the country than women – by 1904 there were twice as many men.[7] The Jewish bachelor who had come to make his fortune, or who could not afford to return to 'the old country' to look for a bride, frequently could not find a Jewish woman to marry and there was considerable intermarriage chiefly with Afrikaans women, or cohabitation with black or coloured women. The latter is a sensitive topic, well known in the oral tradition but not dealt with in South African English fiction until the 1980s. Yiddish literature, which could deal with sensitive material because the language was inaccessible to Gentiles, tackled the subject much earlier.[8]

Describing his reaction to his 'Jewish Sister', Abrahams refers to the 'understanding' Jew for the first time in South African fiction:

> Then suddenly something inside me burst loose. I had never been able to talk to somebody about the things that were important to me. I had never shared my dreams with anybody. I poured all these out in a terrific, fast-moving flood. To all of it she listened, and I knew she understood ... (pp.30)[9]

The supposed Jewish quality of 'understanding' will be reused by writers seeking to create a positive image. The idealised Jewish figure carries a heavy load of symbolism. She is a fellow outcast and a bearer of culture:

> She made me lie down on the couch and went over to the piano and began to play ... "Well, now for this after-noon's talk. I know how you feel. I'm Jewish, and we've suffered about as much as you have. We know what it is to be an outcast people."(p.31)

The coloured man suggests that her specifically 'Jewish' sensibilities enable her to overcome the usual white prejudice against the black: 'A human being with a white skin had treated me, a human being with a black skin, as her equal. That was the important thing.' (pp.29-30), he writes. Significantly, in 'Jewish Sister', Abrahams is still evoking a stereotype, albeit a positive one, that of the compassionate and under-standing Jew, which here is conflated with the kaffirboetie.

A longer story, 'Hatred', is set in a small country village:

> Vlakfontein ... had a population of about 400 people. All Afrikanders. The natives in the location five miles

away were not counted as part of the population. Old
Isaac and his family were not counted either. (p.77)

A comparison is drawn between the Jews and the 'natives', both
considered by the 'Afrikanders' (Afrikaners) as non-people. Written
during the war, in the period of active Greyshirt agitation, the plot is,
in effect, a critique of local anti-Semitism. 'Old Isaac', a kindly Jewish
shopkeeper is treated with contempt by his Afrikaans customers:
' "So-long Ikey. Your shop stinks like a pigsty" ' (p.79), they say.
They complain that the Jew is cheating again: ' "Wonder why these
people cannot do without cheating! In their blood. That's why they
crucified Jesus. Ja. That's why Hitler sent them out of Germany. Best
thing for us to do. Everywhere they go they make trouble. The curse
of God's on them. And such dirty things" ' (p.86).

Max, son of 'Old Isaac', has been lynched by a mob of Afrikaners,
whose frustrations have been whipped up in a speech from their
member of parliament:

> "... And what have we people had from the British? Our
> language is insulted. Our flag is insulted ... Britain is
> fighting for democracy. And where is this democracy?
> The kaffir, the bushman and the Jew. That's where our
> democracy is. Our women are not safe because the British
> encourage their being insulted ... Where does the gold
> from our mines go? To the Jews, and to the Bank of
> England" ... There were more speakers ... They attacked
> the "kaffir boeties" and the "jingoes." They called for the
> expulsion of the Jews. (pp.88-89)

Abrahams perceptively shows how archetypal anti-Semitism and
contemporary political attitudes become fused. In projecting Afrikaner rhetoric concerning British villainy, and the role of the Jews in
contemporary politics, he exposes the muddled thinking of the
Afrikaners. They regard the Jews not only as international bankers –
powerful and exploitative – but also as an inferior species, once again
categorised with the blacks.

The narrator sympathetically identifies with the character of a lone
Afrikaner who defends the Jews and pleads for tolerance and an end

to hatred. Although shouted down, the maverick Afrikaner rescues the wounded young Max and returns him to his family. Afterwards, unable to remain in the village since he has been labelled a 'traitor' and a 'communist' (p.89), he tells his sister that he will spend the night "[w]ith those very nice Jewish people. And I've eaten ... [a] lovely meal. Almost as good as yours." He claims: "The young fellow is really clever. Most probably we'll talk into the early hours of the morning ..." (p.92). The hospitality of the Jews, their intelligence and nurturing qualities are once more the focus of Abrahams's positive bias.

It would seem that Abrahams is bending over backwards in a didactic effort to show victimised Jews in a positive light and at the same time to attack Afrikaner attitudes. As a member of an oppressed out-group himself, Abrahams is in a favourable position to do so.

Even more didactic and symbolic is Abrahams's sketch, 'Brother Jew', which treats a young Jew, Izzy, who has escaped from Nazi persecution. He is a 'nervous little fellow ... possessed with a terrific inferiority complex' (p.17), surely mirroring that of the narrator/ author since this is another of the stories in *Dark Testament* prefixed by the words 'I Remember'. Both in this sketch and in 'Jewish Sister' the titles underscore the author's perception of the close, almost familial relationship between the coloured person and the Jew.

> He came to me one evening. He was very nervous.
> "You write? They told me so? ... I wonder if you'll do me a favour ..." ... His eyes with that peculiar quality which is found in the eyes of all people who have suffered deeply, had fear and expectation in them. (p.17)

Suffering is the keynote of Izzy's being. The narrator points to its parallel in the suffering of the coloured man, discriminated against on the grounds of race, maintaining that '[t]he Colour-Bar had done certain things to me, but not quite what Jew-baiting had done to Izzy' (p.18). Izzy offers the narrator a tract which he has written:

> "Do you know me? I'm Brother Jew ...
> "Wouldn't it be better if it were dirty Jew, stinking Jew, moneygrabbing Jew, everything-evil Jew? ... Slimy and cunning and evil and grabbing?

"Brother Jew Jesus.
Son of doubtful birth,
Did you have a hooked nose and greedy eyes, and did
you come to steal? ...
"... I held out my hands, and I said, Pray let me love.
Let me share in your tears and your joys.

"But they turned away from me.
Jew.

"In their churches they read the book of my fathers ...
And they prayed to a son of Israel, but me they left
outside ...
"They sought what I had and they cursed me ...
"I walked among the poor and hungry. And the rich
pointed me out and said: He is the cause of all your
suffering. And they stoned me, and I had to hide for my
life." (pp.18-20.)

The mawkish self-pity which characterises the passage results from
the Gentile, coloured author's conception of Jewish identity, constructed from his own identification with the Jew. Unwittingly,
however, the passage projects several negative assumptions about
Jews. Although his intention is to refute it, the narrator uses the
discourse of Jew-hatred in all its forms – religious, economic and
social – and the insistent repetitive stress on phrases such as 'dirty
Jew', 'stinking Jew', 'moneygrabbing Jew', 'everything-evil Jew',
emphasises and re-emphasises the shibboleths of anti-Semitism. The
non-realistic, biblical mode evokes the sense of a mythos underpinning the recital. However, in seeking to create a sympathetic
portrait, the narrator draws attention to his own understanding of
Izzy's predicament: "I can understand it [he says] because it's part of
something I've always wanted to say ..." (p.20).

Abrahams uses what he understands as the situation of the Jew as
part of his apparatus of protest. While the protest here seems to be on
behalf of the suffering victim of Nazi oppression and anti-Semitism,
the subtext of the sketch is less about the Jew and more a declaration
of the coloured man's own position in a hostile society. Abrahams

was among the first of those South African black protest writers who, by stressing their own victimisation at the hands of whites, sought to appeal to the morality and conscience of readers both inside South Africa and throughout the world.

The story ends with the mysterious disappearance of Izzy, who having fled to South Africa from Germany, now presumably continues his wanderings to other cities and possibly to death. Reinforced by the biblical cadences of Izzy's lament, this presentation recalls the prototype of the Wandering Jew, a type which, as has been shown, frequently evokes sympathy.

Abrahams wrote *The Path of Thunder* (1948) openly as a protest novel, and was one of the earliest South African works to be influenced by the black American writers of the Harlem renaissance. First published in America and since translated into twenty-six languages, it was an international success.

The main character, Lanny Swartz, is a coloured man, educated in Cape Town, who returns to his home village in the Northern Karoo to open a school. He falls in love with a white girl and, in the attempt to run off together, both are killed by vengeful whites. They invoke the 'path of thunder' – the path of 'prejudice and bigotry running through this racially obsessed society'.[10]

Before the tragic outcome, Lanny and an intellectual black school teacher, Mako, find a friend in Isaac Finkelberg, son of a local Jewish shopkeeper. Like Lanny, Isaac has been sent away to be educated. Once again Abrahams draws a parallel between the Jew and the coloured man. The Jewish shopkeeper and his dreamy, intellectual son challenge the familiar South African stereotypes of the cunning and avaricious merchant, and the upwardly mobile second generation. The kindly shopkeeper is shown adding 'a little shovelful to the proper quota' (p.114), and performing similar acts of charity. He donates meat for Lanny's homecoming, pointing the parallel between his son, the young Jew and the young coloured man:

"This, I think … is the best piece of meat I have… When Isaac returned he [also] did not have one penny. I had to send him the money for the train … And there are those who say, 'Everything the Jew touches becomes money.' They are foolish ones those. They should look at my son and they will know. And now he is writing a book! And even that will not become money!" (p.27)

In deliberate rebuttal of the image of the financial Jew, the figure of the intellectual son, Isaac, is a version of the positive stereotype – educated, cultured, learned and philosophical – invoking George Eliot's nineteenth century Jewish paragon, Daniel Deronda. In his story, 'Brother Jew', the narrator had referred to Sarah Gertrude Millin's novel, *God's Stepchildren*. It is therefore possible that Abrahams also read *The Coming of the Lord* since the situation of the shopkeeper father and the intellectual son resembles that in Millin's novel. In similar manner, in treating Mr Finkelberg's fear of his son's involvement with non-whites, Abrahams shows a restrained understanding of the difficult position of the old Jew, his horror of being singled out for discrimination, and his craving for self-protection. Mr Finkelberg warns his son:

> "You will bring us trouble ... Already the Dutch people are saying things about us because we are Jews. That is how it began in the old country ... You think your father is getting the habits of these Dutchmen and feeling better than the black people. You are wrong. Too long have I been insulted to want to insult others. I am only thinking of you and the store and myself. We want a place where we can live in peace and freedom ... If we look after our own business and leave the others alone, perhaps they will leave us alone."
> His sad, wise eyes pleaded with his son; begged him to understand the centuries of oppression that made him see things as he did. (pp.71-72)

Deliberately evoking sympathy, by using the echoes of the Wandering Jew, the narrator continues:

> Through the open door came the low, muffled voice of his father ... It was the lonely voice of all the Jews everywhere who had been made homeless wanderers over the earth's surface for more than two thousand years; the voice of a Jew who had to leave a home he had built with his own

hands ... who had suffered all insults and indignities and
violences ... who had given much and then received
spittle on his face; a desolate voice that had gained a
quiet, resigned strength and submission ... (pp.75-76)

However, in the figure of Isaac, he presents a new image of the South
African Jew as a fighter for his future, an early Zionist:

Isaac looked at his father and thought bitterly ... The
meek and humble Jew. Two thousand years of oppression and persecution had so crushed him that ... he
seemed to have forgotten how to strike a blow for his
freedom and independence. A long, long time is two
thousand years ... Had their blood run to water in that
time? ... Perhaps they were too civilized ... Too deeply
steeped in the peaceful, commercial, and creatively
gentle art of living. They knew how to build but they
had forgotten how to destroy ... Where was the warrior,
the Jew with the strong arm, schooled in the arts of war
as well as the arts of peace? (pp.72-73).[11]

This is only a fleeting impression, and Abrahams is quick to defuse it
when Mr Finkelberg reacts:

"Yes. I know your thoughts ... You say your father is
weak and cowardly. Perhaps you say to yourself that
your people are weak and cowardly ... It is ever so, my
son. It was thus with my father ... and so it goes back.
So it will go forward too." (p.73)

Where Isaac plays host to Lanny and Mako and sympathetically
discusses their problems of identity, colour and nationalism, he
reverts to another more familiar incarnation – the kaffirboetie.
Possibly Mako makes an oblique reference to the burgeoning State of
Israel, established in 1948, the year this novel was published:

"[The Jews] are like the colored people in one way and
unlike the colored people in another way. The traditions

the Jews have are traditions of suffering. That is really all. That and their religion ... [The Jew's] past and his tradition have been wiped away because he has no land of his own ... I think the Jew must make more of a future and not let the past sit on him too heavily." (pp.88-89)

No conclusions are reached, but these and similar problems shared by coloured people, blacks and Jews, are aired superficially. Mako's stated belief that because the Jew has no land of his own, he is dispossessed of power, is another point of perceived identity between the Jews and the black South Africans. Abrahams powerfully conveys the sense of stigma attached to and experienced by Jews and blacks, all of whom feel themselves to be 'outsider[s], like [people] living between two worlds' (p.135). Lanny explains to the white woman he loves:

"You see, we know that people are always trying to insult us, and to keep that insult away we try to forestall it. We're always looking for it so that we can deal with it ... And when people are as sensitive as that about anything they sometimes see an insult where it does not exist." (p.126)

As in 'Jewish Sister', it is the Jew who offers understanding and compassion. The symbiotic relationship between the coloured and the Jew is suggested, and the author once again powerfully projects a sense of his own understanding of the position of the Jew:

Impulsively, Isaac flung his arm round Lanny's shoulders.
"You don't want to tell me about it, Lanny. You just want someone to understand. I understand." (p.153)

Alan Paton

Another strikingly philo-Semitic text is *Too Late the Phalarope* (1953) by Alan Paton (1903-1988). The novel is a courageous indictment of the Immorality Act of 1927 which prohibited sexual intercourse between people of different races and which had been stringently enforced after the coming to power of the National Party in 1948.[12] A positive image of the Jew is found in the figure of the Jewish shopkeeper, Mr Kaplan, affectionately known as Kappie. Once again, as in Abrahams's *The Path of Thunder*, sex and miscegenation are the primary focus.

The setting is a small Afrikaans country town in the Transvaal in about 1950. The plot deals with the ruin of an idealised protagonist, Pieter van Vlaanderen. He is a police lieutenant who cares about the welfare of the blacks. Driven to 'temptation' by the coldness and naivete of his wife, he forms a brief and furtive sexual liaison with a young black woman. It is less the discovery of his having offended under the Immorality Act and his subsequent prosecution than his extreme sense of guilt that destroys him and his family.

The novel seeks to combat injustice, intolerance, prejudice and discrimination, wherever they occur. Paton was a founder member of the Liberal Association which preceded the founding of the Liberal Party in 1953, the year in which *Too Late the Phalarope* was published. He was also a member of the Society of Christians and Jews, who worked for better relationships between Jews and Christians in order to counter anti-Semitism. In Paton's novel, the saintly and intellectual Jew who befriends Pieter, plays records of classical music to him and cares for and comforts him, derives from his idealisation of the Jew as member of a group which suffers discrimination.

At the heart of the text there is a sense of alienation. Many of the characters are outsiders in the strictly Calvinist community. They include Pieter, because of his gentleness and sensitivity, the fact that he fought in the War against the wishes of his father, and finally because he committed the 'crime' of having sexual intercourse with a black woman. The fact that the author condones the sin of adultery forcibly suggests that his intention is to focus intensely on what he considers to be a political wrong, and to ignore the religious aspects of Pieter's sin.

The narrator, Pieter's aunt, is a spinster, in some way disfigured and described as 'not like other women' (p.9). She is another outsider. Because he is a Jew, Kappie is similarly regarded by the Afrikaners as being 'set apart from the world' (p.218). Yet in spite of this, as the narrator ironically stresses, the Jews were well treated in Venterspan:

For we Afrikaners of Venterspan were not against the
Jews, as they were in some other places, nor do we think
that all shops should be in Afrikaners' hands. We never
had any boycotts or secret plans against the Jews, and for
that the credit must go to my brother, and to Dominee
Stander of the great Church, for neither would counte-
nance any hatred of the Jews. The dominee often
reminded us that our great book came from the Jews,
and that we too were a people of Israel, who suffered
and died to win the Holy Land ...(p.27)

As Salo Rappaport reminds us, because they shared 'the language and
sentiment of the Bible, Christians could not be emotionally indifferent
to the drama of the Holy Land and the "Chosen People".'[13] This aspect
of philo-Semitism is shown in the narrator's admiration of the 'people
of Israel, who suffered and died to win the Holy Land'. This applies
both to the exploits recorded in the Bible, and to the establishment of
the State of Israel.

Underpinning this South African drama of race hatred and
persecution, is the shadow of the Holocaust and the tragedy of the
European Jews. While Paton allows the narrator to cite as social norms
the clichés of Jew-hatred, his intentions, as evident in this passage and
in the tone of the text as a whole, are to refute them. In the light of his
well-known humanist views, Paton constructs his Jewish character with
some affection and even sentimentality. The disgraced Pieter, excluded
from the Calvinist community which closes ranks against him, turns to
the Jew from whom he receives the same aspect of charity as Smith's
Jew-woman offered to the disgraced miller. Kappie is described
as 'understanding some tragic trouble of the soul', and the narrator
adds, 'the Jews understand about the soul ...' (p.123) – a telling satiric
comment on the absence of compassion in the strictly Calvinist
Afrikaans community.

Like Peter Abrahams, Paton stresses the quality of 'understanding', a vague attribute intended to convey a sense of the Jew's
compassion and insight. Paton projects on to the Jew the qualities of
tolerance and sympathetic caring for the underdog which are aspects
of his own liberal humanism; and Kappie, who is hardly characterised and is a collection of qualities rather than a rounded

character, is the mouthpiece for Paton's benevolent propaganda.[14] In many ways, Kappie would seem to be a projection of Paton's own ideas: Kappie 'knew all the ways of the world and judged them not' (p.88). The narrator comments: 'where would [Pieter] have found a man more true and faithful? And where would he have found a man who would better have understood and would not have shrunk from him?' (p.123). The implication is that Kappie's interest in music, his kindness and generosity, not only to Pieter but to his niece whose education he finances, are Jewish attributes.

At the climax of the story, when the disgraced Pieter contemplates suicide, it is the Jew, Kappie, who dissuades and comforts him:

> he came down over the rows of seats, and sat down beside him, and put his arm about him, not round the shoulders, for he could not, being so small a man. And he spoke to him there, as one speaks to a child, as a woman speaks, as most men would fear to speak in the presence of any other person, about friends and courage, and about no one deserving to suffer for ever, and about a plan for man and wife and children to go to some new country, where they could forget the terror and suffering ... He spoke as a woman speaks to her child when sobbing is past, one questioning, the other answering and comforting ... (pp.242-243)

The short stature of Kappie, which may derive from the negative stereotype of the stunted, physically unattractive Jew, is here used for its connotations of gentleness, which contrasts vividly with the fierce fundamentalist creed of the Afrikaners of Venterspan. There are strong parallels between this passage and the one from Peter Abrahams's *The Path of Thunder*, where the Jew, in a gesture of solidarity and compassion, puts his arm around the shoulder of the troubled coloured man.

In Paton's text the outcast condition of the Jew again becomes a paradigm for another outcast from society. The saintliness of the Jew-woman in Pauline Smith's 'The Miller' was similarly directly related to her condition of outsiderhood. In Paton's text, anti-Semitism is reversed in order to focus on what the author views as an equally or more vicious racial attitude – the condemnation of those who have sexual relations across the colour bar. The figure of the Jew is used ironically as an icon of the true 'Christian', as opposed to false Christians – the Calvinists, as Paton shows them to be. The sentimental tone of this passage, however, illustrates the way in which the figure of the Jew as a paragon, carrying the load of the author's moral principles, becomes as much a stereotype as the more popular Jew-villain.

The liberal myth of the Jew as champion of the underdog can be traced throughout the twentieth century in the work of writers who show the Jew as leftist, social worker, doctor or philanthropist. This positive attitude was balanced by the naked expression of anti-Semitism and the projection of negative stereotypes of Jews.

The Anti-Semitic Novelist

Oliver Walker

In 1949 Oliver Walker published a novel, *Wanton City*, about the arrival in South Africa of Peter, a young Englishman, a prospective reporter on a Johannesburg newspaper. This character is obviously modelled on Walker himself who was a well-known Johannesburg journalist. Dealing with Johannesburg life in the mid-century, the text abounds with caricatures of Jews, all fat parvenus or vulgar cosmopolitans. Coming out on the boat from England, Peter meets a number of Jews:

> Peter shared his table with ... a fat middle-aged Jewess whose bosom began just beneath her second chin.
> "Ullo," she said cheerfully when he sat down. Her black button eyes hardly left the plate of nuts she was cracking between the soup and the fish courses. "You must 'urry up or I shall eat all the food ... [The others] should be sick, per'aps," said Mrs Steinbach, with an upward heave of her dumpy shoulders. She added with an air of great slyness, "All the more for us to eat, eh?" and stuffed a couple of walnuts rapidly into her mouth ... (p.17)

The portrait of this vulgar, 'dumpy', gluttonous, sly Jewish woman is echoed in the other Jewish characters. 'Rita Goldschmidt' is 'too fat' (p.91); 'Miss Scholmanowitz' is dressed in a too 'elaborate evening dress' (p.19); 'Mr Guggleheimer' has 'flashing gold-filled teeth' (p.30); the description of a 'big-breasted blonde Jewess' (p.40) is stereotypical as is that of 'a stout, short Jew with a bald, egg-shaped head' (p.50). These figures, especially the women, hark back to Julia Leverton of Westrup's novel *The Toll* (1914), except that in the earlier novel the treatment of the attractive but ill-bred Jewish woman was far less vicious. In Walker's text, however, especially in the echo of Hoggenheimer in the name 'Guggleheimer' and the allusion in 'Goldschmidt' to gold – connoting vulgar materialism and wealth – the images of the ostentatious, acquisitive Jewish men and women are reinforced.

In the voracious greed of Mrs Steinbach, Walker encodes the avarice of the evil Jew. Remnants of the image of the criminal Jew with underground connections can also be traced in the reference to a group of men who are obviously involved in shady dealings. The author cannot resist continuing the motif of the vulgar, rapacious Jew: 'Two of them who kept their hats on while they guzzled a green salad and cold meat, looked Jewish' (p.152). He refers in passing to 'Lisping Lou Behrmann's gang, a mob with numerous assaults and liquor convictions against them' (p.155). Thus at the middle of the century the spectre of the underworld Jew of Johannesburg, even of his connections with the liquor trade, survives.

Walker imitates the earlier Yiddish accent and the lisp both in the name of 'Lisping Lou Behrmann's gang' and the speech of the secretary of the Philharmonic society:

> "Yeth, yeth indeed," answered an excessive lisp at the other end. "Of courth Mithter Lomond ith going to conduct for uth. It vill be on the twenty-t'ird of dith month ... ve hope he can manage more than von ..." (p.127)

Near the end of the novel, the simmering hostility against Jews breaks out into a grotesque statement by the anti-Semitic Carruthers:

> " 'Nother thing I can't stand here are the Yids. I don't mind some Jews, but I bar the Yids. They lift their legs

and Yiddle over everything. The place is lousy with 'em pushing, elbowing 'Vot-you-vanters'. Yiddling over English, over sport, over art – everything. My friend up in Swaziland calls em go-Ghettoes of the twentieth century ... Ha! Ha! Not bad, eh?" (p.197)

The reference to the urinating dog is a continuation of the insulting trope of the Jew as animal. The scatological elision of 'piddle' with 'Yiddle' – itself a pejorative term – reinforces the virulently anti-Jewish tone of the novel. Carruthers satirises what he believes to be the pushiness of the Jew, his comments possibly revealing Walker's resentment of Jewish penetration into many aspects of Johannesburg life. He shows the Jews of the 'wanton city' (Johannesburg) involved in sport, the arts, journalism, and many areas other than the traditional ones of trade and criminality, which had long before acquired a negative label. This antagonism, and envy of the success of the Jew and the way in which his influence expands, may explain the projection into his novel, as late as 1949, of negative stereotypes.

Bernard Sachs attacked Walker for his anti-Semitism, and Walker retorted that he was not to blame for the utterances of his characters. Sachs rebuked Walker for his evasions by replying in print:

> What is the distance between Peter (Oliver) and the repulsive exhalation of Carruthers? That is important. The author, even if he is not the character Peter, cannot remain neutral towards it He must either agree with it and justify it – or disagree and clearly show it either through a character or his own comment. But he experiences no shudder, neither does he rebuke Carruthers.[15]

It has been argued that the author may use a prejudicial discourse because no other discourse is available. Further, it is suggested that, because an image totally uncontaminated by the weight of centuries is irretrievable, stereotypes may occasionally be used for effect by an author relatively innocent of the prejudice which they encode. However, this argument raises an artificial distance between the discourse within which the author works and the author himself. The very selection of certain characteristics and not others for intense focus can only be accomplished when the author connives with what he expects the reader to understand and approve. The author exercises control over his own work, he makes decisions and choices, and to opt to use these images without distancing his narrator or himself is indicative of his own negative attitude towards Jews.

If a comparison is made between Walker's textual anti-Semitism and a glancing reference to anti-Semitism in Peter Wilhelm's short story, 'Dolphins', in *LM and other Stories* (1975), it becomes apparent that by the 1970s, overt expression of anti-Semitism in fiction had been marginalised. A conversation takes place between drunken academics:

> 'Beasley's a clown,' said Robert in a slurred voice. He was drinking brandy and ginger ale, and had already downed eight.
> 'A real clown,' affirmed Madge. Then: 'I should have known better than to have taken a Jew on my staff.'
> ‑'Oh, is he Jewish?' said Robert. 'I didn't know. That explains everything.' He opened his mouth and laughed, playing the professor's little game of anti-semitism.
> It suited Madge's style to hate Jews and he continued to harp on Beasley. (p.50)

Of major importance here is the narrator's ironic attitude. He stresses the drunken professor's 'little game of anti-semitism' from which he, significantly, distances himself. Madge too, plays a game – hatred of Jews is merely a 'style'. In Walker's treatment, however, no sense of narratorial or authorial distance is present, and his text, as distinguished from Wilhelm's, may therefore be read as anti-Semitic.

Hidden Anti-Semitism

A.A. Murray

More insidious is 'hidden anti-Semitism'. A text purporting to be philo-Semitic may, on examination, be found to be just the opposite. A.A. (Audrey Alison) Murray's *Anybody's Spring*, (1959) is a vivid example.

On a superficial reading, the novel seems to be a defence of the Jew, since the plot appears to culminate in a vindication and celebration of Jewish virtues. Murray depicts Isaac Fonk as a kindly Jew, previously a small country shopkeeper in the Orange Free State, who makes money on the Johannesburg Stock Exchange, and becomes very wealthy. Throughout the novel Fonk appears to represent the good Jew. He is tenderhearted, philanthropic and a kindly father, stigmatised and isolated by his family and the anti-Semites. He 'is oppressed with nervous foreboding', and muses:

> The bankrupt man is a Jew and, at once, all Jews are suspect. Even old Fonk ... As always, in adversity, the Jew crystallises out of the melting pot of humanity. The mass draws away from him and he is suddenly isolated, the insoluble body where all is merged and blended into one substance, one race, however divergent its individual origins may be. The stigma of the bankrupt man does not fall upon all other members of the Exchange because they too are stock-brokers, but upon Fonk and certain others, because they too are Jews. (p.259)

While still a poor man, he had married a destitute Gentile girl, who soon draws back in horror from his Jewishness:

> when he surprised her ... her eyes, as they turned upon him, were filled with a sort of startled dismay. Only now, he thought, does she fully realise that she is my wife, and she is appalled. (p.25)

Here is the first instance of the recoil from things Jewish which will be the hallmark of the text.

The Fonks have three children. The violently anti-Semitic daughter, Yelland, discovers at the end of the novel that she is not Jewish at all, her natural father being Mrs Fonk's Gentile lover. She suddenly loses her prejudices against the Jews, and in a scene which appears to be grafted on to the text, she chooses to affirm her solidarity with Mr Fonk, and through him with Judaism. Fonk has paid vast sums of

money to save her reputation and, disillusioned with Johannesburg
life, she returns with him to the country town:

> 'I had to come ... I hope you're not angry, Father ...
> Can you buy me a ticket? Can you get me a seat?'
>   'As it happens I have the compartment to myself.'
>   'But I saw you were booked in with someone else.'
>   He smiled, a little twisted, wry smile.
>   'Oh, he? He tipped the conductor to get him out of
> here. He didn't want to share a compartment with a bally
> old Jew-boy.'
>   He saw tears spurt up in her eyes. She leaned forward
> and placed a hand on his knee.
>   '... When I knew you were not my father you became
> so much more ... I remembered every kind word, every
> indulgence, every affectionate gesture ... I want to see
> the sort of thing you like and get to like it too ...'
> (pp.298-300)

This unrealistic scene, which is nowhere anticipated in the text,
occurs at the end of a novel in which the subtext is strongly, even
offensively anti-Jewish. Throughout the novel Yelland, vocally and
with extreme repulsion, has displayed her hatred of Jews – proffered
by the author as self-hatred:

> 'I hate Jews,' she said ... 'There's something greedy
> about them I can't stand. The way they eat; the way
> they speak about their possessions; the way the hands
> of the women curl inwards as if they were grasping at
> something; the way the fingers of the men fit together
> as though they had been slit down by a sharp knife.
> I hate them. To know that I am one of them makes
> my flesh crawl. Aunt Leah! Oh God, Aunt Leah!' Her
> lips trembled and her nostrils dilated with disgust.
> (p.62)

Aunt Leah is a typical negative image. She is 'fat' (p.27) and
'repulsive' (p.23), with 'dark, protruding eyes' (p.19). One niece says

of her that 'she revolts my eye' (p.8), another that 'she sickens me' (p.9). As expected, Aunt Leah has a Yiddish accent.

The description of the hands and fingers is curious. It revives the image of the malformed Jew of medieval iconography, and projects the physical revulsion felt not only by Yelland – which echoes her mother's revulsion towards her own husband, Fonk – beyond the text, so that the reader is drawn into experiencing the same recoil. Throughout the novel allusions to Jewish religious observances and taboos, to Jewish food, and to characteristics labelled 'ugly' and 'vulgar', are linked for insulting, pejorative effect.

Although most of these anti-Semitic effects are projected through Yelland's consciousness, the narrator does not distance herself from her character, whose change of heart at the end of the novel is entirely unconvincing. There is a complete absence of any authorial distance or irony. Yelland's brother, Mark, concurs with her in rejecting his Jewishness; he defines their disgust as a sickness: '... it is in yourself ... How wonderful it would be to be born into this life quite free ... None of those stigmas of race or creed or faction which now constitute our uneasy heritage ...' (p.63).

The experience of self-hatred is accepted as perfectly natural by both the characters and the author, and by extension is an expected response from the reader as well. It should be read in conjunction with the way the author frequently shows Jewish qualities and characteristics as ugly and unpleasant.

The text abounds with sneers about Jewish wealth, appearance and ostentation. Fonk's second daughter's Jewish suitor is 'a big solid man with a fleshy nose and glittering gold rings on his fingers' (p.294). 'He had a rough, porky skin like a scraped pig' (p.296). A character exclaims: 'I know old Fonk oozes money and all that, but hell ... you don't make friends with people like that. The blighter's a Yid!' (p.14). A house is a 'disgusting kosher monstrosity' (p.14). A 'vulture of a woman' is depicted as a 'Jewess with a beak of a nose and bifocal glasses which made each eye look like an upturned shellfish. Her husband, an immensely fat man with three solid rolls beneath his chin, surveyed the room with subtle contempt in his insolent, dark eyes,' (p.189). The vulture and a shellfish, images of predatory and slimy creatures, are characteristic of anti-Semitic discourse. A girl recoils at Mark's kiss:

> There was a herbal, astringent taste in her mouth as though it had been tainted ... 'I've been kissed by a Jew.' She felt that she had committed a crime against herself, against her family, against her upbringing ... She could picture her mother's unbelieving horror ... And her father. She knew his contempt for the Jews that amounted almost to a mania. She had seen him flush and splutter with anger when he talked of them, hating them for their skill at amassing money in a world where everyone but himself seemed to have a great deal too much of it. (p.121)

Again, no authorial irony is evident, rather a strong echo of the discourse of racial anti-Semitism familiar from Nazi propaganda, as well as the envy aroused by successful economic competition.

Yelland is nearly seduced by a rich Jew, Phillip Pollins, who uses her as a pawn in a sordid matrimonial transaction. Pollins, who has married a Gentile woman, has changed his name from the Jewish sounding 'Pollinsky', and been converted to Christianity.

> His parents had been East European Jews but, some-where in his lineage, Nordic or Scandinavian blood had infiltrated the veins of his forebears to make him tall and fair-skinned, to give him his thick, powerful neck and red, metallic helmet of close, curly hair. His eyes were small, deep blue and set closely on either side of his thick, straight nose.
>
> Men said of Pollins that he did not look like a Jew, yet, knowing him one, it was impossible to see him as anything else. His feet flung outwards as he walked: something about the thrust of his head gave his straight back the appearance of inherent round-shvoulderedness. His hands were small boned and fleshy ... the fingers ... fitted one into the other without a gap. (p.208)

The almost obsessive concentration on physical features is, as has been shown in previous chapters, a characteristic of the anti-Semitic authors of the beginning of the century. In the first paragraph, in every one of the supposedly 'non-Jewish' features catalogued – the tall stature, fair skin, 'powerful' neck, blue eyes and 'metallic helmet' of hair, which encodes the concept of the 'Aryan' warrior – the shadow of the negative image can be found. The reader is invited to take for granted that it is the drop of Nordic blood which has made him tall, fair-skinned and blue-eyed; the short stature, dark skin and dark eyes of the Jewish stereotype are implied.

After listing the so-called non-Jewish features, the author proceeds to conjure up the stereotypical ghetto-Jew – flat-footed and round-shouldered. The Svengali image hovers as well. Pollins woos Yelland with his 'silky' voice (p.210), and by taking her to the opulent John Orr's tea room. Yelland sneers: 'You would [choose John Orr's] because it's got the thickest carpet and the most mirrors. The Jews love it' (p.209). She sees in Pollins 'a cleverly camouflaged unctuousness; the same personal impertinence that she hated in his race, however skilfully he might disguise it ...' (p.238). She shudders: 'He's bought a share in me with one red rose and an extravagant gesture. He's a Jew alright, even if he doesn't look like one ...' (p.207).

Pollins's attempted seduction of Yelland is reminiscent of the relationship between 'the Jew' and Bertie in Olive Schreiner's *From Man to Man*, that of Julius Hermann and May Leslie in Stephen Black's *The Golden Calf*, or Rudolf Feinbaum and Ethel in Westrup's *The Debt*. Pollins is a stockbroker, a figure representing the crooked Jewish businessman, and he confesses: 'I am a strong man whose only lust is power.' He says further:

> 'And the ladder in my climb to it has been the weakness and greed of men who consider themselves models of honesty and rectitude. Do you know how one acquires power from such men? ... They are willing to turn a blind eye to your methods in securing profit to yourself so long as there is also an adequate profit for them ... These men, my co-directors, will whine that they trusted me and that I have abused that trust. Bah! Trust, honour, fair-play, all the trumps weaklings have invented for their own protection! ... I have been a king ... and have bought and sold shares ... to the tune of millions of pounds and not a soul has questioned me as long as there was plenty of money for all ... power ... was as

> necessary to me as life ... To save it I'd do anything. I'd
> kick anyone out of my way. I'd drag them down; I'd
> climb on their bodies if it meant maintaining the
> position I hold precariously today. (pp.250-251)

This is the Hoggenheimer figure in its mid-century guise of the
Johannesburg stockbroker. It resonates with the much publicised
Jewish participation in South African finance, and the growth of
financial empires such as that of the Oppenheimers. Some of the
components of the earlier stereotypes, such as the participation in
IDB or smousing, have been modified or adapted to suit the new
mid-century circumstances.

The novel apparently attempts to avoid overt anti-Semitism but
covertly it betrays the author's bias and wholesale acceptance of
stereotypes. When at times the narrator treats Fonk sympathetically,
the writing is unconvincing. 'He had been a good, hard-working
young Jew, much respected by the villagers' (p.17), is her banal
introduction to the young Fonk, repeating the discourse of those
anti-Semites who refer to the exceptional Jew in order to distinguish
him from what they hold to be the norm. In order to make him
acceptably sympathetic, Murray needs to eliminate Fonk's Jewish
characteristics: 'There was scarcely a trace of accent in his deep,
softly-modulated voice. [He had a] passion to acquire knowledge and
the outward signs of a cultured mind' (p.24). Fonk's truly favourable
attributes comprise significantly his escape from his stigmatising
Yiddish accent and his aspirations to Gentile culture.

− 5 −

ANTI-SEMITISM
AND ETHNICITY

Jewish authors respond

At first the response was only in Yiddish. In a story entitled 'Lost her Head', published in 1939,[1] Morris Hoffman (1885-1940) depicts graphically, from the Jewish point of view, an encounter with the naked anti-Semitism in the Cape during the late 1930s. A young middle-class Gentile man is in love with a Jewish girl who works with him in a factory. Gradually influenced by Greyshirt propaganda, he asks her:

> 'is there any truth in what the Jew-haters write in those newspapers and pamphlets – that the Jews have a secret organisation whose aim is to eliminate all Christians, and that the hatred of Jews for Gentiles is implacable? ... [D]on't you know anything about the book "Talmud" which lays it down as a good deed to rob and ruin Christians? ... [I]n their clutches lies the control of the whole country and all its important enterprises ... [T]he Greyshirts maintain that the Jews build their fortunes by cheating non-Jews with the help of the commandments laid down by the Zionists and the Communists, who disseminate the teachings of the "Talmud", the "*Kol Nidrei*" and the "Elders of Zion" ... [O]ne can't deny that there are Jews who stage fake bankruptcies and even those who burn down their own businesses ... I'm only

repeating what I read a few days ago in the leaflets ...
[that] Jews have all the most lucrative jobs, they are all
rich and happy, while the Afrikaners are poverty-
stricken, toil-worn – they stand in the scorching sun,
with shovels and wrecking-bars in their hands, breaking
up stones, constructing roads ... have you ever seen Jews
doing such hard unskilled labour?' (pp.37-38)

Referring to many of the anti-Jewish grievances propagated by the
neo-Nazi organisations, Hoffman's narrator goes on to allude to
governmental support for Greyshirt agitation:

Their Jew-baiting was becoming unendurable; their
poisonous accusations cut to the quick every human
being with decent feelings; yet the Government turned a
deaf ear and looked on foolishly at the abominable
behaviour of these thugs. The response to every Jewish
protest against the fact that such a gang was permitted
to insult the whole Jewish people was that no law existed
to prohibit the vilification of an entire nation, although it
had always been prohibited to defame an individual.
(p.41)

The denouement of the story occurs when the Gentile man chops off
his Jewish girlfriend's head. The melodramatic ending seems to have
been dictated by the violent emotions evoked in the story.

A later and more affirmative literary response to anti-Semitism was
the flaunting of Jewish consciousness, as in the exploring, publicising
and celebrating of Jewish communal roots in South Africa. At the
mid-century it became a commonplace for Jewish writers in English
to stress their own eastern European origins and their experiences in
South Africa. They did so by sketching the Lithuanian background
of their Jewish characters, or by publishing autobiographical or semi-
autobiographical memoirs.

The parade of ethnicity can be traced both in the development of
Jewish historiography[2] and in the proliferation of family sagas or novels
of nostalgia in which the shtetl is recalled, the vicissitudes suffered by
the immigrants to South Africa and their difficulties with anti-

Semitism memorialised, and their triumphs glorified and codified into a new South African Jewish mythos. A new stereotype, the Jewish immigrant – variant of the archetype of the Wandering Jew – emerges in both autobiography and fiction. Since some Jews feel more comfortable in the new country, they may explore their own difference, or use Jewish stereotypes ironically, or exploit Jewish material for humorous effect.

A negative response to anti-Semitism is also found in the Jewish fiction of this period. Possibly because of self-consciousness in the presence of Gentiles, Jewish authors may feel compelled to conceal as far as possible their own Jewishness, even when their work is clearly autobiographical. A less obvious variation of their self-consciousness is their frequent use of a Gentile pseudonym. They may treat the racial situation obliquely by concentrating on another out-group, in this case the oppressed blacks.[3] More dramatically, the Jewish author, internalising the stereotypes generated by Gentiles, may satirise aspects of Jewish communal experience and project and propagate the negative images earlier constructed by Gentile authors.

Light-Hearted Fiction

My Jewish Clients (1953) and *Jewish Merry-Go-Round* (1959) are M. Davidson's collections of humorous sketches of Jewish life. Davidson writes of immigrants, traders, businessmen, the 'kaffir-eatnik', the 'peruvian' father, the 'idol of Ferreirastown', the stock exchange, barmitzvahs, the celebration of Passover: in fact, a wide cross section of the every day experience of urban Jews. His touch is light and good humoured. Although many of the situations are hackneyed, the author seems to go out of his way to stress that his characters are varied and not typical:

> Berel, a middle-aged, pug-nosed, red-faced man with broad shoulders and a menacing paunch, was not a millionaire … (p.60, 'A Tale of Two Storekeepers.' *Jewish Merry-Go-Round*)

> My client San Nooshein was a wealthy bachelor in the late thirties, not bad-looking, intelligent, fairly

well-educated. (p.69, 'Too Rich to Marry', *My Jewish Clients*)

Some of the characters are presented as rogues, but they are never evil; many, like Mr Berdelowsky, are kindly:

> "I tell you, I'm going to be hard … A *chazer* (pig) gets away with everything. Why be soft? What for? What thanks you get? …"
> I nodded.
> His red eyes lit up. "Will you do me a kindness? Please give this fiver to my sister, Mrs. Cohen. She lives in 72 Upper Staib Street. A sick woman."
> "I thought you were going to be hard."
> "Never mind. She is my sister. Blood is wetter than water, like the Engelsman says."
> (p.26, 'The Kaffir-Eatnik', *My Jewish Clients*.)

There are many Yiddish expressions and allusions to Jewish custom. The fact that there seems to be a certain amount of special pleading, that the focus may fall on the foibles but more often on the virtues of the Jews, and that the later book has a glossary translating Yiddish expressions into English, suggests that Davidson writes for a wider, non-Jewish audience.

A very similar treatment of Jewish experience is found in David Dainow's *Our Schadchan* (matchmaker), (1954). It, too, has a glossary and several humorous illustrations. The offering of in-group experience for out-group inspection, even though it may to a certain extent be sanitised, is an index of how the Jewish author has become sufficiently confident to enjoy his own ethnicity and to share it with a wider audience.

A Half-Way Case

Sam Manion's historical novel of Jewish immigration at the end of the nineteenth century, *The Greater Hunger* (1964), is notable as an attempt to domesticate the image of the Jew and make it acceptable to Gentiles. It is the story of David Mason, originally Manachowitz –

his name had been changed by customs officials on his arrival in South Africa. He is a Jew from Lutzin in the north of Russia. A professional soldier in the Russian army, he is 'over six foot in his socks' (p.19).

After marrying Marinka Dubowitz, a Jewish girl who is 'blonde, her long plaits coiled high on her shapely head in the Russian fashion of the day' (p.13), David emigrates to South Africa to seek a better life. That these characters are Jews seems almost fortuitous. However, there is a sense that the author is watching anti-Semitism over his shoulder, since the positive aspects, which are in fact the seemingly 'non-Jewish' qualities of the characters, are highlighted.

The insistence on the fact that they are blonde and tall, seems a conscious effort on the part of the author to depict an opposite type to the dark, short Jew of popular typecasting. That Manion consciously portrays David and Marinka as Jews who have escaped their background is apparent in David's avowal: 'We belong to a new generation. I can't and don't go to Shul to argue endlessly Talmudic points. And Marinka, Joseph, please God, when he grows up, will be even more remote from this kind of life than we are' (p.19). The implied sneer at 'this kind of life' – the traditional Jewish kind of life – betrays the ambivalence in Manion's superficially positive portrayal of David and Marinka.

The more familiar physical type is the sketch of Abraham Cohen the tailor, a distant relative, with whom David boards when he arrives in Cape Town: 'He was a little man, thin and stooped as if weighed down by the cares of life. His eyes were covered by thick lenses' (p.25). There is also a Jew who is ' a wanderer in a strange land' (p.26), and an immigrant smous, a dealer in bags and bottles, who invests his profits in property, becomes a millionaire and boasts that his daughters '[a]ll three married doctors' (p.65). In South Africa, David follows the formulaic pattern of upward mobility, to the extent of divorcing Marinka and marrying a Gentile woman.

Although Manion evokes Jewish types, he effectively smudges them. Nevertheless, in its attempt to show a new, not very Jewish kind of Jew, Manion attempts to make the Jew acceptable to Gentiles. The rejection of what Manion sees as typically negative aspects represents one type of response to anti-Semitism.

The Jewish Silence

The avoidance or disguising of Jewish material by Jewish authors which is manifested at this period in South African history may have been another reaction to prejudice.

Bertha Goudvis (1876-1965) was born in England and brought to South Africa as a child of five. Her father had emigrated from Poland to England and then moved on to South Africa. With her parents and siblings, Goudvis spent her youth trekking across the country as her father made a living first as a smous, later as a gold prospector and tavern keeper in Barberton before moving to Bulawayo, Rhodesia. Living among both English and Afrikaans communities but belonging to neither because she was Jewish, she was in a unique position to record early colonial attitudes. After her marriage, she was manageress of hotels in Lourenço Marques (now Maputo) in Mozambique and Natal, worked as a freelance journalist for several newspapers and wrote short stories, plays and a novel, *Little Eden* (1949).

While Jewish material features in two of her plays – *A Husband for Rachel* and *The Aliens* – written during the 1920s and 1930s and unpublished during her lifetime, and a few short stories, it is not found in her novel, *Little Eden* (1949), set in Natal, where she lived for some time. The main action concerns the visit of a Rand magnate to inspect the minerals on a farm. Mr Karlsbach, an upright man, is, in fact, Jewish but is treated in a cursory though sympathetic manner: 'He's a family man himself and [very] concerned about his own wife when she's in that condition. Jews are like that, you know' (p.138). Karlsbach himself is the butt of cheats and, in a reversal of the familiar situation, is 'verneuked' by the Gentiles (p.134).

As the novel is based on the facts of her own life, Goudvis constructs a narrator closely resembling herself, with a family identical to her own in many respects but whose religious affiliation is not stated. It is implied that the family are Christians. The novel was written in old age, after a period when Goudvis had been involved in Jewish affairs. She had been an ardent Zionist, acting as the first treasurer of the Johannesburg Women's Zionist League.

In her unpublished autobiography, *South African Odyssey*, written during the 1960s, she mentions the 'difficulty' (p.63) and restrictions she experienced because she was Jewish. At another time, writing of her school days in Burghersdorp she records:

> Because mother had told Mr. White that I was Jewish I was excused from morning prayers and New Testament instruction. I was the only Jewish child in the school but did not feel my isolation until one day a classmate named Maria approached me in the playground. She was a big girl and towered over me as she made her accusation: 'You are a Jewess and the Jews killed Christ.'
>
> 'Oh no!' I replied, 'the Romans did that.' 'It's a lie: the Jews crucified Jesus,' she cried, and so saying struck me with such violence that I fell to the ground ...[4]

She writes of a slightly later period:

> Jewish social life in Barberton followed the usual pattern. English-speaking families kept together ... Nearly all had some non-Jewish friends but the more sensitive were conscious of a social bias against our people and reacted in the usual way, so that there was a kind of self-segregation.[5]

Goudvis reverses the concept that 'some of my best friends are Jewish', recording that the Jews 'kept together' and merely 'had some non-Jewish friends'. She suggests that this self protective attitude is the Jews' reaction to their perception of the Gentiles' 'social bias' against them. Her experiences of religious anti-Semitism and social discrimination obviously left a deep impression. Elsewhere she has written:

> It has been said that in those early days there was no anti-Semitism in South Africa and that Jews and Christians mingled freely in social life. My own experience is that when a few Jewish people live in a non-Jewish community they are accepted for what they are themselves and if their appearance is agreeable and their manners show good breeding they may become as

> popular and respected as any other people. When, however, the Jewish population increases and includes, as all populations must do, a certain obnoxious section, the non-Jews begin to show anti-Semitism, classing good and bad Jews together in their race hatred. Consequently the Jews draw apart and form their own cliques amongst themselves ... Sensible Jews, who are well aware of the way in which history repeats itself in this connection, make their own social life with or without non-Jewish friends ...[6]

In her own acceptance of the idea that the Jew ought to have 'an agreeable appearance' and manners which 'show good breeding' in order to be acceptable to Gentile society, Goudvis seems to be conniving in the Gentile perception of Jews and of internalising the negative stereotype of the ugly and uncouth Jew. Elsewhere she remarks approvingly that her father did not look Jewish, having blond hair, blue eyes and 'the straightest nose I have ever seen'.[7] Her rejection of 'Jewish' Jews is further evident in her demarcation of 'sensible' Jews as those who 'draw apart' from the 'obnoxious section'.

A reason for Goudvis's reluctance to identify herself as a Jewish author may be the very need she describes to be 'popular and respected' by Gentile society. The passage indicates the extent to which she has been influenced by the value system of the Gentile world. Possibly for this reason, or because of the peculiarly ambivalent situation of the Jew at mid-century, she clearly did not, in the late 1940s, wish to tackle the problem of the position of a Jewish woman in colonial society, preferring to concentrate on examining her own burgeoning feminism. At about the time she was writing her novel she was asked by the Johannesburg newspaper, *The Star*, to write a weekly column of Jewish interest, which she did for ten years, but it is revealing that she felt the need to conceal her name – and her gender – and used a pseudonym, Daniel.[8]

A further example of this 'silence' may be found in *Strange Odyssey*, (1952), Betty Misheiker's novel based on the life of her mother in eastern Europe – her marriage, the birth of her children and her emigration to South Africa. In this book Misheiker entirely omits Jewish reference. The family's place of origin is given as 'Shavli in

Imperial Czarist Russia' (p.8). Although this is a large town in Lithuania from which many Jews emigrated to South Africa, this fact is never mentioned, presumably because to write of emigration from Lithuania would be to disclose the Jewish content of the account.

One or two clues, however, alert the Jewish reader. 'My brother admits to having placed an outsize Lithuanian pillow on my face,' (p.7) she writes, betraying the true place of origin of the family. Further, she reports how her mother meets a Russian doctor named Kallin who admits he is the son of an elderly lady named Kallinsky. He had changed his name from the Jewish sounding 'Kallinsky' to the Russian sounding 'Kallin'.

By Russianising her characters and their origins and by carefully censoring any reference to Jewish custom, religion or language, Misheiker would seem to be intent on expunging the image of the Jew from her work. Although these are minor touches and the intention may well have been to universalise the subject, Betty Misheiker is well known as a Jewish woman and this fact is nowhere stated in the text.[9]

Nadine Gordimer dealt with Jewish experience in some of her early writing (which will be discussed in Chapter 8) After 1953, however, for over thirty-five years she did not in any serious way tap the potential of Jewish material in her work. When she does so in her novel of 1987, *A Sport of Nature*, she resorts to the use of stereotypes.

In-group Treatment of the Jew – the Internalisation of Stereotypes

Albert Segal's novel, *Johannesburg Friday* (1954), depicts a day in the life of a suburban Johannesburg Jewish family – Mr and Mrs Leventhal's twenty-fifth wedding anniversary. The suburban lifestyle of Jews becomes, especially for Jewish writers, a parallel to the lifestyle of the ghetto of some fifty years before. In Segal's novel the familiarities of South African Jewish life of the early fifties is explored, not in depth but in breadth. Reference is made to immigration and the father's relentless accumulation of money. He then loses interest in wealth, runs a small bookstore, and becomes a member of a Benevolent Society. The image slides round the spectrum from the acquisitive, ruthless immigrant, to the learned, philosophical and kindly Jew.

The children are more assimilated, some of them professionals, all of them driven by their parents' desire to see them educated and upwardly mobile. Once more there are relationships between Jews and blacks, and references to the illegal liquor trade, anti-Semitic incidents, and the daughter's involvement with a Gentile man. The most fully realised of the characters, Mrs Leventhal, is the closest we have in South African fiction to the 'Yiddishe Mamma'. However, this sentimentalised type – found in Yiddish literature, introduced into American mythology by Sophie Tucker in 1925, and retransformed in the 1940s into a martyr who nevertheless induces guilt in her children – has never been popular in South Africa.[10] Despite her concern with food and her children, Mrs Leventhal is not a true 'Yiddishe Mamma'. For one thing, she is not an eastern European immigrant like her husband. She comes from the East End of London. Then, too, she knows hardly any Yiddish.

While in Segal's novel there is very little attempt at characterisation, the specifically Jewish aspects of the family's daily life – the preparations for and celebration of the Sabbath – are exploited for local colour. There are touches of anti-Jewish feeling scattered throughout the text. Mrs Perlman, a Polish immigrant, is described with heavy satire:

> Toothless though she was, Mrs. Perlman did not find the pletzel [a sweetmeat] any the less tasteful. As she ripped it to shreds with her gums, ignoring the beads of spittle that trickled down her chin, she fumbled in the folds of her dress for a cigarette ... Words tumbled from her mouth in gusts of Yiddish and Polish. With them splattered particles of food, sprays of liquid and spirals of smoke. (p.48)

The voracious and ugly Jewess, a feature of Oliver Walker's *Wanton City*, is echoed here by a Jewish author, and demonstrates again a high degree of internalisation of Gentile prejudices. Nevertheless, the ostensible subject is a benign exploration of the daily life of a typical Jewish family, and the negative aspects are tentative.

Victor Barwin's *Millionaires and Tatterdemalions*, published in 1952, is a collection of short pieces dealing with differing experiences of

Jews in South Africa at the start of this century. The first story, 'The Emigrant Ship', describes the departure in 1902 of the cattle ship, *Baltik*, from the Latvian port of Libau with a hundred Jews on board. They come mainly from 'the border state of Lithuania, from ... Kovno, the district towns of Ponvesh and Shavli ... in the Jewish Pale' (p.13). The stereotype soon appears; the author writes of the Jews that they 'resembled the eternal symbol of Jews wandering from land to land' (p.13). Jews, praised for their diligence, are shown as superior members of the human race:

> The majority will forge ahead, fail perhaps, but will get up and start again, and never drift or go under.
> For there is grit in them; ambition, and the will to succeed. The relentless persecution that drove them from their old homes, that ground them down in poverty and squalor, has not broken them ... It gave them hardihood, taught them patience, and developed in them those mental powers which were their supreme attribute. If individually there were some to be criticized, taking them collectively, these Jews ... were a pulsating, living mass of people, thinking, loving, hating, feeling, as only superior members of the human race can, and will. (p.18)[11]

Like many other fictional good Jews they are musicians: ' "Most peculiar," said the captain to the officer by his side as they turned to go, "and I thought these were the rabble and dregs of the Pale. We have listened to a concert which was equal to the best talent in our own Riga" ' (p.28).

The Jewish immigrant is glorified. But while the author's intention might have been to construct a counter-myth to that of the dirty, evil, cunning immigrant mythos, the discourse of the text recalls that of other South African writers who construct images of Jews not from any close observation or perception but from worn out characteristics and situations inherited from previous centuries.

In 'Gold from Ophir', for example, he treats the familiar 'rags-to-riches' theme. In this story Loeb Hiram travels to Kimberley where he takes a lowly job clearing a claim. 'Loeb kept his job for six months, during which time he learned thoroughly all that was necessary to know regarding picking, washing, gravitating and sorting … ' (p.50). Soon 'he found a stone worth one hundred and fifty pounds' (p.51) and his fortune was made. Aari Hiram, previously referred to as Aari Solomon, prospers on the gold fields by becoming a smous. He invests his profits in property: '[a]ssisted by substantial loans from the local banks, Aari built twenty houses on his plots' (p.62). Soon he too is a millionaire.

Two other stories in this collection deal with apostasy in the Jewish community as a consequence of the drive for upward mobility. In 'A Convent Jewess' a young girl is sent to a convent school by her ambitious mother:

> "I will not allow our child to remain in the common Jewish school and mix with all the scum of Fordsburg and Ferreira. We must send her to a high-class convent school and make a grand lady of her." (p.81)

The scathing term 'scum', previously commonplace in the derogatory treatment of the Lithuanian immigrants in newspaper articles and reminiscences, thus makes another appearance in fiction. When the daughter tells her parents of her intention to marry a Gentile, they react with shock:

> "A non-Jew! Did you say a non-Jew?"
> "Yes!" answered Sonia with provoking contempt, "a Gentile, a gentleman and not a Shylock."
> "But a Gentile – and you, my daughter, a Jewess!"
> "I am not a Jewess!" she protested; "not by education and sentiment at any rate."
> …
> "But such folly! Such disgrace! To marry out of your faith, away from your God, and against the continuity of our people for which millions have sacrificed their lives in all generations."
> "The chain is broken," answered the girl.
> "Then go! I will not look upon a renegade," cried the father wildly. "Go!"
> "I'll go, of course I will," retorted Sonia, an ugly

smile twitching at her lips; "who will stay with Jews like you?"

...

"Sonia!" [her mother] cried, throwing up her hands in agonized appeal, "Stay! Come back! Don't go, darling. Don't leave me! Your mother – " And then her voice was silenced.

Sonia slammed the door on her parents and went away – away to her lover. (pp.96-97)

If Barwin's intention was to expose the wrongful thinking both of the mother who, through her snobbish attitudes allowed the situation to develop, and of the treacherous Sonia herself, he ruins his opportunity through the use of cliché and melodrama. This provokes an uneasy sense of at least the partial endorsement of stereotypical thinking.

'The Call' is an overly sentimental tale of a 'mighty magnate of the stock exchange' (p.101) who lives in a 'palatial Parktown mansion'. He has married out of the faith and 'Mammon was his god' (p.104). He ignores the Day of Atonement, but when his wife prepares to take the children to church to *Nachmaal*, he offers to take his son to the synagogue:

The Christian mother jumped up from her chair and rushed to her son as if to save him from the peril of his life. She tore him away from his father's arms and pressed the boy to her side.

"Come away," she exclaimed. "Your father is a Jew!"

That his father was a Jew was quite a revelation to the boy, who had never been told ... The only man he knew as "a Jew" was a bearded, shabby-looking man who occasionally came to the back door shouting for old clothes, whom the housemaids addressed in an insolent manner and upon whom he considered it great sport to set the dogs barking and biting. That his father should be like that man almost terrified the simple child...

And the father saw and understood. He saw and understood the hateful look which his wife threw at him as she led the children out of the room.

He was left alone – an outcast in his own home.
(p.107)

The magnate is finally reconciled to his religion by a well-timed letter from his dying mother. But any emotionally satisfying effect is cancelled, as in the case of the previous story, by the possibly unconscious evocation of anti-Semitism. In an exaggerated and ludicrous manner the Christian mother wrests her son from the figure of the Other, the bogeyman Jew, his father.

The use of anti-Semitic discourse has a double effect. The intention might have been to provoke sympathy for stigmatised Jews while at the same time satirising the apostate. But the powerful presentation of recoil from Judaism and Jews is all the stronger for the use of the hostile negative stereotypes. By this time entrenched as part of the mythos, they become emotionally more effective than the author intended and the consequence is highly ambivalent.

Arthur Markowitz uses even more stridently anti-Semitic discourse. His novel, *Facing North* (1949), focuses on a Jewish family and follows the fortunes of the daughter, Maxa. It is a cautionary tale of her disgrace after her sexual affairs with both a Gentile and a coloured man. In Peter Abrahams's 'Jewish Sister', sexual attraction between a Jewish girl and a coloured man was the vehicle for the author's depiction of a sympathetic identification between the two. However, dealt with by Jewish writers, the stock situation brings disgrace and invokes a taboo. In *Facing North* Maxa becomes a fallen woman, no better than a prostitute – a fate from which her father rescues her by arranging a marriage with an immigrant Jew.

The author's point of view is complex. His treatment of Maxa's fate is not without irony. Markowitz satirises the parents' reaction to Maxa's disgrace – the hasty procurement of a husband who is only acceptable because they believe she has spoiled her chances of any respectable match. But the narratorial voice shares with the university-educated Maxa her repulsion from her husband who is a Jewish immigrant shopkeeper. His Yiddish accent is savagely guyed by the narrator: 'Doin't be afreid, mine sveet,' he wheedled. 'Doin't cry, mine vife, I lov you ... doin't cry ... ' (p.400). In this text the Jewish characters show this form of snobbish disdain for those less assimilated and educated than themselves. In his failure to negate the negative impression, the author seems to share this attitude.

Victor and Yettah Freye, Maxa's parents, are immigrants from eastern Europe:

> Thirty years ago, when he arrived in Cape Town ... Victor knew only one ambition. He wanted security and all that came with it: respectability and social position among his fellow men ... he changed his name from Freydberg to Freye. It sounded less foreign and he wanted to be a good South African.
>
> With a clearly defined aim before him [he] had gone up-country in an ox-wagon to barter and trade with the farmers as so many of his compatriots were doing at that time ... when he had saved some money, he opened a store. (pp.15-16)

Victor is a smous whose upward mobility, change of name and bid for respectability are, by now, commonplaces in South African fiction. The familiar element of criminality is soon introduced in the form of his wife's sharp dealing with the 'Natives' and the Afrikaners:

> It had all started on one of those busy afternoons when the trains from the north brought back a load of Native mine-workers on their way home ... Yettah had taken to pottering about her husband's store after closing time ... and showed particular interest in the stacks of secondhand clothing ... (pp.17-18)

Yettah – the typical wily Jew – deceives the Natives into believing that the farthings she has planted in the linings of pockets are hidden sovereigns, luring them into paying exorbitant prices for trashy goods. Although Victor has some qualms about this dishonesty, he soon agrees with Yettah that '[h]e would want to give ... his children ... the best education that money could buy' (p.21). With heavy-handed irony, the author shows Victor conniving in various acts of dishonesty. He next opens a 'kaffir-eater', vowing that once he has made money he will join the committee of a Benevolent Bureau. He does so; but

Markowitz savagely satirises the activities of the Bureau, whose double standards in withholding aid from a destitute unmarried mother are an ominous foreshadowing of the fate that could have awaited Victor's own daughter.

Other more subtle disparagements drain sympathy from Victor's character. The irony is most obvious when Victor buys a house named *Ish-Tov* (the righteous man) 'in the most select of Cape Town's suburbs' (p.24). But Victor's 'righteousness' is scrutinised and demolished throughout the text. Victor acquires the property of a bankrupt Gentile grocer by guile at bargain price. Knowing that the site has flat rights, he erects a large block of flats on it and makes an enormous profit. This episode is an ironic allusion to the allegation made at the beginning of the century that Jewish shopkeepers bought up cheaply the property of bankrupt Afrikaners, a practice documented in newspaper reports and touched on by Pauline Smith in her story, 'Anna's Marriage'. The ruined grocer later joins the Greyshirts, the possible implication being that the Jews themselves, through sharp practices in the course of their ruthless upward mobility, may have been instrumental in giving rise to the anti-Semitic movement.

This novel, which appeared in the 1940s before Albert Segal's *Johannesburg Friday*, is the first recorded instance of a Jewish writer using the negative image of popular mythology in order to satirise the Jews of mid-twentieth century South Africa.

It will be shown in Chapter 6 that Dan Jacobson also has a critical attitude to some aspects of Jewish behaviour. But while Jacobson attacks the notion of prejudice, Markowitz sets out to expose his perceptions of Jewish elitism and Jewish business malpractices by manipulating the stereotypes of the foreign Jew, the dishonest Jew, the assimilationist Jew – the commonplaces of earlier fiction – in a text which could arguably be used to fan anti-Semitism. This was a bold move at a time when the Jewish community as a whole and its business practices in particular were under attack from press and pulpit. In his indictment Markowitz shows a high degree of self-confidence. He has evidently internalised some of the norms and prejudices, if not of the Gentile, at least of the assimilated towards the foreign Jew.

A second novel, *Market Street* (1959), has a similar tendency. The theme is the stock rags to riches situation. Jacob Silber is an impoverished immigrant from Lithuania with 'his eyes on the main chance' (p.21). He has a strong Yiddish accent and his speech is riddled with Yiddish expressions. There is, however, a redeeming sense of irony as when Jacob reflected: 'Funny how they [South African Jews] call the *shocherdike* (blacks) dogs an want to tritt them like pipple' (p.38).

With the money he has made in various ingenious ways, Jacob surreptitiously buys up unproductive land belonging to an Afrikaner Free State farmer, as he suspects that the ground is gold-bearing, but decides to withhold his motives. Of course, he has guessed correctly, and becomes a millionaire. This presentation differs in few respects from that of Gentile writers and journalists at the turn of the century. Jacob Silber is a literary descendant of Abraham Goldenstein, the main character of Stephen Black's play, *Helena's Hope, Ltd*, who is similarly a smous who makes a fortune through slyly buying up gold-bearing land. The conflation of the markers of appearance – signalled by the bulbous nose (p.13) – with the Yiddish accent, double dealing and ascent to wealth, especially at the expense of the Afrikaner, recalls the stock figure of the Boereverneuker. That this concept is present in the author's mind becomes explicit in an Afrikaner's emphatic comment concerning Jacob; he said that he 'was not going to be *verneuked* by a little Jew …' (p.74).

There is, typically, a love affair between a Jewish man and a black (Indian) girl. Other stock characters are Mrs Melman, 'a sagging, heavily built, middle-aged woman' (p.31), a young Zionist, and a beautiful, convent-educated young Jewish girl, whose 'body was slender with only a suggestion of coming voluptuousness about her bosom' (p.123). Although the character of the feckless Len Melman, a young Jewish man who has *not* made money, is treated with some humorous sympathy, he is merely a foil for the far more powerful figure of Jacob Silber. Markowitz points to the prevailing anti-Semitism in the country as Len Melman muses:

> You are hated for becoming assimilated or remaining unassimilated, for being a liberal or being an extremist. You are called a traitor and a deserter, a *kaffirboetie* and a jingo, a Judas, an enemy of the people. And you are hated … (p.180)

Attested by the stock situations and exaggerated behaviour of Jacob Silber, the satire is directed at all Jews and is by far the controlling feature of the text. This pattern was to be followed by other Jewish authors who, scorning their own background, sought to exorcise a sense of inferiority and to ingratiate themselves with the dominant culture by using the very discourse of anti-Semitism in constructing and often savagely mocking Jewish characters.

The fiction of Markowitz, Segal and Barwin gathers together some of the elements of the earlier negative images, and grafts on to them new aspects and new emphases which are specific to the situation of the South African Jews of the mid-century. It would seem that at this time the mythos is being subtly altered, and the treatment of the Jew becomes substantially a Jewish concern.

In texts written by Jewish authors, the Jew is no longer a figure of the outsider, unless, as in the case of Barwin's 'mighty magnate' the intention – though not the result – is to treat the image sympathetically. Usually the stereotypical situations are dealt with from the inside as part of an in-group perception. Variations of the original negative prototype modified on the diamond fields, together with the ambivalent images surrounding the figure of the smous, emerge here as the immigrant who makes good, the apostate, the Jewish businessman. In the texts dealt with so far these types are neither scrutinised nor, in any serious way, interrogated by the authors. This interrogation will be found in the work of Dan Jacobson, and to a lesser extent in Lewis Sowden's *Kop of Gold* (1955).

–6–

INTERROGATING
THE STEREOTYPES

Dan Jacobson

During the 1950s Dan Jacobson wrote a number of short stories and novels concerning inter-group relationships, a subject which, at that time, had hardly been treated at all by South African writers. During the period after the National Party's victory in 1948 with the statutory hardening of racial and group prejudice, Jacobson was involved in a fundamental examination of his own position as a white, a Jew and a writer. In his non-fictional writing at this time, Jacobson claimed to be a 'liberal', but he was also candid about what he uncomfortably acknowledged as his own personal, inbred racial prejudice, which he castigated as a 'blur of ignorance' and 'failure of the imagination'.[1] For him the exploration of racial prejudice and group animosity had become a moral imperative.[2]

Most of the chief characters of his early fiction are Jews, many of them marginal and alienated. Critics have recognised the pervading sense of alienation in Jacobson's work,[3] but it has never been clearly categorised either as an aspect of Jacobson's own moral dilemma, or as a function of his fictional representation of the Jews' familiarity with the condition of stigma, their consciousness of being, like the blacks, members of a permanent out-group. Jacobson, however, also believed that the Jews, in the course of their upward mobility, had assumed 'an unheroic posture', being overly protective of their own group or self interest and failing to support other victims of discrimination.[4] In many of his early works he explores Jewish issues in the

South African context, and his focus includes a consideration of the obligations of one minority group towards other groups.

The seemingly anecdotal short story, 'A Day in the Country',[5] presents, in almost diagrammatic fashion, a paradigm of the triangular group relationships between Afrikaners, Jews and blacks.

The narrator, a young Jew, travelling with his family on a country road, encounters a number of Afrikaners apparently torturing a helpless and terrified black child. In symbolic terms, the child represents the powerless black group, with the Afrikaners – identified by their language – as oppressors and bullies. 'They were laughing ... white face after face all bared in smiles' (p.21). The cruel animal image is present in the word 'bared'. Employing a shorthand typical of categorical thinking, Jacobson consciously and ironically makes use of those colonial stereotypes in which physical cues are vital to the process of stereotyping. He describes an Afrikaner as 'big and strong, with enormous bare arms folded on his chest ... wearing a grey shirt' (p.25), thus deliberately evoking the spectre of the Greyshirt movement.[6]

Jacobson also sketches the Jews with reference to stereotypes and stereotypical situations. They take advantage of their position of isolation and protection in the self-imposed 'ghetto' of their motor car, not merely to signal their disapproval, but to avoid a direct confrontation. Conscious of their situation within their own minority group, the Jews identify neither with the dominant Afrikaner in-group nor with the persecuted black out-group. Yet, because of their experience of oppression, they empathise with the persecuted rather than with the persecutors.

By their silence and their moral cowardice born of a fear of diverting the Afrikaners' hostility to their own group, they connive in a symbolic act of oppression. In this way they tacitly ally themselves with the powerful in-group to avoid being recognised by the Afrikaners as Jews, members of a vulnerable out-group. Jacobson illustrates the way in which, by vacillating between group positions, the Jews experience an acute sense of discomfort and guilt.

In the further development of the plot the Jews drive away without interfering on behalf of the black child. The Afrikaners overtake them, and shout out of the car window some hostile, derogatory words which no one catches. Yet the Jewish father is incensed: 'I know well enough what he shouted' (p.24), he declares belligerently, making, or seeking an excuse to make the assumption that they have been the victims of anti-Semitic prejudice. His heated response to what he merely supposes is an attack on his own group position, stands in striking contrast to his apathetic reaction to the observed attack on the child. Although Jacobson investigates the quality of Jewish compassion, his attitude should not be confused with self-rejection. The narrator is critical of both sides, and the tone is neither angry nor bitter. Jacobson's own compassionate insight ensures that he points out the moral without condemning any group.

The story continues: imagining that his group is being insulted, the Jew pursues the Afrikaners and catches up with them. He accosts them: 'You can't go round bullying everybody [meaning 'the Jews'] like you bully that Kaffir child' (p.26). The pejorative word, 'kaffir' signals more clearly than would 'native' or 'African' the Jew's complicity in race-colour denigration. He adds: '*You people* make me sick', and the Afrikaner retorts: 'You have no right to talk like that about *my people*' (p.26 emphases added). Thus the opposition presented here is not the traditional one between white and black but between two white groups. Both groups fear rejection and desire approbation in order to maintain their prestige.[7] The narrator makes this point in the following passage:

> and then I realised that our fear – the fear that we would be called 'Bloody Jews', the fear which perhaps had kept our mouths closed when we had seen the picannin being tortured – was his fear too. He, the Afrikaner ... felt that my father was sitting in his car and despising him for the race he belonged to, and judging him and his race by what we had seen on the road ... he wanted us to think well of his race. (pp.26-27)

The reference to 'fear' signals the operation of a blocking device – in the conflict of group positions a stalemate is induced by rival prejudices. At the end, in a reversal of the expected outcome, the fragility of each group's status unexpectedly keeps the balance of power between them.

The reader must be alert to the author's ironic presentation, and avoid being misled by the seeming exercise of prejudice in his use of such terms as 'Jew', 'Dutchman', 'kaffir', 'bloody swine', 'despising', 'judging', 'damning', 'condemnation'. The apparent deployment of familiar racial stereotypes is also misleading. Jacobson's purpose is clearly not to reinforce stereotypes; on the contrary, it will be shown that the thrust of his work is to interrogate and ultimately to attempt to implode them. He skilfully and subtly exploits the discourse of prejudice, while creating a text which seeks to subvert the concept of prejudice itself.

The story ends quietly and ironically. There has been a conflict, but for neither side has there been a 'victory'. Jacobson leads the reader to this conclusion through the irony in the last paragraph: 'Everyone was feeling depressed and beaten, though, as I have explained, the victory was ours. But we had all lost, so much, somewhere, farther back, along that dusty road' (p.30). The bleak and arid 'dusty road' symbolises not merely a spatial but a spiritual location. Here Jacobson draws attention to the way in which the desire for acceptance conflicts with the values of justice, compassion, innocence, and integrity, and compromises them.

'The Zulu and the Zeide'[8] is another powerful short story concerning relationships between groups in South Africa, this time between Jews and a black man, as a prototype of wider relationships between whites and blacks. Here prejudice and group antagonisms are addressed obliquely through irony, opposition and parallelism, as is evidenced by the alliteration in the title. Analogies are drawn between the vulnerabilities of age and race – representing two outgroups. Once again, as in the previous story, the central characters are a Jew, who also represents the white man, and a black man.

The plot centres on Harry Grossman, a middle-aged and prosperous Jew, who employs Paulus, a young Zulu fresh from Zululand, to look after his immigrant and now senile father. The central relationship depicted is that between 'the Zulu' and 'the Zeide' (the grandfather), neither of whom speaks each other's tongue or, for that matter, English, but between whom a bond of compassion and dependence develops.

Although the narrator describes Paulus as a 'muscular, moustached and bearded African' (p.107), who looks 'like a king in exile' (p.109), and has 'the face and figure of a warrior' (p.116), he is referred to by Grossman in the common South African terminology as a 'raw boy' (p.107). Again Jacobson uses the precise discourse of prejudice with the intention of undermining it. The name Grossman – in English 'gross man' – with 'gross' connoting 'uncouth', is chosen as a negative signifier. Since Grossman is described as a 'thickset, bunch-faced man with large bones' (p.103), Jacobson once again uses for subversive purposes the methodology of non-Jewish writers who use names and physical characteristics as correlatives for moral qualities.

There are many parallels in the text. Through senility, the old man has reverted to childhood, and the dignity due to his age has been withheld by his own group – Grossman's wife and children have nothing to do with the old man. As a result, he has lost his status as a white man, and has become 'a butt and a jest to the African servants'(p.102).

Because of his race, the Zulu, in South African terms, is auto- matically disqualified from full political and social adulthood – hence the designation 'boy' – and is treated with contempt. He is expected to behave submissively and, conscious of the impotence of his group position, he connives in this behaviour, standing 'with his hands behind his back and his bare knees bent a little forward, as if to show how little he was asserting himself' (p.108). The old man and the young Zulu thus occupy a similar situation of humiliation and marginalisation, and the text hints at the wider issues of group dominance. In this instance, Grossman, the Jew, is ironically seen to occupy the position of a member of the dominant in-group, a position usually reserved for the Afrikaner in South African group relations. He says:

> 'You'll always be where you are, running to do what the white baas tells you to do. Look how you stand!' ... and then with contempt, using one of the few Zulu words he knew: '*Hamba!* Go! Do you think I want to see you?' ... Harry gestured him away, and had the satisfaction of seeing Paulus shuffle off like a schoolboy. (p.117)

Grossman's relish in assuming the position of the 'white baas' in his power relationship over the Zulu, and his 'lust' (p.116) to humiliate and dominate are graphically demonstrated. Paulus is given food 'three times a day after the white people had eaten' (p.109), paralleling in humiliation the experience of the old man who has to submit to being treated as a patient, and is similarly bullied and patronised by his son. Jacobson satirises these derogatory and prejudicial attitudes when Grossman is made to point the parallel: 'I think the old man has just found his level in *der schwarzer* (the black man) – and I don't think *der schwarzer* could cope with anything else' (p.114).

In the description of the developing relationship between the two, wider symbolic and prophetic implications for the South African situation are subtly suggested. At first the old man 'took immediate fright' at Paulus (p.110). 'After some bewilderment Paulus simply went along with the old man' (p.110).

> At first he did so cautiously, following the old man at a distance, for he knew the other had no trust in him. But later he was able to follow the old man openly; still later he was able to walk side by side with him, and the old man did not try to escape from him. (p.110)

Finally, Paulus picks the man up in his arms. Initially fear and caution characterises the approach of both men, there is 'no trust'. After a period of time the black comes to 'walk side by side' in a position of equality with the white man, who, as has been suggested, has been stripped of his power – literally, through his senility – who accepts him, and 'does not try to escape'. Still later the black man, himself powerless, is shown to physically support and protect the white man in an intimate gesture of caring. Thus, in a highly symbolic fashion, a reversal of the expected racial relationships between white and black – of hostility and amity, power and impotence – is played out.

In this tale of recognitions the old man and Paulus, each in his own way, recognises the other as a *döppelganger*. The political overtones, suggesting the alienation of both the Jew and the black, attest the marginalisation of vulnerable out-groups in South Africa, by ironically emphasising the parallels:

> The young bearded Zulu and the old bearded Jew from Lithuania walked together in the streets of the town that was strange to them both ... They could not sit on the

bench together, for only whites were allowed to sit on
the bench, but Paulus would squat on the ground at the
old man's feet ... when they crossed a street hand in
hand — there were white men who averted their eyes
from the sight of this degradation, which would come
upon a white man when he was old and senile and
dependent. (pp.110-111)

The outcome contrasts the situation of the old Jew and the young
Zulu. Like most of his generation, the old man had been expected to
save money to bring the rest of his family from Lithuania to South
Africa, but he had been neglectful and irresponsible, shifting the
burden on to his children.[9] The Zulu, however, has taken on the job of
nurse, so foreign to his upbringing and physique, in order to earn the
money to bring his wife and children from the Zulu kraal to the 'white'
South African town. When Grossman hears what Paulus has done
'[his] clenched, fist-like features suddenly seem[ed] to have fallen from
one another, [and he] stared with ... guilt and despair at Paulus, while
he cried, 'What else could I have done? I did my best,' before the first
tears came' (p.121). Jacobson's stories often turn on epiphanic
recognitions. Here Grossman recognises the parallels, and realises that
Paulus – powerless and discriminated against – has succeeded with
dignity, while both he and his father have failed in the performance of
their duty. Perhaps Harry Grossman's 'guilt' consists as well in a
recognition that he has become selfishly corrupted by prosperity and
the racist attitudes of the dominant group.

Jacobson intends his readers, both Jewish and Gentile, to share in
these recognitions, and if the cap fits, to wear it. Throughout this story
there are deliberate resonances for the wider community of South
Africa, and part of Jacobson's fictional intent of the 1950s is to suggest
that South African Jewry, overly concerned with protecting its own
group position, and in its affluence and relative security, may, like
Grossman, have become infected with a spurious sense of power and
have lost sight of duty, compassion and humanity.

'The Example of Lipi Lippmann'[10] deals more closely with the
issue of stereotyping itself. The poverty-stricken Lipi, an elderly
immigrant Jew, is ambivalently viewed by the local inhabitants of the
town of Lyndhurst:

In Lyndhurst, if a Gentile spoke enviously to a Jew about how rich the Jews of Lyndhurst were, how clever they were, how well they did in business, the reply was often made – 'Well, it's not really true about all the Jews. Just look at Lipi Lippmann!' No one, not even the biggest anti-Semite in the world could say that Lipi Lippmann was rich or clever or did well in business.

Lipi Lippmann once said that the Jews of Lyndhurst should pay him to remain poor, his poverty was so useful in arguments. But the joke was received in silence; it was felt to be in bad taste. The Jews of Lyndhurst were ready to use Lipi Lippmann's poverty to propitiate an envious Gentile, but they were ashamed of him nevertheless … Every other Jew in town was a licensed wholesaler or a licensed hotel-keeper, a licensed dentist or a licensed doctor … (p.62)

As has been suggested, the image of the upwardly mobile, rich, successful Jew, which Lipi contradicts so usefully, is closely based on the actual demographic situation of the Jewish community during the first half of the twentieth century, which evoked Gentile jealousy and exacerbated anti-Semitic feeling. Paradoxically, however, as a poor Jew – jeered at by the Afrikaans children as a *Koelie-Jood* (p.63) – Lipi is an embarrassment within his own community. Designated as belonging to an out-group, albeit a group within a group – '*Koelie* being an insulting term for an Indian' (p.63) – he would appear to emphasise the marginal status of the Jewish group itself. If, as the colonial authors of the diamond fields have emphasised, the Jew strives to achieve social acceptance through financial success, Lipi conspicuously does not fit this paradigm. Within his own group, his usefulness as a counter-Jew is undercut by the way in which he uncomfortably reminds his community of their out-group status.

After his house is burgled, he untruthfully lets it be known that his life's savings, with which he was planning to visit the Holy Land, have also been stolen. At once the attitude of the Jewish townspeople changes:

For Lipi had become a hero, even something of a martyr … If they felt any embarrassment or shame in connection

with him now, it was only because they had been
ashamed of him and embarrassed by him in the past.
His poverty now appeared to them noble; his ambition
to visit Israel exemplary … There was none among the
well-to-do Jews of Lyndhurst who did not feel himself
humbled by Lipi's humility, shamed by his selfsacrifice
… (p.68)

While at first Lipi had challenged the image of the upwardly mobile
Jew, in the mind of the townspeople he now epitomises and validates
the stereotype of the 'good Jew', the humble, pious martyr. However,
the passage contains key words – 'embarrassment' and 'shame' – which
encode the precarious and uncomfortable nature of the Lyndhurst
Jews' relationship with the wider community. Because Lipi has drawn
attention to himself, and thus to the Jewish community, the community feels threatened. It must now make a propitiatory gesture
which will draw favourable notice from the Gentiles. The Jewish ex-
Mayor of Lyndhurst relishes enacting the role of the Jewish benefactor
in leading a drive to raise funds to send Lipi to Israel.

Filled with regret for the deception he has perpetrated, Lipi suffers
emotional torment:

Lipi's rage had been directed against himself; against his
own poverty and powerlessness; against the lifetime he
had spent toiling in the sun, for so little reward, for a
house that ten minutes could despoil, for possessions
that ten pounds could buy. (p.69)

In 'a frenzy of regret and self-hatred' (p.69), he accepts the original
negative image of himself held by his own community. He confesses his
untruthfulness to the ex-Mayor, whose anger is aroused. Firstly, he
has had to revise and rerevise his own categorical thinking, an
uncomfortable process. Secondly, if the deception were to be made
known, he, as a public figure, would be vulnerable to the ridicule of
both the Gentile and the Jewish communities. Thirdly, he has striven
to promote and preserve 'the cordiality of what he called "inter-faith
relations" in Lyndhurst' (p.71), and Lipi threatens to expose himself
as a cunning and perfidious Jew, an image the ex-Mayor has

endeavoured to counteract. Furiously dismissing Lipi, he insists on his silence, and orders him to play out the charade, leave for Israel immediately and never return.

After Lipi throws himself under a train, the ex-Mayor, like Harry Grossman in 'The Zulu and the Zeide', feels deeply guilty and remorseful. He realises that in seeking to preserve his own self-image as a prosperous and successful Jew, and a public benefactor, and in endeavouring to protect the reputation of the community as a whole, he has lost sight of common humanity. Like 'A Day in the Country', the story is a telling indictment of how thinking in stereotypes and the drive towards self-preservation may corrupt morality.

Jacobson's full length novel, the humorous fable, *The Price of Diamonds* (1957), is also set in the Karoo town, Lyndhurst. It deals only marginally with the South African political situation. The Yiddish expressions, the frequent use of questions, and the reproduction of Yiddish verbal patterns and inverted speech rhythms are significant. They suggest that beyond its whimsical fantasy, the deeper concerns of the novel are the experiences of the Jews as a social group, in which prejudice and power dynamics are once again fundamental.

The chief characters, Mr Fink and Mr Gottlieb, immigrants from eastern Europe, are business partners in a firm of manufacturers' representatives. Gottlieb, who is timid and childlike in personality, feels impelled to assert himself over the dominant Fink, and in so doing becomes unwittingly involved in an IDB intrigue.

In the construction of Gottlieb, Jacobson unobtrusively blends and manipulates a number of Jewish stereotypes. One concerns the compulsive involvement in IDB. Jacobson uses this situation in order to mock it, since the over-scrupulous and timid Gottlieb forms a strong, even ludicrous counter-image to that of the unscrupulous and sinister IDB operator of diamond field fiction.

In creating a counterbalance to the myth of the powerful demonic Jew, Jacobson depicts Gottlieb as alienated, easily duped, and conscious of his own powerlessness, both as a personality and as a member of an insecure out-group. Gottlieb talks to himself, he rehearses conversations in which he outshines the intimidating Fink, he dreams of showing off to Fink and, in general, lives in a state of self-conscious indecisiveness through which a vein of comedy runs very strongly. He is, in fact, a version of the figure of the ironic man. This image of the *schlemiel* (fool) partly derives from the comic potentialities of the medieval negative prototype – which was ridiculed and mocked as well as being hated and derided.

In her study of the figure of the schlemiel, Ruth Wisse traces its origin in Yiddish folk culture, humour and literature. After being taken into American popular culture, it only emerged in serious fiction in America after the Second World War. Here it was re-created in I.B. Singer's *Gimpel the Fool* which was translated into English in 1953 only four years before the publication of Jacobson's novel. Thereafter, when writers began to explore the nature of their Jewishness, the type became immensely popular in American Jewish fiction. When America as a whole began to experience itself as a 'loser' after the war and during the 1950s, the schlemiel figure – the quintessential loser – took on a symbolic national importance. The ironic schlemiel, however, is a comic anti-hero rather than a villain.[11]

Gottlieb is a typical schlemiel. He is a good-natured, ineffectual 'little man', a bumbling but sympathetic figure of fun, the humorous, modernist, bourgeois anti-hero of which Charlie Chaplin and Woody Allen are well-known manifestations. The reader is drawn into humorous complicity and identification with Gottlieb in his embarrassed relationships with more self-confident or powerful characters:

> while Gottlieb would have enjoyed telling Fink about the day's encounter and his visit to the police station, he expected far more to enjoy showing Fink the little box and its contents ... Fink talked; but Gottlieb was silent, cool, a man to whom things happened; Fink would see the very next morning what kind of man Manfred Gottlieb was. (pp.26-27)

Furthermore, in showing Gottlieb's need to compensate by asserting his dominance over his wife, Jacobson may be drawing the parallel between the Jew and the woman. Both are assumed to accept the legitimacy of the inferior status imposed on them by the power structures of society, and both endeavour to deflect aggression by deference and submission. In a reversal of the relationship with Fink, but not the situation, Jacobson shows Gottlieb's bullying exchange with his wife:

'And I am a man whose words mean something.'
'Yes, Manfred.'
'I am a man that people must listen to.'
'Yes, Manfred.'
'I am not an ordinary fellow.'
'Oh no, Manfred.'
'I have my powers, and my ambitions too.'
'I suppose so, Manfred.' (p.86)

Through his irony and humour, Jacobson obtains extra tools with which to dissect power relationships. Humour evokes enjoyment but, more significantly, reflects deeper levels of meaning. It can also be one of the most revealing expressions of the relationship of an out-group both with itself and with the more powerful and hostile in-group. Operating essentially through ambiguity, and functioning as a decommitment, it enables a member of an out-group to behave aggressively towards a member of a more powerful in-group yet deny harmful intention. It also allows him to dissociate himself from the responsibility of his own behaviour.[12] The larger humorous and ironic sense with which Jacobson holds up for inspection and mockery aspects of stereotypical thinking, while at the same time using the very stereotypes he examines, constitutes what can be termed 'Jewish irony'. Sartre has defined 'Jewish irony' as the way in which the Jew, 'because he knows he is under observation, takes the initiative and attempts to look at himself through the eyes of others'.[13]

Albert Memmi takes a similar view. In rejecting the claim that some have made for what has been termed 'Jewish humour' as an expression of 'unshakeable ... optimism' he suggests that it should rather be regarded as being 'based on a painful awareness in the Jew of his real condition ... [of] oppression and accusation'. Jewish humour, he believes, is ambivalent, being an amalgam of pity and mirth. It should be recognised as a defence mechanism which can take the edge off hostility and disarm the aggressor by laughter. After all, he suggests, 'what is funny can not be very dangerous'.[14] In soliciting the audience's sympathy, the schlemiel figure – of which Gottlieb is a variant – is a defensive and multivalent image – victim and fool, humorous and alienated.

Despite the comic elements, a pervading consciousness of alienation and vulnerability is present in much of Jacobson's fiction. Sheila

Roberts has suggested that 'Jacobson's characters are alienated not because life in South Africa is untenable but because they are acutely conscious members of the late twentieth century'.[15] When Jacobson portrays this alienation as central to the Jewish experience, however, it more specifically represents that of a stigmatised out-group. In the case of Gottlieb, what is clearly evident is his sense, as a Jew, of being marginalised in an alien society:

> In the lounges of hotels, the stoeps of bars, in the drive-in yard ... Gottlieb could not feel at ease ... He could only feel ... in these unfamiliar and distant parts of the town, so far from his solid house – a stranger, a curiosity to the others there, most of whom he suspected of regarding him as an object of scorn, kindness, anti-Semitism, or help which he did not need. (pp.91-92)

Gottlieb regards his own home as the only 'solid' referent in his environment. It is a place of security, while all other places – 'hotels', 'bars', 'yards' – are potentially alien and hostile. For the first time in the novel the term 'anti-Semitism' is used to signify this specifically Jewish experience. The anxiety from which Gottlieb suffers is part of his need to find and establish 'his place'. The narrator comments:

> there was not a province in the country in which Gottlieb had not worked ... always he had moved on, for ... in none of them had he been free from ... an anxiety, a pressure upon him, that ... was associated with his boyhood in the old country ... he had had to win for himself, in the harsh African sunlight ... *his place, his certainty, his establishment* ... (pp.169-170 emphasis added)

In another story of this period, 'An Apprenticeship',[16] Jacobson significantly reveals through the impressionable eyes of a child the Jew's sense of being an outsider:

> 'I envied [the Gentile children] because they seemed so much safer, so much more secure, than our selves. The Palling boys did not have to read in the newspapers

about the massacre of their fellow-Jews in Europe; they
did not have to protest against anti-Jewish remarks made
by boorish schoolmasters or uglier things said in the
playground by schoolboys.' (p.77)

This is the same kind of anxiety and alienation felt by Gottlieb, but
here it is more closely linked to the Holocaust and to the sense of
sinister anti-Semitism then active in South Africa.

'Through the Wilderness',[17] has the first person narrator looking
back to his childhood experience, when he 'associated the Hebrew
language with being alien, set apart, exposed; implicated in what [he]
was convinced at an early age was a continuing, unendurable history
of suffering and impotence' (p.9). Here Jacobson shows the Jew
himself aware of the stigma marked out by language.

Written only a few years after the Holocaust, some of the stories
refer to Nazi Germany and stress the trauma spread by the Holocaust
among Jews all over the world. As the young Zionist in 'The
Promised Land'[18] declares:

> 'For ten, twelve, twenty years people have been doing the
> most hideous and unspeakable things to Jews: they have
> been shot, whipped, gassed … lamp-shades have been
> made out of their skins and ornaments out of the gold in
> their teeth … As for the Jews who were lucky enough to
> be outside Europe, they have known only *humiliation,
> impotence, rage and despair …*' (p.175 emphasis added)

The interplay between power and prejudice, humiliation and dignity,
is an important subtext of 'Droit de Seigneur,'[19] a domestic tale of
marital infidelity set in a seedy Braamfontein hotel where the Jewish
hotelier, Mr Gellin, makes an immense fuss of two guests who are
Polish counts, thereby arousing the jealousy of the others. Jacobson
extends the parameters of his story to include ancestral memories of
anti-Semitism. Speaking of the counts, Mr Gellin tells his guests:

> 'You must understand that there is a history behind those
> two. And what a history, a terrible history! Those men –
> and their parents, and *their* parents … were like gods in

the country where they came from ... And if the count
didn't like the Jews, then the Jews suffered ... So you can
imagine what it is for me, when I have a memory of such
things, to have them here ...' (pp.13-14)

The hotelier has lavished attention on the counts in order to
humiliate them. He tells them:

'... Do you think I don't know what you've been
thinking of me? Do you think I couldn't see how you
looked at me – how you didn't look at me, as if your eyes
shouldn't fall on such an object as me? ... Do you think
it's for love that I gave you a table for yourselves, and a
fine room, the best room in the hotel? Do you think ... I
don't know what this hotel is? And that's why it was my
pleasure to have you in it, for exactly what it is, this hotel
in Braamfontein – *not* for what you could do to make it
grand, but for what the hotel could do to make you
bitter and humble. Do you think I don't remember? Do
you think I have ever forgotten what you people were?'
    'Jew!' Count Jezviecks said, turning.
    'That's right,' Mr. Gellin said ... (p.20)

The exclamation 'Jew!' announces the count's anti-Semitic bias. Mr
Gellin accepts it because he intends to reverse its implications of powerlessness, stigma and humiliation. He claims the upper hand, glorying in
'what the hotel could do to make [the counts] bitter and humble'. The
Jew, a member of the despised out-group, has scored what appears to be
a moral victory. However, Jacobson's irony adds a further dimension:
Gellin has reversed but not transcended the parameters of prejudice.
His moral victory sounds empty and hollow. Prejudice, Jacobson shows,
remains unacceptable, whether it is directed towards Jews or Gentiles.
    Indeed, an exposure of prejudice is an important subtext of *The
Price of Diamonds*. Jacobson subtly satirises any form of prejudice
through ironic reversal:

At Christmas-time they had given her a bonus and
a raise in salary ... and then Miss Scholtz wept and

> said that there was nothing in the world better than
> a good Jewish gentleman. 'A good Scotchman is also
> a fine man,' Gottlieb said distressed ... (pp.60-61)

Here the reader has to be alert to Jacobson's ironic dialogue: Miss Scholtz's epithet 'good' has an implied opposite, the 'bad' Jewish gentleman. Gottlieb, himself, alludes to a 'good' Scotchman, implying that most Scotchmen are not 'good', and underscoring Jacobson's intention to interrogate all forms of stereotyping.

As Memmi reminds us, almost all Jewish jokes when told by Jews are some kind of special pleading and all Jewish jokes told by non-Jews are anti-Semitic.[20] In this novel, the comedy and humour encompass a sidelong glance at the anti-Semitic variety as well:

> With a solemn, snub-nosed face, Groenewald essayed
> his first joke. 'You wouldn't be much good for a
> customer for me when I'm in the pigs, would you, Mr.
> Gottlieb? It's lucky not everybody thinks like you
> people, isn't it? Because then where would the pig-
> farmers be?'
>
> Groenewald waited for Gottlieb to smile ... Gottlieb's
> pursed mouth and frowning brow did not relax into a
> smile ... 'So much money a man like you must have,'
> [Groenewald] mused. (p.220)

Jacobson shows that the stock Gentile references to pigs and to the money that Groenewald attributes to Gottlieb – 'a man like you' suggests 'a Jew' – do not amuse Gottlieb who recognises, behind the ostensible good humour, the underlying workings of anti-Semitism. As in the other texts under discussion, Jacobson does not spare Jews in his exposure of their own prejudice and racism. Gottlieb himself uses racist platitudes and claims class privilege in relation to his black servant: 'Look, Sylvia's been with us a long time, I'm happy with her, she cooks well, everything. But I also like people to be what they are, not to try to be what they aren't' (pp.28-29). 'Sylvia was a "girl" of thirty-five', (p.29) the narrator comments ironically .

Jacobson's *The Beginners* (1966) is the only full-length novel of literary merit in which Jewish experience is central and is affirmed and explored on a large scale. The plot concentrates on the family of Joel Glickman – his immigrant father and mother, his brother and sister, and over forty other characters. Joel returns to South Africa from war service in 1945, resumes his university studies and becomes involved with a group of young Zionists who are preparing to emigrate to Israel. After a short period in Israel, Joel returns to South Africa but eventually emigrates to London where he meets and marries a Gentile woman whom he had known in South Africa.

Countless facets of Jewish experience are explored: aspects of early immigration from Lithuania, Jewish trading, the suburban Jewish family, Greyshirt activity, Jewish alienation after the victory of the racist Nationalist government, Jewish involvement with radical politics, the Zionist experience, snobbery, upward mobility, the lure of assimilation and the changing of the Jewish name, intermarriage and first-hand experience of the Holocaust related by a survivor.

Although these often repeated situations form the background of Jacobson's novel, he does not use them in order to focus on them or merely to provide local colour and authenticity or to satirise them. His object is chiefly to explore the troubled consciousness of the main character against a wider canvas of the life of a Jew growing up in South Africa at the mid-century. *The Beginners* is also the first South African novel to express the impact of the founding of Israel on the Jews of the Diaspora.[21] In it Jacobson greatly expanded the themes of his work of the 1950s. The self-questioning chief character, Joel Glickman, explains the South African Jew's situation:

> 'We are trying to cure ourselves of all the false, negative ways of being set apart that we suffer from, the wrong kinds of specialness. Or loneliness.'
> 'Loneliness?'
> 'Loneliness, marginality – I don't know what the word is. But I know what the state is: to be a kind of demi-European at the bottom of Africa, to be a demi-Jew among the Gentiles. Other people have other ways of suffering from it.' (p.194)

And Joel applies, as does Jacobson himself, the measure of the Jews' European experience to their current political attitudes in South Africa. Again Glickman is starkly critical:

> 'Look how we live. There's been a bloody great war, they killed six million Jews like flies, they dropped atomic bombs on Japan. And look at South Africa ... Look at this country, with the kaffirs living like pigs and the white men kicking them around. And what do we do about it all? Nothing! I come back and find that we just go on and on, in the same house, doing the same things, thinking the same thoughts, as if nothing at all had happened. How can we do it?' (p.58)

In this passage, the white man, the black man, and the Jew are again a triangular focus of examination. Questions are asked, but no answers are given. Once again the point is made that prejudice, as Jacobson indicated in his account of his own situation,[22] cannot easily be purged or imagined away.

After *The Beginners*, Jacobson's fiction no longer concerned itself so closely with the themes of group hostility, racial prejudice, or the ambivalent group position of the Jews in South Africa. His work in the 1950s had broken new ground in an area which was then virtually untouched, and is in the vanguard of the literature of political awareness which was developed more fully in South Africa by Gordimer, Fugard, Coetzee, Brink and others.

There is a striking contrast between the richness of Jacobson's focus on Jews and the paucity of their treatment in almost all the earlier and contemporary texts in South African fiction. This can largely be attributed to the fact that Jacobson is not content with merely reproducing stereotypes even when dealing with group affiliations. His method is more complex and infinitely more subtle. In investigating racial prejudice, including anti-Jewish prejudice, he manipulates the stereotypes he constructs in order to create a situation in which the reader is led to confront the ironies and complexities inherent in them. Like Sarah Gertrude Millin before him, Jacobson contributes significantly to an understanding of the problems of Jewish interaction with the wider South African society.

Lewis Sowden

Lewis Sowden's humorous *Kop of Gold* (1955), deals with the rivalry between two sections of a small Afrikaner community, and with the discovery of gold. The tone of the novel is similar to that of Jacobson's *Price of Diamonds* in its whimsicality, its air of fantasy and in the ironic attitude of the narrator.

Playfully using the language patterns of the Afrikaners, he gently satirises the categorical attitudes of the simple country folk. The characters are all stereotypes; among them is a Jew – a shopkeeper, sharp in money matters, concerned with the welfare of the blacks and to a certain extent ostracised and alienated. Sowden uses this material in a spirit of mockery. The social distance the Afrikaners feel from the Jew is subtly presented. The narrator speculates on where the young lovers could have met: 'It couldn't have been at the Jew-store because Jansen de Wet never used to call there ...' (p.5). On the other hand, where convenient, ostracism is ignored:

> Selina had sent for a dozen bottles of sweet wine from the Jew-store without making any secret of it, and Jan had not dared to utter a single word in protest. Truly, Jews and Englishmen had their uses ... (p.3)
> It was remarkable how Jews and Englishmen found their way into all sorts of corners of the world ... one could always recognise a Jew or an Englishman, yes-no? ... talking and laughing with everyone as though the country belonged to them ... (p.12) the Englishman ... belonged to the Anglicans, and that was nearly as unfortunate as being a Jew. (p.233)

Here the Afrikaner's perception is of the Jew and Englishman as united in one out-group as it was in Scully's *The Harrow* (1921) and Nash's *The Geyer Brood* (1946). However, in Stephen Black's *The Dorp* (1920), Peter Abrahams's 'Hatred' (1942) and Pauline Smith's 1914 diary entry, Jews are specifically contrasted with the English. In Sowden's text Jews are inevitably referred to in connection with profit and money. A character says of a Jew: ' "In any case, he'll make money afterwards, like all lawyers." "And the same holds for all Jews" ' (p.109). But it is a Jew who offers to double the amount paid to the blacks for their land, and thereby plays the role not only of the shrewd shopkeeper but also of the kaffirboetie. The story ends amicably with everyone sharing in the spoils of the gold find. Sowden ironically mocks prejudice in a text which hides a serious, satiric intention under a light-hearted and amusing manner.

THE STEREOTYPES
PERSIST AND
CHANGE

When they appear in historical novels, Jews continue to play the roles assigned to them in the early colonial texts.

The Historical Novel

Shortly before the Second World War, when economic conditions in the country were still unfavourable, and when anti-Alien agitation once again strongly threatened the Jewish population, Stuart Cloete published *Turning Wheels* (1937), the tale of the Great Trek of 1836. When a smous – a 'wandering Jew' (p.206) – is briefly introduced, the portrait contains the familiar negative markers of appearance and shrewdness:

> The Jew came, as such traders always came ... following his hooked nose into the depths of the country ... flattering, expostulating, and complaining that if he took such prices as they offered he would be ruined ... Quick and vivid as a bird among the phlegmatic Boers he overpowered them by his animation ... (pp.204-205)

A minor character, a Prussian, has nothing but contempt for the Jew:

> [S]peaking to him in his own tongue, [the Prussian] had called him a Jewish swine ... Like vermin, these people penetrated everywhere; too insignificant to be killed they

swelled gradually on the blood they sucked till at last they became dangerous, holding the very lives of many men in their hands, squeezing them between their fingers till the juice of their property ran out ... Hit them and they cringed, succour them, and before long they bit the hand that fed them. A people without a land, a people without the capacity for gratitude, to whom money was a god. (p.205)

Although his novel is set in the first half of the nineteenth century, Cloete seems to be harking back to the stereotype of the avaricious, 'blood-sucking' smous which was prevalent at the end of the century. The displacement of point of view on to a Prussian may be a result of Cloete's consciousness of the prevailing Greyshirt anti-Semitic feeling in the country at the time the novel was written. However, the author does little to counter the impression created, although when the smous and the farmers share a joke, the satire is equally directed against both the Afrikaner farmers and the Jew:

This idiosyncrasy of his about gold the smouse [an alternative spelling] explained was due to a different racial outlook, and one of which in time, after a longer residence among them he would not doubt become cured.

Ja, jong, time will cure you, they said, for cattle are true riches. See how they increase and multiply and can gold do that? they asked laughing.

"Ach, how right you are," he said. "If only gold would increase as do your herds, how wonderful that would be."

And thus they talked, each laughing in his sleeve at the stupidity of the other. (p.207)

Another historically based novel appeared during this period featuring a Jewish character in an ambivalent way. *The City of Gold* by Francis Brett Young (1884-1954) was published in 1939. Brett Young was an Englishman who spent over twenty years researching his novel. The result is a construction based not so much on his own perceptions as on the reminiscences he absorbed.

The novel concerns a group of characters who make or lose fortunes on the diamond and gold fields, and are instrumental in the founding of Johannesburg. An important character is Meninsky, a 'little Jewish smous', called 'the Peruvian', who comes to South Africa from Poland by way of Whitechapel (p.61):

He was a shrimp of a man, with a short body and relatively long bow-legs whose thinness ... suggested those of an insect. His face, too, was against him. Though he shaved himself regularly, his cheeks and chin were always dull blue-black, prolonging the shadow of coarse, close-cropped black hair as stiff as a dog's which grew low on his forehead above large brown eyes, super-ficially lustrous yet oddly opaque. It was in some ways an animal ... face ... [H]arsh experience had given it a look of cunning and wariness ... His mind, too, was quicker in its reactions than the minds of most of his customers ... but though this agility made many fear his shrewdness, Meninsky was not, as were many of his kind, rapacious. (pp.61-62)

The animal images directly derive from the discourse of anti-Semitic writers. Brett Young also points out the Jew's exoticism, stressing his 'Oriental exuberance' (p.115), opaque eyes and foreign accent, although in this case the accent is ironically Cockney. Another stereo-typical marker is Jewish cunning: Meninsky is a 'smart little Yid' (p.108) with an 'eye to the main chance' (p.114). The author is at pains to qualify his construct by drawing Meninsky sympathetically. Like Schreiner's 'Jew' in *From Man to Man*, Meninsky suffers from the effects of 'a humiliating childhood':

On his arrival in South Africa as a penniless immigrant, his first thought had been to restore the self-respect which had been crushed out of him in a humiliating childhood ... [He established] a reputation for honesty, rare among the vagrant foreigners ... in his dealings among the simple, unprejudiced folk of the high-veld, who had found him a man of his word who gave value

for money and not one of those *Boerverneukers* who lived
on his sharper wits and exploited their ignorance. (p.62)

By default, the author implies that the character escapes the attribute
of the dishonest 'Boerverneuker' – who is, however, the standard
against which he is defined. A lengthy and ambiguous anecdote is
related to show Meninsky reversing the expected verneukery. He
prevents a Boer farmer from buying a watch he had previously tricked
him into believing was made of gold. Meninsky, in fact, tries to teach
the Boer how not to be cheated in the future. Brett Young seems to be
leaning over backwards in order to modify what at first glance would
seem to be a negative image.[1]

Researchers identify two broad classes of stereotypical attributes:
the use of identifying cues which are usually physical, and ascribed
attributes, including expected patterns of behaviour.[2] Both aspects of
the stereotype are used in *The City of Gold* and the reference to
expected attributes, in this case the expected dishonesty of the smous,
confirms the author's reference to categorical thinking. On the other
hand, Meninsky's 'radiant vitality' (p.63) is emphasised, and his
energy, cheerfulness, and intelligence are strongly featured. He works
hard with pick and shovel, and remains uncorrupted although he
makes a fortune.

Since the novel is dedicated to 'Florence Phillips and to the memory
of Lionel Phillips', it is possible that Brett Young based his character to
a certain extent on the figure of Lionel (afterwards Sir Lionel) Phillips,
one of the Johannesburg Randlords who had initially made a fortune
on the Kimberley fields, and whose career is not dissimilar to that of
Meninsky.[3] Thus Brett Young continues to promote the ambivalent
image of the smous well into the twentieth century.

In 1946 Thirza Nash (1885-1962) published a family saga, *The
Geyer Brood*, set in South Africa in the second half of the nineteenth
century. Max Coleman, from London, born Maximilian Kuhlmann,
'was a mixture of Jew and German, the Jew predominating in his
features and stature, in his avid mind that seized on every opportunity that offered itself on the diamond fields for making money'. As
a diamond buyer, he was rapidly becoming wealthy.

There are stereotypical references to appearance – Max's child by
his Afrikaans wife has 'his father's nose, and looked like an Israelite

indeed' (p.85) – and to name changing, Jewish apostasy, and marriage out of the faith. In other respects the portrait is almost entirely positive. Max is 'gay, likeable, generous ... Women liked him, men admired and respected him.' (p.67). The narrator asserts that he 'was one of the men on the fields who saw the wealth there not as something to be grabbed for selfish purposes, but as a potential factor in the fate of the country and of the Empire' (p.76). Here the narrator makes a direct rebuttal of the hovering negative image. After the death of his child he returns to Judaism, and in the closing pages is rewarded by the British with a knighthood. By showing successful 'interracial' marriages, the novel sets out to illustrate the different strains in the Afrikaner 'nation', and to recommend the unity.

Like Scully's *The Harrow* and Sowden's *The Kop*, the novel demonstrates the close association of the Jew with the Englishman. *The Geyer Brood* differs from Stephen Black's *The Dorp*, in which the Jew remains outside the main Afrikaans and English groups, and shows the integration of the Jew simultaneously into both these groups – by marriage on the one hand and by loyalty on the other.

Jewish involvement with the diamond fields, and particularly with IDB, remained a fascinating subject throughout the twentieth century. In 1962 F.C. Metrowich published a 'biography', a recreation of the life of one of the diamond fields' most colourful characters – *Scotty Smith: South Africa's Robin Hood*. The first anecdote recounts how Scotty observes a couple of Jewish merchants who attempt to smuggle diamonds across the frontier by feeding them to a horse. Scotty steals the horse, kills it and recovers the diamonds. The second anecdote concerns his encounter with 'a notorious Jewish diamond thief' (p.51). Scotty offers a pedlar a lift on his transport wagon. Police pursue them and the pedlar hides. Scotty directs the police elsewhere and discovers that the pedlar has slipped a packet of diamonds into his pocket. While the Jew remains hidden, Scotty hides the diamonds, denies their presence and shakes off the Jew. The Jewish villain/ Gentile hero dichotomy is again evident here. Scotty Smith is engaged in the same illegal trade as the Jews – after all, in both instances he ends up with the illegal diamonds. Yet he is constructed as a hero and the Jews are shown as shabby, ignominious, cowardly and cringing.

Daphne Rooke's novel, *Diamond Jo* (1965), again reverts to the diamond fields as the setting for an exploration of the rags to riches theme. The narrator is a Jewish immigrant from Whitechapel, Mannie Bernstein, who at first makes a modest living as a smous. Later he travels to the diamond diggings and becomes a 'kopje walloper who used to trudge from claim to claim buying diamonds' (p.7). He is nicknamed 'Ikey Mo', and partly through practising IDB, amasses a fortune and becomes the rich, well known Sir Emanuel Bernstein.

Once again the Jew is sympathetically drawn. This is due to a number of factors. The novel was written after the Second World War and the establishment of the State of Israel, when the anti-Semitism of the 1930s and 1940s was less vociferous. The image of the more assimilated second and third generation Jew had become familiar, and was replacing that of the foreign immigrant. The harsher components of the Jew-villain stereotype were being smudged and eroded. The anti-Semitic and xenophobic cartoons of Jews that had appeared in the press before and during the Second World War were no longer popular fare, and were discouraged by a government on the whole sympathetic to the Jewish state and tolerant of South African Jews. Further, the Jews belonged to the white in-group as opposed to the black out-group, and were thus racially acceptable in a society increasingly dominated by the differences between black and white. Rooke uses Bernstein to explain:

> We came as poor people to Africa. Poverty in Africa though was different from poverty in England. Here we were not so greatly despised, for men were judged not only by wealth and breeding but according to colour; poor Jews we might be but we were Europeans and beneath us were the Indians, the Coloured people and the Kaffirs. (pp.87-88)

In this text, perhaps because he is the narrator, Bernstein does not speak with an accent, nor does Rooke provide a stereotypical physical description. While Jewish authors frequently use Gentile narrators, this is one of the very few times in South African English fiction that a Gentile author has chosen to use a Jewish narrator. In order to give verisimilitude to the character, the text abounds in Yiddish expressions. The Yiddish accent used by other Jewish characters is associated with business dealings:

'There's nothing here I can deal in.'
'Except diamonds,' said Solly. 'Vot, he is jokink for sure.' He winked at Mrs. Reuben. 'Lookink for something to invest in? My poy, look arundt you ... No, Mannie. My wibe and me make a libbing. Bring in a partner, bring in trouble ...' (p.51)

She projects further perceptions of the Jew, ironically through what a black man tells Bernstein: 'There's some call you that young turkey-cock of a Jew and there's some call you that robbing swine of a Jew ...' (p.92). Bernstein recalls:

... an astonishing change had taken place in my father ... he had diamond fever ... And when he picked out a diamond – oi yoi yoi. His hands shook, his body writhed, it was like an orgasm. This was a terrible thing for me to see in him, as though in his old age he had lost all sense of decency and had exposed himself in public. (p.86)

The sense of embarrassment which is evoked is attributed to Bernstein but reveals the author's perception of reactions to Jews. Although Rooke clearly does not associate these negative characteristics with Bernstein, they do provide examples of the propagation of anti-Jewish prejudice.

Appearing almost at the same time as Rooke's novel, is a vastly more popular treatment of South African history – Wilbur Smith's block-buster, *The Sound of Thunder* (1966). This text demonstrates a favourable attitude towards Jews. It is the first novel of the Anglo-Boer War to feature a Jewish woman as one of the chief characters, and it is the first in which a Jewish man is shown to be a brave, though not very competent, fighter. Also, this is the first time that an historical novel avoids using the figure of the smous or diamond dealer.

Rose Friedman, twenty-one-year-old wife of Saul, is the stereotypical beautiful Jewish woman. Dark, voluptuous and exotic, she is so powerfully sexual that when she appears for the first time, within a few pages, she seems to conjure up a storm, during which – despite her married state – she has a passionate encounter with Sean

Courtenay, the swashbuckling hero. Saul Friedman, is a 'little Jewish lawyer' (p.65) who has joined the Natal Corps of Guides. The narrator shows him as 'thin and hairy', and comments that 'in a pleasant sort of way he was extremely ugly' (p.66).

Notwithstanding Smith's attempt to portray a beautiful and good Jewish woman, and a new type – the likeable Jewish soldier – he finds the Jewish potential of his characters irresistible. Ruth's uncles, the Goldberg brothers, are wealthy Jews, whose family has interests in shopkeeping, minerals, hotels, meat factories, and a brewery. Benjamin Goldberg uses several Yiddish expressions – 'Oi Yoi Yoi!' (p.121) among them – and lives in some splendour. During the course of the novel, Saul is conveniently killed, leaving Ruth available to marry the victorious Gentile, Sean.

More recently, James Ambrose Brown's novel, *The White Locusts* (1983), treats the founding of Johannesburg. The subject is remarkably similar to Brett Young's *The City of Gold* – published forty-four years before. Brown's novel documents the fortunes of immigrants on the Kimberley diamond fields and in Johannesburg, notably Leonard Penlynne whose Jewish father's name was Penzlovsky. A swashbuckling adventurer who makes good, Penlynne represents the fully assimilated Jew. His Jewishness is nevertheless finally thrown in his face by a mistress whom he deserts: 'You bloody swine,' she screamed. 'You rotten Jew bastard. Get out!' (p.318).

A second Jewish character, Isadore Isaacs, is a waif from the Russian Pale of Settlement who has grown up in Whitechapel. His fortune is made largely through illegal liquor dealing, and he is last seen smoking a cigar, checking his gold watch (p.204), looking down on the 'peruvians' from Lithuania. 'Surely you don't despise your own people?' (p.208) asks his religious sister after he has sent for her from London. The answer he evades giving is 'yes'. The narrator comments: 'Christmas, yes. Yom Kippur, no. He had had enough of ritual piety while his father lived' (p.205). Hearing the new immigrants in the streets of Johannesburg speaking Yiddish, which he remembers from his early childhood in the Pale of Settlement, makes him 'cringe' (p.205). He thinks: 'There had been too much shame and abasement. Here he spoke only English' (p.205). Isaacs is the typical assimilationist Jew, with aspects of the Barnato image. Indeed, Barnato is mentioned several times in the text as a role model for immigrant Jews.

In this portrait Brown shows a greater sensitivity towards Jewish assimilationist tendencies than many other writers dealing with this theme. Throughout the text there are scattered references to anti-Semitism from which the third person narrator stands aloof. Nevertheless, the unfavourable aspects of the Jewish presence in early Johannesburg are all paraded: illegal trading, particularly in liquor, insanitary living conditions, outlandish appearance and accent.

In Stephen Gray's satiric novel, *Caltrop's Desire* (1980), the original diamond fields image of the IDB with a Yiddish accent is used differently. The narrator purports to write the 'memoirs' of Caltrop, an 'old campaigner' born in 1867. Caltrop is an orphan who grows up in Kimberley and who 'remember[s] ... Barney Barnato' (p.11). While reporting on IDB for the *Diamond Fields Advertiser*, he meets Ikey Moses 'the greatest [fence] of them all .... Of the three tons of sparklers winkled out of the Great Hole, you could count on 10 per cent going Ikey Moses's way' (p.11). The name 'Ikey Moses', and the connection with IDB, are stereotypical. The Jew is, however, projected ironically, although there is a standard reference to short stature and a glancing reference to the Yiddish accent and expressions:

> 'Oi young John ... you are a fine, a fine yunk man.' (p.12)
> Ma Moses coached me on the back veranda. 'Mozart, little John,' she said, 'you spell M-O-Z-A-R-T mit a T.'
> 'Schubert,' I'd say.
> 'Mit a H, she'd say. 'Now yunk man, come and have your clothes washed. If you vant to play the schlemiel, play it in fresh clothes, I'm tellink you.' (p.13)

Both Ma and Ikey Moses are kindly nurturing figures. Caltrop refuses to betray Moses's IDB activities: 'I liked Ikey Moses too much to want to do a thing like that to him. He was the nearest, you see, I came to acquiring a father' (p.13). The ironic treatment of the Jew in this text reflects a new literary self-consciousness in South African literature. Stephen Gray is actively involved in the retrieval of early South African texts and is so familiar with the literary constructs of the past that he is able to use stereotypes with a measure of detached amusement as part of a quasi-historical satire.

It may well be argued that the image of the Jew in the historical novel provides a particularly cogent example of the way in which authors may deliberately choose to incorporate into their texts, as historical verities, those very stereotypes and stereotypical situations which have by now become almost mandatory, believing that these images are readily recognisable and provide local colour – hence the popularity of such images as the smous, the digger, the merchant, and the assimilationist. Nevertheless the author controls the way in which images are projected. Over time, the presentation of the Jew in the historical novel has softened considerably. The demonic aspect of the anti-Jewish type has by the late twentieth century substantially eroded, although the markers of appearance and accent are still firmly in place.[4]

The Image of the Jew Domesticated

Throughout the twentieth century the images of the evil Jew, the Wandering Jew and the good Jew persist in attenuated and even domesticated form.

At times, however, the image ironically remains that of the Other. In 'The Wanderer's Coin' in Hein Wicht's *The Mountain* (1966), a mysterious stranger gives the narrator a lucky coin which he says he was given by 'the Wandering Jew himself!'

> He was an old man and he looked like a Jew, and he spoke of things that had happened centuries ago – spoke like an eye-witness. He came to our farm in rags, begging for something to eat and a place to sleep. My father wanted to set the dogs on him, but I felt sorry and got permission for him to sleep in the wagon-house. (p.18)[5]

More often, however, writers project versions of the stereotypes already established in South African fiction, such as the trader and the kaffirboetie, or new images of the professional – chemist, doctor or lawyer. Frequently only the Jewish name and occupation are stated.[6]

Further naturalised images are found in Bryce Courtenay's *The Power of One* (1989). There are several minor Jewish characters: a friendly Jewish storekeeper, a beautiful, helpful Jewish teacher and her intellectual, chess-playing father; and a major character, Morrie Levy, a school friend of the main character, Peekay. Although the narrator treats Morrie with affection and admiration, both negative and positive stereotypes come into play as well as the well-established clichés of Jewish experience.

Morrie's immigrant parents from Poland 'escaped being rounded up by the S.S. by pretending they were Roman Catholics' (p.323). He is obsessed with Hitler's persecution of the Jews and suffers vicariously: 'Morrie had never known any racial prejudice, yet he had a strong sense of alienation [and] ... guilt' (p.330). Unusually for a non-Jewish author, Courtenay is sensitive to Jewish alienation. In *The Power of One* the narrator comments: 'I sensed his Jewish alienation and I understood the intelligent, clear-eyed pessimism that seemed a part of everything he did. He had inherited loneliness' (p.360). After his persecutions in Germany, Morrie's father makes a fortune in South Africa. But Morrie is troubled:

> Believe me, being rich, in a Jewish household anyway, isn't a lot of fun. Everything is overdone. Too much love, too much money, too much food, too much care, too much reminding you that you're different, that you're Jewish ... You can have my twelve bedrooms and six bathrooms. I'll swap you my old man's five cars and three chauffeurs ... (p.377)

An excess of money and food and expensive motor cars are, as has been suggested, typical adjuncts to the image of the Jew in the late twentieth century. Another typical characteristic is Morrie's cleverness:

> "I'm a Jew, remember. We're supposed never to forget ... It took two thousand years of persecution ... to make me smart ... Persecution is the major reason for a Jew to exist. If it didn't happen we'd be as intellectually inferior as your lot ..." (pp.335-337)

Morrie imitates his grandmother's Yiddish accent and mannerisms, and is exceptionally adept at making money. Yet he is terrified that he will be taken for a money-lender, saying rather precociously and unbelievably, ' "the whole purpose of my education at this *goy* school is so that sort of stigma can be removed from my Jewishness ... I've already had several hundred years' training in usury!" ' (p.351). In these and like statements it is easy to isolate the special intervention of the author and his intention to make statements about Jews. Morrie is also a kaffirboetie. Caught with Peekay teaching blacks in a night school, he is berated by a policeman: ' "Okay, Jewboy ... don't think you seen the last of me. I know a *comminist* when I see one" ' (p.451). This touch is very reminiscent of Hugh Lewin or Denis Goldberg's testimony concerning their prison experience.

The Kugel

Towards the middle of the century, apparently new images appeared. Close examination, however, demonstrates that these are merely versions of the earlier types. One of the most frequently recurring has been the kugel. Usually a woman, she is a variation on the sexually attractive, large-breasted Jewish women prevalent in the earlier literature. This has passed into recent South African mythology as a striking type – the upwardly mobile, wealthy, spoilt, almost invariably Jewish young woman, overly interested in materialism and ostentation, living in an up-market suburb, driving a flashy car, and speaking with a nasal inflection and whine.

The figure of the kugel took shape around the mid-1950s and was popularised by Adam Leslie in his satiric revues of the 1960s. From the 1970s onwards it began to appear frequently in newspaper and magazine articles, freely used, by Gentiles and Jews alike, to satirise upwardly mobile, suburban Jewish women. This stereotype is a local version of the Jewish American Princess, the JAP, which Letty Cottin Pogrebin defines as:

> a spoiled, materialistic, vapid, demanding, self-absorbed brat who twists Daddy around her little finger and stalks a husband who will support her in the style to which her father has made her accustomed. She's trendy, sexy-looking, but, alas, frigid. She's tired, has a headache, sex is inconvenient; she prefers shopping. She's a clotheshorse,

an inveterate home decorator, a collector of furs,
jewelry, and vacations. She loves to entertain but hates
to cook ...[7]

Originally created by Jewish comics, the JAP figured in several
American movies, such as *Marjorie Morningstar* (1958) and *Goodbye
Columbus* (1969), and circulated not only in the media but in
ordinary conversation. Riv-Ellen Prell argues that these representations of women became part of the mythos at the time of the entry
of American Jews into the consumer culture, coinciding with the
moment when consumer culture came to dominate the American
economy.[8]

The South African version, also a product of the move of South
African Jewry towards suburban affluence, is strikingly similar. There
are, however, two additional components – the stigmatising whine,
which is a residual reference to the foreign accent, and the mandatory
big breasts derived from the female exotic type. Also, the kugel is not
frigid. In his first novel, *A Separate Development* (1980) Christopher
Hope showed a lascivious kugel:

> I'd slipped out for a bit of nose to nose with this big
> giver called Jennifer Katz ... They said she was more
> precocious than most, being Jewish. An incredibly
> pretty girl, her father had said that she wasn't going to
> marry no ruddy goy. That's why he sent her to the
> convent: Catholics didn't count. Jennifer was making
> the most of things before she went off to join the Israeli
> army. (pp.9-10)

In another story, 'The Kugel' which was first published in his volume
Private Parts (1982), and republished in *Learning to Fly* (1990), Hope
analyses kugels several times:

> the kugels (deceptively named ... from those sweet
> heavy puddings stuffed with raisins) ... flashing
> hungrily across town in their Italian sports cars, stood
> strategically poised on the library steps sunning their
> breasts and reactivated the marriage market with a

vengeance, hunted down medics, dentists, and lawyers-to-be without quarter, and cursed all politicians. (p.110)

A few pages later he writes:

> The kugels ... are those rich girls with names like Lorraine, and Wanda and Michelle, usually driving Alfa Romeos, whose brothers are clerks on the Stock Exchange or studying to be dentists and whose fathers are rich business men in the shady suburbs; they don't come to university to take a degree, they're here to become known, to look around and have fun and find a husband ... Usually they have big breasts. (p.114)[9]

One kugel, Melissa Dworkin, is mockingly described as 'a rag princess, sister to the famous Clara who had gone to live on a kibbutz and had actually shot an Arab during an attack on the settlement, which caused a considerable stir when news came back since Clara had never shown the stamina needed to pass first year sociology' (p.117).

South African Jewish writers have taken up the stereotype. In 1982 Illana Hitner Klevansky published a satirical paperback, *The Kugel Book*, a light-hearted send-up of Jewish kugels and their families. In Barbara Ludman's *The Day of the Kugel* (1989), although not specified as Jewish, kugels are described by one of the characters:

> Kugels are mostly from the wealthy northern suburbs of Johannesburg ... If you're a kugel, you're doing a BA degree while you look for a medical student to marry ... You are mainly interested in looking terrific. You spend hours on your hair and your clothes ... You usually talk about clothes and motorcars ... You are not interested in any boy who does not drive an Alfa Romeo or better. A Lancia will do fine ... If anybody asks what you're going to study at varsity, tell them psychology. Or sociology. You can teach, as long as it's English ... you must care about the conditions of the blacks you know ... You wish the men didn't beat their wives. You wish the government would stop hassling your maid. (pp.8-10)

The details are very similar to Hope's construction and prove that the figure has entered the South African mythology in a consistent way. When used by Jewish writers, however, the image is an aspect of Jewish irony or self-satire. Although, at times, the satire would superficially appear to be light-hearted, the effects are far-reaching.

While a few Jewish women are constructed as leftists, and one or two as suburban housewives, no other image of the Jewish woman in South African fiction or in the media is anywhere near as powerful as that of the kugel. The strong impression of the wealthy, selfish and overdressed Jewish woman predominates and controls the way in which at least the female half of the Jewish community is viewed by the general population, including Jews themselves.[10] This may contribute to an attitude of self-rejection among those Jewish women who dissociate themselves from the stereotype. Although Jews themselves often create and enjoy images of kugels, there seems to be a lack of awareness of the damage which can be wrought by the cumulative effect of these stereotypes, not only on Jewish women's self-image but on Jewish males' attitude towards Jewish women, and on the view that society as a whole holds of Jews. Pogrebin makes this point in relation to the JAP image:

> The JAP idea seems to be the dumping ground for a lot of garbage from everybody with a problem – non-Jews who hate Jews, men who hate women, Jewish men who hate Jewish women, and Jewish women and men who hate themselves. Male novelists, screenwriters, comedians, or "innocent" tellers of JAP jokes seem to be projecting their own Jewish self-hatred onto the JAP character. By attacking Jewish women, they can believe they are attacking *women* and not the Jewishness they despise in themselves. The woman who collaborates in this game may unconsciously hope to deflect attention from her own Jewishness or femaleness onto the JAP target, thereby asserting that she is a better class of Jew or woman ...[11]

The plot of Hope's story, 'The Kugel', unusually concerns a male kugel. It deals with a homosexual episode between a black man and a rich, apolitical student, Joel Wolferman – a materialistic, flashy Jew who owns a Porsche and whose family's money had been made through exploiting the blacks. The description of his luxurious apartment continues to conjure up a sense of fabulous wealth:

> People fell silent in Wolferman's enormous apartment, gazed at the thick, white wall-to-wall carpet, the massive hi-fi, the steel and leather chairs and whispered about the huge four-poster bed, shook their heads over the money it must have cost ... (p.115)

The main theme of the story, however, concerns Wolferman's homosexual relationship with the black man. Here Hope seems to hint glancingly at the bond between the black and the Jew which was a feature of the work of Peter Abrahams and will reappear in various forms in some black writing as well as in texts where a Jewish author seeks to draw a parallel between Jewish and black experience.

Ethnicity in the Work of Jewish Authors

In the work of some Jewish authors, Jewishness is used for ethnic and historic flavour, humour or satire – the writings of Clarissa Jacobi and Barney Simon are examples. Later, in the novels of Rose Zwi, Lynn Freed and Denis Hirson it is also explored for the possibilities of nostalgia.

Only one text from this period directly confronts the issues of anti-Semitism and ethnic pride. The story, 'The Messiah', from Lionel Abrahams's semi-autobiographical 'novel in 18 stories', *The Celibacy of Felix Greenspan* (1977) deals with the experience of a young Jewish child at a school for the physically handicapped. The adult narrator records how he attended Christian services and became sufficiently impressed to toy with the idea of becoming converted. At the same time, however, he was also exposed to anti-Semitism:

> He was 'Jewboy' and had to hear about Jews having long noses and being stingy and cheats, all because Jesus got crucified by those old Jews – even though it was the Romans who really did it.

> The old carpenter boy, Moses ... who ... was so kind
> that everybody loved him ... said one day, while Felix
> could hear him: 'No, I don't like Jews. They killed Jesus.'
> The boys were always saying that and Felix felt half cross
> and half ashamed. But when Moses said it, it was much
> worse: it seemed to be true, and Christians and Jews had
> to hate each other. (p.27)
>
> One Sunday morning Mr Fergusson preached the
> Bible story of Joseph and his brothers ... 'When the eldest
> brother, Reuben, saw the traders,' said Mr Fergusson, 'he
> said to the others, "Why should we kill Joseph when we
> can sell him as a slave to these traders?" Well, Jews, you
> know, are always ready to sell anything, even their brother
> – so they agreed to do as Reuben said ...'
>
> Felix gave a little jump, The boy on the bench next to
> him nudged him and he saw two other boys turn to look
> at him with quick grins on their faces. (p.30)

Despite the initial reaction of shame, the young child becomes
conscious and proud of his Jewishness:

> Nurse Verster came past on her way to the dormitories.
> When she saw him she said, 'Hullo, Felix. Why aren't
> you at service?'
>
> Felix tried to look up at her but the sun shone into his
> eyes. 'Because I'm Jewish,' he said. (p.30)

Clarissa Jacobi's story, 'A Real Kavalsky', was first published in her
native Dutch in Holland in 1966 and reissued in South Africa in
1972. Jacobi has grafted on to the delicate theme of birth and
confinement moving references to the Holocaust and the experience
of Dutch Jews, some of whom were deported to concentration camps
and gas chambers. This is one the few texts in South African fiction
where the experience of the Holocaust is used not merely for
historical, but also for aesthetic reasons – to contrast the experience
of death with that of new life, which is the main topic. However, the
author also introduces sly satire which evokes the familiar upwardly
mobile suburban Jew:

My brothers-in-law come and congratulate me … My
mother-in-law has first ordered them to shul, then dragged
them back here. The afternoon holds more in store for
them. Lunch: chopped herring, chopped liver, soup with
kreplach (dumpling containing meat). Tradition served in
abundance on silver platters and Royal Doulton … I sense
their longing for the cool lounges of their exclusive sports
club, the undulating green of the golf course, whisky-and-
sodas … My sisters-in-law … are good-looking women …
Ripe and somewhat oversized … The shantung and linen
of their expensive imported suits and dresses hug their
rather massive hips … which they attack … with a wide
variety of weapons: diets, rowing machines in their
Empire-style bedrooms, visits to health farms … My dear,
voluptuous sisters-in-law. (pp.40-41)

The patronising 'dear' notwithstanding, the sisters-in-law are, of
course, kugels.

Barney Simon does not use Jewish material either in order to make a
point about Jewishness or to explore the ethical or philosophical issues
in the South African Jew's response to anti-Semitism, but for its orna-
mental qualities and humorous potential. Here Simon is following a
trend already noted in South African fiction of the mid-century and
which has been identified in American fiction after the 1950s, where
the author responds to the tremendous interest in the Jewish home
background. It becomes fashionable to use Yiddish words and expressions and to explore Jewish folklore and culture in literature, the
movies and on television.[12]

Simon's story 'Our War' in *Joburg Sis!* (1974), is a fantasy about an
unspecified and undated South African 'war'. All the characters, who
feature only briefly, have Jewish names: Rochella, Leiba, Zaidah and
many others. There are further references, obviously used for the
possibilities of their ethnicity, to shul, Yom Kippur and Jewish foods. A
tale is told – a version of the story of the three little pigs – in which
many Yiddish, sometimes broken Yiddish or German phrases are used:

… a big white bear came to the door. "Kinderlach,
konderlach, lost mir arein," the bear said, "children,

children, let me in …"
"Nein! Nein!" The children called, "Mir haben alein!
We have our own!"
"Kinderlach, konderlach," the bear began again, "lost
mir arein – ich et dir gebben putter mit breit! Butter and
Bread!"
"Nein, nein mir haben alein!"
So the bear gave a graiser forts – a big fart – which
blew down the door and he ran in and swallowed all the
children. (p.172)

By this time the Jewish presence in South Africa had become
naturalised enough for it to be possible for Jewish authors, feeling
reasonably secure, to use the memories of parents and grandparents,
and even to use vulgarities, without any sense of shame or
embarrassment.

During the 1980s Rose Zwi wrote three novels forming a trilogy –
Another Year in Africa (1980), *The Inverted Pyramid* (1981) and *Exiles*
(1984). They are strongly based in nostalgia, concerned with the
retrieval of the past, and have a vigorous Zionist bias. They detail the
life of Ruth Erlich, the daughter of Jewish immigrants, from her
childhood in a suburb of Johannesburg before the outbreak of the
Second World War, to her involvement in the Zionist Youth Movement
and her immigration to Israel. Like Dan Jacobson's *The Beginners*,
these novels constitute part of a tradition established in America of the
family novel or 'saga of the generations'.[13] Zwi documents as many
aspects as possible of Jewish life in a working-class suburb, with a heavy
reliance on stereotypes and stock situations.

Frequent allusion is made to shtetl experience, mainly through the
narrative device of Ruth's nightmares, recalling the memories of her
grandparents. On every page of the first novel there are copious
references to Jewish customs, food, festivals and idiosyncrasies, and
even glancing allusions to typical appearance – '[l]ittle wonder I've got
such a long nose' says Berka, 'all my emotions are filtered through it'
(p.13). There are many Yiddish expressions, almost always with an
English translation following. Several songs are given in the original
Yiddish, and there is an extensive glossary of Yiddish terms at the end
of the book, suggesting that the book is intended for a general

audience. Clearly, it is a parade of ethnicity and indicates the author's pride in her past and confidence in her Jewishness.

The characters, however, are all stereotypes. Berka Feldman, the shoemaker, had arrived in South Africa in 1892. He had worked for his uncle in his concession store and 'kaffireatnik' and had also been on the diamond diggings. He is a version of the Wandering Jew having 'started on his life of wandering' (p.9) plying his trade among the Afrikaners. The uncle becomes a man of property, and buys a house in Houghton. A Jewish butcher 'gives short weight' and a Jew who owns a second-hand shop is 'a miser' (p.16). At Ruth's school one school-boy taunts another: 'Bolshie! Bolshie! Isaac is a Bolshie! (p.36), and '[w]hen Annatjie made a movement towards Ruth, her sister jerked her back roughly. "You can't play with them," she said loudly. "They killed Jesus Christ" ' (p.83). Reverend Benjamin had 'a liaison with a Boer woman and progeny of several daughters' (p.52). The upwardly mobile Joel becomes ashamed of his origins:

> On the Mayfontein tram ... he sat in a sweat of embarrassment as the immigrants talked loudly to one another in Yiddish ... He would watch in acute discomfort as an Englishman lowered his newspaper and smirked at the foreign sounds emitted by Joel's co-religionists, as unselfconsciously as though they were still in their shtetl. It was even worse when they trotted out their ridiculous version of English. (p.101)

Joel goes to work for his Uncle Feldman, makes money and, in the second volume, appears as a millionaire. Berka's daughter marries an Afrikaner. Her father had warned her: ' "Don't go with him, Raizel. Stay with your own kind ... You'll never be one of them .... he'll call you a bloody Jewess ..." '. She replies: ' "He won't, Dad. I'm converting" ' (pp.138-139). This melodramatic scene is reminiscent of that in Victor Barwin's 'A Convent Jewess'. It also recalls Old Nathan's advice to his son Saul in Sarah Gertrude Millin's *The Coming of the Lord*. Dovid Erlich, Ruth's father, member of the Jewish Workers' Club, attends a meeting in the City Hall to protest against Nazi atrocities and is beaten by fascists chanting, 'Slay the Christ killers!' (p.147). Some conversations are merely a paraphrase of contemporary Jewish issues:

'Look at Germany: Jews thrown out of jobs, property confiscated, schools closed, people shut up in ghettos ...'
'They let some Jews into South Africa from Germany.'
'And are drafting the Aliens Act to keep others out. They hate the Jews as much as the Nazis do ... This isn't the same South Africa you knew in the old days. All those stories you tell of Boer hospitality and respect for the people of the Book. When they're in the book they're all right, but when the farmer's crops fail and he comes to borrow from the Jewish storekeeper at interest, it's a different matter. When the Jew was a smous ... they tolerated him. When he holds the purse strings or he's in competition, they fear him. And where there's fear, there'll be persecution ... what do you think the Greyshirts are planning? ... [W]e need a home of our own, without Aliens Acts and without anyone's kind permission to exist.'
'Spare me the Zionism ...' (p.14)

Zionism, the Zionist Youth Movement and immigration to Israel are the main subjects of the second and third novels in Zwi's trilogy. The image of the committed Zionist had first featured in Jacobson's short stories of the 1950s, made a brief appearance in Arthur Markowitz's *Market Street* (1959), and was expanded in Jacobson's *The Beginners*. Zwi focuses intently on the inner affairs of the *hachsharah* (training farm in South Africa) and its counter-attraction, the Communist Party. While the first novel of Zwi's trilogy has a measure of charm, and the central character, Ruth Erlich, is well developed, the work as a whole is marked by some folksy sentimentality and Zionist propaganda.

In her construction of the Frank family – Durban Jews involved in the theatre – in her novel, *Home Ground* (1986), Lynn Freed touches on stereotypical Jewish issues to provide local colour and authenticity. A telling use of the fairy-tale device – 'once upon a time'

– evokes a sense of the by now familiar immigrant background and upward mobility of the family:

> 'Once upon a time in a country called Lithuania, there lived a poor Jewish family ... One day the father heard that there was a country at the bottom of Africa where people, even Jews, could go and find diamonds and gold and riches ... when they arrived at the bottom of Africa ... the husband opened a trading store to sell blankets and tobacco to the natives. Soon he had enough money to buy a whole house for his family ...' (pp.30-31)

Throughout the novel the Jewish narrator alludes to Jewish family customs – the Sabbath meal, a Jewish wedding, the Jewish Youth movement. The stigma of the Yiddish accent is represented, in the case of South African born Jews, by a 'whine'. The physical descriptions have not changed during the century: a grandmother has 'a big bust and a big nose' (p.34), and Mrs Goldman 'shrank her short neck even further into her hunched shoulders. She cupped her jewelled hands before her like a mendicant' (p.69). In a satiric allusion to assimilated Jews and name-changing, the narrator recalls:

> Edwina had never invited me over before. My mother said that they would have nothing to do with Jews since her father had married a Gentile and changed his name from Slomowitz to Sloane. My mother loved to expose this sort of treachery. 'Oh?' she would say when I mentioned Edwina, 'That Slomowitz girl?' (p.127)

This snobbery of the more assimilated Jews towards other Jews is further suggested in the Frank parents' disdain for the members of the Jewish youth movements, who have '[g]hastly speech ... ghastly manners' (p.112).

Denis Hirson's quasi-fantastical autobiographical short novel, *The House Next Door to Africa* (1986) similarly retrieves family memories to reconstruct mythology. Here a Jew's service in the Russian army and pogroms are recalled in a dreamlike sequence:

Grandpa Zalman has a dream. He hobbles along ... among hundreds of other prisoners ... A Jew softly wishes them luck from the side of the road, hoping his children have met with no worse a fate at the hands of the Russians ... (p.21)

In come Bolsheviks ... Out goes Granny Toba's mother ... to distract them from Granny Toba who is in the cellar with scarlet fever ... On discovering Granny Toba they say it's not girls they want, only gold. 'My daughters are gold to me,' says Granny Toba's mother softly. They leave with the sacred knives and scrolls. (p.28)

The novel ends with the present-day family preparing to leave South Africa for a second exile in England after the father, a political activist – another, and this time South African bolshevik – has been released from detention. So far, this is the only novel by a Jewish author to deal with the emigration of Jews for political reasons.

In all these texts the authors construct plot and character from family or communal memories, demonstrating a good deal of self-confidence, a measure of self-criticism, and a belief in the wider public's interest in Jewish material.

—8—

JEWISH
SELF-REJECTION

After the middle of the twentieth century, the anti-Jewish stereotype recedes from the work of most Gentile writers, only to be
replaced by an equally negative image in the work of some Jewish
writers. Perhaps the way in which Jewish authors portray Jewish
characters depends, either directly or indirectly, on the effect of anti-
Semitism on Jewish society. One response, as has been shown, has
been the celebration of the Jewish past and of ethnicity. Another may
be that the Jew sees him or herself reflected in the distorting mirror of
the majority culture, becomes influenced by its prejudices and
assumptions, and may suffer from problems of personal identity.[1]
Like some of the diamond field writers, the Jewish authors under
discussion in this chapter, in their fictional treatment of Jewish
experience, show symptoms of just such a problematic and fractured
sense of identity.

Nadine Gordimer

Perhaps the most memorable of the few Jews in Nadine Gordimer's
work is the attractive Joel Aaron, one of the central characters in *The
Lying Days* (1953).

Despite being the son of poor owners of a concession store on the
mines, Joel is extremely well educated. He is cultured, bookish and
caring. A close friendship develops between Joel and Helen Shaw,
the narrator. Joel introduces Helen to a world of art and beauty,
previously unknown to her. He is one, she says,

with whom I was hearing live music for the first time in
my life; who ... pushed me before him on the tram to
town to see exhibitions of painting and sculpture,
showed me the inside of the municipal art gallery ...
from whose books and whose talk I was even beginning
to see that the houses we lived in ... did not make use of
space and brightness and air ... (p.126)

Although Gordimer develops the character of Joel in some detail, the
singularity of the portrait lies in its projection of Otherness. Joel is
Jewish, therefore he is different. When, as an adult, Helen meets Joel –
whom she had first glimpsed when they were both children – she
remarks on his 'different' appearance:

Of course this was a different face. There was no place,
no feature, no bone one could point to and say: Here,
this is where it is; yet the face was different. The faces
that had looked in at me when I was an infant ... the
faces that had been around me all my life had differences, one from the other, but they were differences of
style ... This face was built on some other last ... He
smiled ... that expressive smile that had an almost nasal
curve to it ... (pp.110-111)

Perhaps, in the reference to the smile, lurks the shadow of the hooked
Jewish nose. Gordimer has said of her own craft: 'My method is to let
the general seep up through the individual.'[2] In this instance the
'general' image of a Jew would seem to 'seep up' from Joel's individual and 'different' face.
   At several points in the novel the narrator refers to what is clearly a
racial difference in Joel's features. 'There was a fascination about the
way he looked,' she comments, 'the fascination I had felt in the faces
of Indian waiters serving food in Durban hotels.' (p.119) And later
Helen tells Joel:

"... You look like an Indian, you know."
"Yes, I know I'm black."
"No, an Indian in a hotel we used to go to in Durban

> ... [with] a skin that looked quite liquid, like some kind of metal that had just been poured smoothly over the bones ..."
> "Right. I'm greasy, too." (p.140)

Here Joel himself, in a rare flash of humour for the character – and the author – recognises and points out the stereotyping. The 'black' reference is resonant.

Helen's meeting with Joel's mother, and her visits to Joel's home, are marked by a sense of Otherness and unease. She observes: 'I felt acutely the fact that I was ... in the house of strangers. This I felt in relation to her, and to Joel, the embarrassment he must feel at the accent, her whole foreignness before me ...' (p.115). Helen's parents, too, show a typical distance from Joel simply because he is Other:

> My father spoke to Joel about "your people" and "the customs of your people" with the same air he used to surprise the Portuguese market gardener with a few words of Portuguese, or, when once we drove through Zululand, a Zulu tribesman with a brisk question in his own language ... "That's a well-mannered boy," my father informed me. "They know how to bring their children up to respect older people. And of course they're clever, it goes without saying." (p.120)

The implication of xenophobia, hidden under the father's apparent approval and good manners, is indicated in yet another passage. Helen remembers a conversation: 'You are a very *clean* people, of course. Who said that? Daddy to Joel, the first time ... Of course, all Jews are circumcised; but my father hadn't meant that ...' (p.142). Helen's mother, sourly disapproves of her friendship with Joel. When Helen telephones her from the Aaron's house, her disdain and covert anti-Semitism is starkly and economically conveyed :

> "It's all right, I'm having supper here."
> "Supper? Where?"
> "At Joel's. With the Aarons."
> "With the *Aarons*?" There was a pause. (p.154)

It might be argued that here Gordimer has analysed certain Gentile attitudes concerning Jews. Indeed, in her recent study of Gordimer's work, Kathrin Wagner attributes Gordimer's dissection of anti-Semitism to what she calls 'her own part-Jewish heritage'.[3] The error Wagner makes in claiming that Gordimer is 'part-Jewish' is extremely revealing. Perhaps it was Gordimer herself who, in several of her recorded interviews and articles, blurred the fact of her Jewishness.

At approximately the time that her early works of fiction were appearing, Gordimer wrote of her childhood influences in an article which appeared in the *New Yorker* in 1954. There she records how she was sent to a convent school and regarded herself as belonging not to the Jewish community but to 'our little colonial tribe, with its ritual tea-parties and tennis parties'. She relates how her mother distanced herself from her 'particular [Jewish] section of the community'. 'She got on much better with the Scots ladies of the town ...' she said, and she describes her 'working (or, rather, baking) like a beaver for the annual cake-and-sweet sale in aid of the Presbyterian Church'. She adds: 'Our life was very much our mother's life'[4]

It is apparent that Gordimer felt alienated from her father, a Lithuanian immigrant watchmaker, who was not able to pass as a member of the 'Scots' community. In a brief, dismissive reference she mentions that he pays dues to the 'ugly little synagogue' (p.116), thus extending the key anti-Semitic epithet 'ugly', with its strong suggestion of Jew-hatred, to the very religious observances of Jews. In 1991 Gordimer expanded this theme:

> I never had much sense of identity with the Jewish community ... Although [my father] had a normal Jewish village religious upbringing, my mother more or less forced him to abandon all that. We kept only the Day of Atonement ... He had a new suit about every two years and off he would go to fast and my sister and I would be sitting in our shorts in the car, waiting for him, looking at these people coming out of the synagogue![5]

The father is shown as some sort of scapegrace, while the sisters, who are deliberately dressed in a way that heaps contempt on Jewish religious observance, watch the worshippers mockingly. The tone of this passage, culminating in the dismissive reference to 'these people' echoes that of the anti-Semitic writers, and reveals a certain recoil from things Jewish.

In the same year that she wrote this passage, in an interview with Natan Sharansky in *The Jerusalem Report*, she spoke with some bravado of the way her 'very much assimilated [mother] despised [her] father's background ... We didn't ever go to synagogue ... We didn't keep kosher – we ate bacon.'[6]

Judie Newman is another who has been deceived. In her study of Gordimer, she claims: 'Gordimer was ... the daughter of a Jewish jeweller and a mother of British descent'.[7] It may be that Gordimer herself has colluded in these versions of her status, or rather her non-status as a Jew. It would seem that, like many other assimilated second and third generation Jews, she feels a sense of marginalisation, of being suspended between the Jewish community into which she was born, and Gentile society with which she would seem to feel a greater kinship.

In her early fiction, there is a similar narratorial recoil from Jews. In *The Lying Days*, the child, Helen, has made a forbidden visit to the mine stores, the 'filthy kaffir [concession] store ... [o]ther children called them the Jew stores' (p.18). Here she sees a Jewish woman 'sitting on an upturned soapbox pulling at a hangnail on her short, broad, thumb ... her fat ankles, in cotton stockings, settled over her shoes ... [she] looked up puffily ...'(p.20). The child's feelings are analysed: 'I passed her with a deep frown, it was on my face all the time now. My heart ran fast and trembly ...' (p.20). Although the source of the anger and fear are unidentified, it is clear that it is a negative response to a particular Other represented by the Jewish woman.

Several components of the physical description of this Jewish woman are repeated in the description of Joel Aaron's mother:

A short round woman stood in the doorway: she held her hands in front of her in the attitude of someone coming for instructions. They were puffy hands with hardened flesh growing up round small, clean but unkempt nails, the ragged-cuticle nails of domestic workers or children ... Her body in a cheap silk dress ... was the incredibly small-hipped, thickened body of Jewish women from certain parts of Europe, the swollen doll's body ... She sat down near the door on a straight-backed chair and her swollen ankles settled on her shoes. (pp.115-116)

Both these are merely variants of a sketch of yet another Jewish woman, who appears in a short story, 'The Defeated', published at the same time in Gordimer's collection, *The Soft Voice of the Serpent* (1953), and which bears many similarities to the beginning of the novel. Once again there is a Gentile narrator, not dissimilar to Helen Shaw. She sneers at Mrs Saiyetowitz, wife of a concession store-keeper, who has 'fat insteps leaning over down-at-heel shoes' (p.196), recurring symbols of defeat and demoralisation. Other physical stigmata recur. The narrator claims that Mrs Saiyetowitz has

small, pale eyes narrowed into her big, simple, heavy face ... and she had always to peer at everything ...
I saw that she was very ugly. Ugly with the blunt ugliness of a toad ...
She had the short stunted heavy bones of generations of oppression in the Ghettos of Europe; breasts, stomach, hips crowded sadly, no height, wide strong shoulders and a round back. Her head settled right down between her shoulders without even the grace of a neck ... (p.198)

Jewish and animal ugliness are conflated in the image of the toad – the symbol of disgust identical to that found in the work of anti-Semitic colonial writers, which continued to be used as a mode of disparagement of Jews throughout the century.

In *The Lying Days*, the narrator similarly describes Jews in terms of animals: 'Whenever I met Joel's parents they seemed to lapse into a kind of heaviness ... I could not imagine them more at ease, any more than I could imagine the demeanour of the lion I saw blinking behind bars ...' (p.138). The movements of Joel Aaron's mother are 'slow, heavy and insistent as her voice ... like a horse who keeps up the plod of pulling a load even when he is set free in the field' (p.116). The father is 'hunched' and 'grunting' (p.149), and has a 'hoarse, coarse voice' (p.151). The narrator comments: 'He reminded me of some heavy, thick-skinned animal, a rhinoceros or a boar' (pp.151-152).

The stock epithets appear again in 'The Defeated' in her treatment of the storekeeper, Mr. Saiyetowitz. The narrator says of him that he has a

> disgruntled, dispossessed air ... He lurked within the depths of his store like a beast in its lair, and now and then I had seen the glimmer of his pale, pasty face with the wide upper lip under which the lower closed glumly and puffily.' (p.201)

He bullies and 'spiritually maltreat[s]' (p.203) the 'natives', to whom he appears as a 'beast'. The Jewish storekeeper in *The Lying Days* is, predictably,

> a short ugly man with a rough grey chin ... he looked at me with screwed-up eyes, irritably, and did not see me. His shirt was open at the neck and black hairs were scribbled on the little patch of dead white skin ... as I came to the door of the eating house, a crescendo of heavy, sweet, nauseating blood-smell ... assailed me ... and a big white man in a butcher's apron [was] cutting a chunk of bruised and yellow fat-streaked meat from a huge weight impaled on a hook. (p.19)

The vivid expression of abhorrence, encapsulated in the key word 'nauseating', is even more powerful because the Jew is elided with a butcher. The 'blood-smell' from the meat 'impaled' on a hook encodes cruelty, and a possible faint allusion to the spectre of Shylock. The Jewish storekeeper is stereotypically 'short' and 'ugly'. Significantly, the epithet, 'ugly', becomes habitual in Gordimer's early work. In 'The Defeated' the narrator derides the very name, 'Saiyetowitz': 'I remembered it because it was ugly', she comments (p.197). Sarah Gertrude Millin's similar preoccupation with Jewish 'ugliness' is recalled here.

In *The Lying Days*, the older Helen visits the Aarons' house for Sunday-night supper. The narrator's repugnance is displaced metonymically on to the food – 'Mrs. Aaron ... was spreading a mess of grey wet fish on a roll ...' (pp.150-151). Helen compares the Jews' messy delicatessen foods with the wholesomeness of her own family's eating habits:

> my parents had a horror of what they called 'made-up' foods and we always ate simple, fresh things, home-cooked; on Sunday evenings we had ham-and-tomato sandwiches, eaten with milk (beer for my father) on the veranda in summer, or with cocoa before the fire in winter. (p.149)

The deliberate stress on ham followed by milk – an allusion to two of the major prohibitions of the Jewish dietary laws – is a device the narrator uses to signal her distance from all things Jewish. The suggested unwholesomeness of the Jewish diet represents, again metonymically, the unwholesomeness of the Jews themselves.

In these instances it cannot be argued that Gordimer merely constructs anti-Semitic narrators, or innocently uses anti-Semitic discourse, from which the author herself is aloof. There is no implied distance between the author and the attitudes towards Jews attributed to the narrators, especially when these narrators may be regarded as reflecting and not merely experiencing. There is also no analysis of the Gentile characters' perception of Jews, other than a brief reference at the end of the novel. Joel asks wryly:

> "... Helen, they did seem pretty impossible to you, didn't they? – My mother and father."
> There was a second's hesitation before I answered.
> "Yes," I said. "Impossible for *you*."
> "You mean the store and the things that make up their life and the way they look?"
> "Yes – yes, I suppose so. I have to admit that's what I really mean. You're so different. Money is their standard. – No, that's not it – money is their civilization."
> (pp.351-352)

Helen's prejudiced perception of the Jews' appearance, their connection with the store, their addiction to money, is not challenged, and stands as the last word on the determinants of the Jews' 'impossib[ility]'.

Wagner considers that in *The Lying Days* Gordimer has directly addressed the issue of prejudice. She discusses Gordimer's depiction of 'the undercurrents of anti-Semitism common in the mining communities of the East Rand', and would have us believe that Gordimer's political radicalism – 'her identification with the marginalised, the oppressed and the excluded may be understood to have originated not in any intellectual analysis of the magnitude of black oppression in South Africa but in her own early experience of difference on a variety of levels'.[8] But this is not an idea that Gordimer shares. In the interview with Sharansky, she was adamant: 'I don't think that my Jewishness is an influence [on my writing] and I get rather annoyed when people say that my opposition to racism comes from being Jewish.'[9] The projection of difference in Gordimer's work demands to be probed more fully.

In the early fiction there are passages in which a generalised fear of difference, of the Other, is projected through the experiencing consciousness of the narrator. In 'The Defeated' the child visits the concession store and observes the black people surrounding it:

> I was careful not to let them brush too closely past me, lest some unnamable *something* crawl from their dusty blankets or torn cotton trousers onto my clean self, and I did not like the way they spat, with that terrible gurgle in the throat, into the gutter, or, worse still, blew their noses loudly between finger and thumb, and flung the excrement horribly to the air. (p.196)

But this is the only occasion where physical distaste appears in relation to the blacks. Here it is immediately qualified by the recording narrator, who refers to black exoticism and vitality, with a striking change of tone. From the distance of time, the narrator recalls her childhood admiration for '[t]he clamor of their voices – always shouting, but so merry, so angry! – and the size of their laughter ...'. They become transformed into story book characters: 'I felt vaguely the spell of the books I had read ... markets in Persia, bazaars in Cairo ...' (pp.195-196).

In a similar passage in *The Lying Days*, the child, Helen, visiting the concession store, at first makes a connection between the Otherness of both Jews and blacks: 'There were people [Jews] there, shadowy, strange to me as the black man' (p.20). But she goes on to describe how

> native vendors squatted besides braziers offering roasted mealies and oranges arranged in pyramids. They sat comfortably, waiting for custom to come to them; they gazed levelly out at the Mine boys ... The gramophones from the stores made music and there was gossip and shouting above the tiny hammering of a man who sat cross-legged beating copper wire into bracelets ... a boy sat with a sewing machine, whirring the handle with his vigorous elbow jutting. Beside him were khaki and white drill trousers, neatly patched ... (p.23)

Their food differs markedly from the offensive, putrifying meat, emblematically impaled in the 'Jew-store'. They convey a sense of purpose, vitality and artistry, opposed to the defeat, poverty, dirt and ugliness inscribed in the construction of Jews.[10]

Helen later becomes conscious of a bond she shares with a black girl, Mary Seswayo:

> She is a girl, the discovery came, like me. It was not the rather ridiculous statement of an obvious fact, but a real discovery, a kind of momentary dissolving of obvious facts, when the timid, grasping, protesting life of my own organism spoke out, and I recognized its counterpart in her, beneath the beret and my kindness and her acceptance. (p.142)

The friendship ultimately fails. Helen comes to recognise the gap between Mary's social context and her own. She considers that for Mary – 'how useless it must all seem, how impossible to grasp, the structure of the English novel ... with the woman making mealie porridge over the fire, the man carefully preserving the dirty bit of paper that is his pass ... ' (pp.186-187). But this discovery does not negate the bond between the girls, which is set against the difference Helen has always felt – despite the admiration and attraction – in her relationship with Joel Aaron, the Jew. Furthermore, there is no sense of mockery or disgust in the portrayal of the commonplaces of the black shop or the black home.

Thus, while, in the early work, both Jews and blacks are constructed as Others, there is a significant difference in the authorial treatment of these Others. The reasons for Gordimer's idealisation of one out-group – the blacks – and the disparagement of her own out-group – the Jews – may be more complex than has been observed.

Stephen Clingman has identified a number of 'split positions' which Gordimer occupies by nature of her colonial background, and in her attempt to overcome the class and race structures of apartheid while simultaneously being contained in them.[11] It would seem that there are further 'split positions' to be considered, especially those associated with her fractured personal identity. One such position concerns her identity as a Jew in a Gentile society.

The ways in which Jews relate to the majority culture in which they live became particularly problematic at the time of the process of acculturation and assimilation during the period of the Enlightenment. Their close bonds with their own community were weakened, but freedom from the constrictions of the ghetto did not lead automatically to social integration. Because they were never accepted as anything other than a minority group, some Jews became influenced by the assumptions and prejudices of the majority culture. Often they became marginal people with a confused sense of identity, feeling themselves inferior and stigmatised by their Jewishness. They came to believe that they suffered from what Erving Goffman has described as a 'spoiled identity'.[12]

In their attempt to rid themselves of this barrier to the fullest participation in the life of the majority, many Jews adopted Christianity. Others, as Sartre put it, became 'inauthentic',[13] attempting, in ways short of conversion, to deny or escape from their Jewishness. Those Jews in particular who accepted the validity of the hostile Jewish stereotypes generated by Gentile society, suffered from self-doubt, frustration and aggression. Unable to direct these feelings against the logical target, the high-status Gentile group which remained an ideal, they might turn them inward onto the self. Hence arises the pathological condition known as 'Jewish self-hatred', that loathing in oneself of what one believes to be specifically 'Jewish' and desires to eradicate.[14]

This particular 'split position' has already been noted in Gordimer's attempt to reconstruct or at least rearrange her own biography to suggest membership of the Gentile in-group. In her early fiction she imaginatively reconstructs herself in the Gentile narrators she chooses, who nevertheless reflect much of her own thinking.

There is a further 'split position' hinted at in her comments about her family background in South Africa, and inscribed in her fiction: that between the station held by her father, the lowly foreign immigrant Jew, and the 'superior' white anglophone culture to which her mother aspires, and to which her own upbringing, education and sympathies predispose her.

This split is fictionally treated in a recent story 'My Father Leaves Home', from *Jump and other Stories* (1991), where she writes of a visit to an eastern European country, and the memories of her immigrant father evoked in the narrator. Given the known circumstances of Gordimer's family background, this story appears to have an autobiographical content. In terms very similar to Gordimer's published interviews, the narrator relates:

> If the phylacteries and skull-cap were kept somewhere the children never saw them ... He went fasting to the synagogue on the Day of Atonement and each year, on the anniversary of the deaths of the old people in that village ... went again to light a candle ... In the quarrels between him and his wife, she saw them as ignorant and dirty; she must have read something somewhere that served as a taunt: You slept like animals round a stove, stinking of garlic, you bathed once a week. The children knew how low it was to be unwashed. And whipped into anger he knew the lowest category of all in her country, this country.
> *You speak to me as if I was a kaffir.* (p.64)

Narratorial sympathy for the father, stigmatised by the mother as a member of a socially devalued out-group, is opposed by the chilly tone of the passage. The children appear to share the mother's contempt. Later, the narrator's distant attitude towards her father becomes overt:

When I began to know him in his shop ... he shouted at the black man on the other side of the counter who swept the floor and ran errands and he threw the man's weekly pay grudgingly at him ... I saw there was someone my father had made afraid of him. A child understands fear and the hurt and hate it brings. (p.66)

Deliberately reversing the categories of in- and out-groups, she implies that the Jew, despised by others, even by his wife, for his Jewishness and ascribed a low social status equal to that of the black, lacks insight and compassion. Like Dan Jacobson's Grossman in 'The Zulu and the Zeide', he revels in a relationship in which he has power over someone he considers to hold a status inferior even to himself. Thus the Jew, stigmatised on racial grounds, becomes himself a racist.

In this story, perhaps unconsciously, Gordimer crystallises the 'split position' she occupies as the assimilated daughter of an immigrant father. The father's anxiety – '*You speak to me as if I was a kaffir*' – expresses the Jew's fear of social slippage. It is obvious that Gordimer was acutely aware of her own situation in South Africa in the 1950s, a period when anti-Semitism threatened the status of Jews in a country increasingly polarised between black and white. As a group, Jews were particularly vulnerable to losing their fragile purchase on the white hegemony, since earlier in the century anti-Alienism had identified Jews with Asians, and more recently Nazism had once again imputed to them a racial impurity.[15]

The fear of slippage from a position barely acceptable because it is acculturated, might lead Gordimer herself to displace those prejudices and hostilities which are part of her colonial inheritance from the black – most obvious candidate for the role of the Other, but unacceptable to her in terms of her developing liberal sympathies – to that hidden Other in her own inheritance. This hidden and repressed Other, infinitely more shameful and more difficult to deal with, is not merely the Jew as such, but the foreign, Yiddish speaking Jew, typified as ugly and reviled as 'scum' in the South African mythos.[16] A similar sense of embarrassment concerning lower and better class Jews was expressed by Millin in her non-fictional writing of the 1930s and 1940s, periods during which hostile attention had been focused on Jews.

When interviewing Gordimer in 1991, Sharansky discovered her lack of interest in things Jewish: 'When we spoke of politics, she was passionate and idealistic;' he wrote, 'when we touched on her Jewish background, she seemed distant and analytical'.[17] Perhaps this rejection of Jewish involvement may be attributed, not only to a specifically South African context, but also to what Letty Pogrebin has identified in certain American Jewish women activists as the 'Rosa Luxemburg syndrome'.

Pogrebin suggests that because of the internalisation of negative Jewish images, there is a high incidence among these women of what she calls 'Jewish shame' or lack of ethnic pride. Having chosen to dissociate themselves from the negative stereotypes firmly imprinted on their minds, they tend to ignore what she terms 'our special Jewish sorrows', because they consider them too self-serving. She ponders the way in which those women who are full of compassion for oppressed groups have nothing but contempt for their own group. It would seem to her that traditionally both women and Jews have been reluctant to confront their persecutors. She believes that Jews are good at self-criticism, and are better at fighting for the rights of others than at standing up for themselves. 'Rather than identify as Jews', she argues, 'they had preferred to count themselves as feminists, anarchists, leftists, Marxists, civil rights workers, defenders of minorities and oppressed peoples. They did not recognize in their own denial of Jewish oppression proof of the impact of anti-Semitism.'[18]

As her career developed, Gordimer's work was to become more sharply focused on the evils of apartheid and on charting South Africa's social and political 'history from the inside'.[19] Her treatment of Jews, however, remained compromised by a failure to move beyond those stereotypes assembled in South African fiction over the century.[20]

After a silence of over thirty years, in her novel of 1987, *A Sport of Nature*, Gordimer finally returned to the treatment of some 'Jewish' material. One of the Jewish characters in the novel is Olga:

On summer mornings she oiled herself, spreading her toes to get at the interstices and twisting her neck, over which a string of pearls bobbled, while the four youngsters played waterpolo in the pool. When they came out to dry off ... her attention slid from her *Vogue* or Hebrew grammar ... (p.5)

Olga is a kugel. Like all kugels, she devotes much of her time and energy to beautifying herself:

> Olga's hair, pulled with a crochet hook through holes in a rubber cap, was being tinted in streaks while her nails were steeping in tepid oil ... [She was] reading a manual about isometric exercises a friend had brought from New York. Every now and then ... the empty shape of her shantung trousers as she pulled in abdominal muscles stiffly ... showed she was putting theory into practice. (pp.6-7)

Business guests are entertained at Olga's pool:

> in Olga's pavilion beside the pool Jethro carried round a whole poached salmon – the stately pink corpse laid out with the cook's radish roses and swags of golden mayonnaise – and Hillela was allowed a glass of the French champagne ... Arthur['s] ... head hung forward from his thick shoulders while he chewed – like an ox, yes. (pp.63-64)

The opulence of the pavilion, the decorated salmon and the French champagne are contrasted with Olga's Jewish husband's 'thick' appearance and ungainly manner of eating. The animal reference – 'ox' – provides an important clue to her projection of embarrassment concerning Arthur's Jewishness. Earlier Arthur had been described scathingly by another character as *'that circumcised ox Arthur who will soon be rich enough, that's for sure, to climb on top of her in a bed that used to belong to the Empress Josephine ...'* (p.49). Both passages, connected through the image of the ox, serve the purpose, once again, of devaluing Jews.

The main character is Olga's nice, Hillela Capran, who wishes to pass as a Gentile. She rejects the Jewish association of her name 'Hillela' – derived from Rabbi Hillel – and calls herself 'Kim' at her

English boarding school in Salisbury. Both her parents have remarried, to Gentiles.

Hillela is expelled for forming a friendship with a coloured boy. The Jewish woman as sexual predator is strongly endorsed in this text: the sexuality of both Hillela and her mother is emphasised. As a first stage in her sexual history, Hillela seduces her young cousin: 'He touched her breasts a little; he had noticed, living with her as a sister, that her breasts were deep and large' (p.32). Indeed, Hillela makes her way through life trading on her sexuality. In her wanderings through Africa, eastern Europe and America, she conforms to the myth of the Wandering Jew, and – the apotheosis of the kaffirboetie or bolshevik – commits herself to the African struggle, marries two black revolutionaries in succession, and returns to South Africa for that country's independence celebrations.

Another aunt, Pauline, who with her lawyer husband, Joe, are 'politicals', are further examples of bolsheviks. They send their son to a non-racial school 'over the border in a neighbouring black state' (p.19). With his ultra-Russian name, the son, Sasha is another strong bolshevik image, an activist who is detained for political offences. Thus in four characters in this text Gordimer stresses the Jewish/bolshevik nexus. In treating this extended family, Gordimer makes a significant mistake in a passing reference to 'Olga's Friday night *seder*' (p.52). No one with any connection with Judaism, however tenuous, could confuse a Friday night (Sabbath) meal with the Passover *seder*. That a Jewish author should perpetrate this mistake invites an inference that there may be a subconscious desire to conceal her own Jewish origin by seeming ignorant of even the most fundamental aspects of Jewish tradition.

Reviewing *A Sport of Nature*, Michael Wade suggested that here Gordimer finally 'addresses and celebrates the Jewish component of her identity'. In noting the frequent use of biblical or rabbinical names in the novel, he asserts that Gordimer runs a hidden allegory concerning the 'historical meaning of the Jewish experience in South Africa'.[21] But Wade fails to take into account Gordimer's attitude towards her Jewish characters which, as has been shown, is satirical rather than celebratory. As late as 1991, after the publication of *A Sport of Nature*, Gordimer made it clear to Sharansky that she was not interested in Jewish issues.

Wade identifies the source of the plot of Gordimer's novel as the story of a non-political Jewish girl who, in 1960, served a jail sentence for contravening the Immorality Act, went to Dar-es-Salaam and married a black political exile who rose to prominence after his country was liberated from colonial rule. It would seem that Gordimer used the historical fact that the girl was Jewish as an opportunity to exploit Jewish material for local colour and, more specifically, for satiric effect, but this has nothing whatever to do with the 'historical meaning of the Jewish experience in South Africa'.

Although the attitude towards Jews in the later work is less strident than that in of her earlier work – the word, 'ugly' has been discarded and disgust has given way to disdain and satire, it is obvious that Gordimer finds it impossible to deal with Jews other than as stereotypes of one sort or another.

Jillian Becker

Another assimilated Jewish woman, writing at a similar period, also shows evidence of an animus against Jews. On the surface Jillian Becker's novel, *The Keep* (1967), is a satirical treatment of an upper middle class Johannesburg family. One subtext, however, is an icy rejection of all things Jewish. The family Leyton – the father a member of parliament, the mother a refined, bored lady with artistic pretensions – is based on the known circumstances of Becker's own parents; and the consciousness of the child, Josephine, and the narrative voice are therefore close to her own. The great-uncle, Fred Kronowsky, is an immigrant:

> Uncle Fred's African studies had begun when he'd 'smoused' through the Free State and the Transvaal with the customary donkey-cart (that *motif* of the pioneering days so common that along the frieze of the century it fits between the oxwagons as a Greek triglyph between the metopes). (p.15)

The comparison with Greek art highlights, with rather obvious irony, the presence of a mythos. Not only is the uncle a smous, but he also becomes those other stock figures, the prospector and the illegal liquor dealer:

> he had turned prospector, exercising his hopes with a sluicepan ... [he made his] fortune in partnership with the owner of a mining store who'd had a side interest in brandy and a side-door which the mine boys preferred to the other ... (p.15)

Further, his upward mobility, his assumption of the trappings of English gentility and his attempts to assimilate into the general society, are also stereotypical. Freda Leyton, Kronowsky's niece, has a father 'who'd been in gold ...' (p.21) – a glancing reference to the figure of the magnate.

Thus far, the author has ironically exploited stereotyping to construct a background for the family. However, in order to dramatise Freda Leyton's snobbish, disdainful attitudes, Becker introduces an aunt who crudely embodies the old negative images. With an exuberance, a relish that goes far beyond the necessities of the narrative, she dwells on this character:

> 'Vos is dos?' Aunt Lydia growled. (p.21)
> 'Nu, Freda, vere's the kinderlach?' she quizzed. She had a voice like a cheese-grater ...
> 'Nanny will bring them down,' Freda Leyton assured her and smiled. Great-Aunt Lydia, who expected skewers if anything from her niece, stared at her a moment suspiciously before going on.
> 'He's vell, bless him, Simy?'...
> 'Gott tsu danken ... he must learn not to vorry his Mama.' Up and down the phrases went. Consonants fell in grains. Unaware that she was a dessicator, she persisted in trying to improve matters by working away with voice and words ... 'Come here Josy ... Come here my kind ... You must give your Aunty a kiss. Fffffpfa ... Now look what I have here for you. Schocalutt ja?'
> [Chocolate] came to remind Josephine so strongly of Great-Aunt Lydia's cheddar-coloured, freckled skin ...

> that she lost all taste for it ... [yet] [k]nowing that her
> distaste for this great-aunt was unfair. (pp.33-34)

Here the narrative voice parades several variations of prejudice and distaste: that of the child, Josephine, that of her mother, Freda, and most powerfully that of the narrator herself. The Yiddish accent is anatomised into 'phrases' and 'consonants', so that the very essence of the language, beyond the meaning of the words, is derided. Moreover, Aunt Lydia 'growls' like an animal. The word 'cheese-grater', which is echoed later in the passage by 'cheddar-coloured', vividly and metonymically suggests how the 'Jewish' qualities of Aunt Lydia 'grate' on Josephine's and, by implication, the narrator's sensibilities. Josephine's physical repulsion is irrational, her 'distaste', she admits, 'unfair'. Nevertheless, it very powerfully expresses Jew-hatred, of which only a portion is projected through the characters.

The narrator shows Freda Leyton's similar attitudes:

> [Freda thought] if only her aunts were thin ladies with
> white hands who smelt of lavender and wore pearls!
> When she had been a boarder at St. Catherine's School
> how she had wished on visiting days that her mother
> (bringing boxes of teiglach) would not talk so loudly ...
> (p.41)

Obviously, Freda desires a Gentile background and rejects her 'fat' (implying 'Jewish') aunts. As the novel proceeds, Freda Leyton's Jew-hatred becomes more hysterical:

> She went to Muizenberg only for the surfing. It was a
> horrible place, crowded with vulgar, loud, ugly people
> whose grammar was worse than her Aunt Lydia's. They
> came down every year from their tasteless houses in
> Johannesburg, fat women with red lips, moustaches and
> diamonds, and fat men with wet lips and flashy cars who
> stood about in indecent bathing-trunks talking at the
> tops of their voices about money and business. They had
> spoilt whiny children. They spread their gorged flesh
> everywhere over the beach which they had ruined with a

hideous pavilion and concrete promenades. Gross, grega-
rious, philistine *Jews!* (p.104)

Anti-Jewish discourse blares: the gross manners and appearance,
vulgarity, bad grammar, and display of diamonds recall vividly the
negative diamond fields image. This is grafted on to the image of
repulsive, moneyed Jews – the despised and envied Jewish upwardly
mobile syndrome. Freda Leyton's irrationality and uninformed
animus is shown by her blaming the Jews of Johannesburg for the
misdeeds of the Cape Town City Council who were responsible for
the Muizenberg pavilion and promenades.

In assessing this anti-Jewish bias, one must acknowledge that the
main authorial attack is against Freda Leyton herself who is treated
throughout with sharp, even malicious, satire. The hatred of Jews
expressed by this central character does not necessarily correspond
with that of the narrator, and, arguably, it cannot entirely be imputed
to the author. It is partly a strategy used in devising a satirical
portrait. However, the author uses no satire or irony *against* Josephine
her contempt for Aunt Lydia's 'Jewish' qualities, therefore it must be
assumed that Josephine's point of view is very close to that of the
author.

In general in this text the boundary between the attitudes attributed
to the characters, that of the narrator, and Becker's own attitude are
blurred. Moreover, the flavour of the satire invites comparison with the
novels of Oliver Walker and A.A. Murray. Becker, a Jewish author,
projects the same disgust as do the Gentile authors. Perhaps, since her
background is Anglicised and acculturated, like Gordimer and many
Jews, especially those at the beginning of the century – she distances
herself from the 'dirty proletariat' in order to protect her own standing
in the eyes of the community.[22]

Antony Sher

Antony Sher is a second generation South African Jew who
emigrated to London in 1968 at the age of nineteen to make a career
on the stage. He has since become one of Britain's most acclaimed
actors. He has been celebrated as a 'Renaissance man', being
simultaneously a director, actor, writer, playwright and artist.

In 1988 he made a confession: 'For twenty years,' he admitted, 'I have been living in England, hiding what I saw as my shameful South African identity'.[23] In the same year he published a novel, *Middlepost*, loosely based on the facts of his grandfather's emigration to South Africa from Lithuania at the beginning of the twentieth century.

Middlepost is a picaresque tale of a Jewish simpleton, designated throughout as 'Smous'. His real name, Zeev Immerman, had been changed to Zeev Zali, according to the custom among the Jews of eastern Europe at the time, in an attempt to avoid conscription into the Russian army. In 1902 Smous is sent by his family in Plungyan (Plunge) to South Africa. Having disembarked at Cape Town, he travels into the interior of the Cape with a bushman (San) woman in tow, attempting briefly and unsuccessfully to trade as a smous and seeking his relatives in Calvinia.

In constructing a character named 'Smous', Sher makes ironic allusion to the ubiquitous smous who features as a Wandering Jew in so much South African Jewish historiography and mythology. But this is where the similarity ends. He is no ordinary smous.

After some time, Smous finds himself in the village of Middlepost. Here live an Englishman and an Afrikaner – former adversaries during the Anglo-Boer War – an erudite Xhosa, and a number of misbegotten local or visiting rogues and crazies. The novel is a chronicle of their grotesque and sometimes obscene misadventures, involving exploitation, torture, murder, maiming, miscegenation, infanticide, rape and absurd copulation. The village is peopled by a gallery of caricatures and gargoyles.

Several reviewers have pointed out that the novel's vividness and energy result from its being essentially an actor's book; it derives from the actor's vigilant catching of tics and gestures which disclose character and his skill at mimicry and exaggeration for effect.[24]

One of the peripheral characters back in Plungyan is Elie, Smous's brother, who 'grotesquely mimick[ed] Jewish behaviour in a way which was doing little for his popularity in the town' (p.49):

> 'Oi veh,' said Elie grinning, 'pardon me for breathing, such a carry-on ... doctor-schmocter, do me a favour ...'
> (p.73)

Recently ... Elie had started to wear a smudge of coal
dust on the end of his nose to shorten its hooked shape
and so de-Jew himself ... because he had started studying
at Count Dolrogulsky's Musical Academy ... [He]
described a favourite pastime among the Dolrogulsky
servants: mimicking Jewish behaviour and speech. 'This
is what we look like to them,' he said, burying his head in
his shoulders, gesticulating wildly with his arms, then
rubbing his hands together in greed. 'Oi-yoi-yoi, business
schmusiness, what a to-do, such a carry on, do me a
favour!' They also say that we torture our animals in the
most unspeakable way when we slaughter them, that we
then smear their fat on our hair and on our bodies to
keep warm, which is why we look so slimy, that we drink
human blood ... But worst of all is how we breed.'
    'Breed?' Smous gulped, 'What? How?'
    'Prepare yourself,' warned Elie. 'The man puts his fruit
in the woman's mouth and then after a while she swallows
it, and then a year later she vomits out more Jewish
babies.' (pp.42-43)
    ... the Russian lettering [on a violin] was gently sliced
away with the razor ... 'Here, you want a Russian fore-
skin?' asked Elie, offering him the sliver of gilded spruce,
and Smous pulled away screaming ... (p.44).

Here Sher has created a Jewish character who recites a catalogue of
anti-Semitic shibboleths. These include the stock anti-Semitic
disparagement of Jewish appearance – the hooked nose, the slimy
complexion; verbal patterns and expressions representing Jewish and
specifically Yiddish dialogue – 'oi veh', 'oi-yoi-yoi', 'business
schmusiness', 'do me a favour' – and typical bodily mannerisms such
as the rubbing of hands together 'in greed'. There are also allusions
to ritual murder, unnatural sexual practices, ritual slaughter and circumcision. In constructing Elie's mocking conversation, Sher has
ransacked the stock of anti-Jewish markers, the commonplaces of
Gentile superstition and anti-Semitic categorisation.

In response to Elie's chatter, his father reprimands him: 'And you,
shut up! ... All day long in the wagon I have to listen to that stupid

voice you put on, and your stupid laugh. Who are you laughing at? You're laughing at yourself'(p.84). As his father suggests, Elie's mockery of Jews turns inward on to himself. Significantly, he attempts to 'de-Jew' himself by altering the appearance of his nose, betraying a high degree of Jewish self-consciousness. He is, in fact, a self-hating Jew and, it will be suggested, functions in the text as a surrogate authorial voice.

Even before Sher himself provided clues as to the nature of the novel, the most perceptive of the South African reviewers, Robert Greig, noticed its pathological nature, pronouncing it an 'imperfect working out of some private obsession'.[25] Indeed, *Middlepost* demands to be read as a case study, as a fantastical enactment of psychological trauma. It was only in 1990 that Sher publicly admitted that his sense of the stigma of being South African had been reinforced by having to face up to two other areas of stigma – being Jewish and being gay. These aspects, he confesses, 'were all aspects of myself that I tried desperately to escape from and have had to come to terms with'.[26]

Sher's novel is the literary expression of his 'spoiled identity'. He made this clear when he told an interviewer, in 1991, that the novel was written at 'a time of me facing up to my background; and through the medium of art, of writing, confronting the question of roots and cultural identity'. He explored the Jewish aspect of his background at some length: 'I suppose my first consciousness of being an *outsider* in any sense, was as a Jew. You know, just in the banal ways in that at school you're aware that you're having other holidays than the majority of kids.'(emphasis added) More profoundly shocking to him was the time spent in the South African army, where he was taunted as a '*Jood, vokken Jood*'. It was an experience of being aware that 'racially you were not the right thing'.[27]

This is a stronger expression of the consciousness of the 'not-quite' element, the 'step-child like status' of the Jew in South Africa that Sarah Gertrude Millin had addressed. Like Millin, Sher seems to be echoing Heinrich Heine who, tormented with ambivalence about being Jewish, characterised being Jewish as an untreatable and profound illness.[28]

In his studies of Jewish self-hatred, Gilman has argued that a member of a group stigmatised as the Other, who accepts the reference group's stereotypes, and recognises in times of anxiety a repressed element of that very Other in himself, may invest this repressed figure with all the qualities which he would normally seek to deny in himself.[29] Remarkable in Sher's own statements concerning his 'spoiled identity' is his sense of anxiety. He writes that he 'desperately' tried to escape from the triple stigma of being South African, Jewish and gay. In creating, or enacting, a fictional world he is partly able to deal with his anxiety by manipulating figures representative of the Other, and thereby exercising a measure of control over his fictional, if not his real, world. He, himself, admitted this. 'Yes, I suppose I am attracted to the outsider,' he told an interviewer. 'That is something to do with being South African, Jewish and gay.'[30]

Because of their strangeness, eccentricities and location outside social norms, all the characters in *Middlepost* can be characterised as Others. Although they are all presented unsympathetically, except the obvious victims – the outcast San woman, a tortured ostrich and a slaughtered lamb – conspicuously, none of the Gentile characters is treated with the relentless mockery and sustained physical disgust with which Sher portrays the Jews. Thus, possibly, Sher's frequently expressed fear and shame concerning the repressed Other in himself is projected on to those who remind him most forcefully of himself.[31]

On first being introduced to the reader, Smous wets his trousers. He is described as smelling bad (p.8), being long-nosed (p.245 *passim*), 'hirsute' (p.10), 'runtish' (pp.10, 78), a 'freak' (p.78) with 'a black mould creeping over his skin' (p.82). The buffoon-like friend of his youth, often assumes a hideous 'Face' – 'his eyes seemed to retract – the closed lids, the whole bulge of the eyeball pulling back and flattening, sucking into the skull, while his mouth stayed half-open and he made little popping noises in his throat' (p.40).

In his zeal to project physical disgust, Sher has surpassed in inventiveness previous negative images of Jews in South African fiction. Onkel Lazar has 'an imposing top hat which he always wore, indoors and out, day and night ... lodged between his huge flapping ears' (p.41). Her [*sic*] Immerman, Smous's father, is 'dumpy and short, his mouth fixed in a desperate grin' (p.12). Smous's grandmother is a cross between Punch's Judy and a rat:

> She lived in a small dark room half way down the passage and only appeared at meal times. Her mouth

was so sucked in it looked as though she carried a small lump under her nose, not unlike a dwarf's fist, which punched back and forwards as she chewed her food. (p.49)

Later: 'He passed his grandmother's room and heard the familiar scratching, rustling noises within, like a large rodent in its nest ...' (p.75).

Pinchvinch, a Hebrew teacher, is 'repulsive ... a pink frog of a man ... so named because of his favourite method of punishment. One clammy hand was probed into the clothing of the guilty party to search out their most sensitive spot' (p.50). Again he uses a discourse which employs animal imagery – the elephant encoded in the flapping ears of Onkel Lazar – the rat, the frog, recall previous anti-Semitic models. In a virulent passage – in which possibly two of Sher's vulnerabilities are involved – Quinn, a homosexual Englishman, regards Smous lustfully and speaks obscenities in the knowledge that Smous does not understand the language:

'It is heavenly, you know,' he informed Smous, 'to be able to sit here and say these things to your face. That hairy face with its glorious organ of flesh sticking out, catching the light just so, its sheen neither slack nor rigid, a face so reminiscent of the lower visage, the lap visage, the loin visage ...' (p.245)

This is a singularly tasteless variation of the stereotypical reference to the Jewish nose. Perhaps Quinn's conflation of the Jewish nose with a penis can be read in Freudian terms. It may be an authorial expression of recoil from those very aspects – the 'Jewish' nose and the circumcised penis – which mark him in his flesh as a Jew. It is thus another expression of hatred for his own condition of Jewishness. Sartre has referred to the flesh itself as an important locus of self-hatred. He argues that the 'inauthentic Jew' 'makes himself an anti-Semite in order to break all his ties with the Jewish community; yet he finds that community again in the depths of his heart, for he experiences *in his very flesh* the humiliations that the anti-Semites impose upon other Jews'(emphasis added).[32]

A further reference to sexual deviancy occurs when Smous enacts a ludicrous pseudo-copulation with the San woman. Sher symbolically situates this scene under a crucifix, in this way further underscoring the striking contrast between the symbol of Christianity aloft and the simple-minded Jew and outcast black woman, both degraded, grovelling on the floor beneath. Ignorant even of sexual behaviour, Smous wonders whether he has practised 'Jewish copulation' (p.251). Here Sher refers back to the brother Elie's lewd repetitions of Gentile allegations that Jewish sexual practices are unnatural and deviant – a commonplace of medieval anti-Semitic propaganda. In this single incident Sher encapsulates Smous's incompetence and stupidity, setting it in the wider context of South African mythology in which the Jew becomes sexually involved with a Gentile or black.

In *Middlepost* not only physical appearance but custom and religious practices are derided. A description of the *cheder* (Hebrew school) and synagogue combines mockery and embarrassment:

> There was only one Bible, around which the boys crowded, and some, so the joke went, learned how to read Hebrew not only from right to left but upside down as well ... Even more terrifying was the synagogue. Here Smous would have to stand for what seemed like hours, a dark sea of adults rocking above him, the men muttering and whimpering as they bound themselves in the black strips of their tfillin ... (pp.39-40)

All the Jews in *Middlepost* are especially stupid and embarrassing in their relations with Gentiles. When visiting a Gentile Russian linguist,

> Her [*sic*] Immerman forgot to remove the purple handkerchief from his hat. He resembled a simpleton at the best of times ... how could he not realise that the handkerchief made him look even more foolish? ... Now it was Smous's mother who became embarrassing, when she refused to part with her soaking shawl ... A quilted jacket in mauve velvet ... was her best garment, but since its last airing years earlier it had grown too tight, and her stocky frame was bursting through ... (pp.12-13)

In describing a religious family on board ship, who are mockingly known as the 'Pious ones', the narrator sneers at their strict Jewish food taboos:

> This family ... refus[ed] to trust that the [ship's] food was truly kosher ... [they] sat on the deck boiling water and concocting soups out of lumps of goose fat, onions and matzos they had brought with them. Watching them, people would shake their heads and say, 'They give us a bad name, no wonder the sailors think we're animals.' (p.67)

Here Sher ironically disparages one of the stereotypes he himself uses.

It may be argued that the tone of the novel is humorous, that the situations are often farcical, that the characters mock each other and are ridiculed by the author. But what we laugh at, and how we laugh, is determined by our own sense of self. Because the author's sense of identity is 'spoiled', he laughs at his characters without affection. A.M. Ludovici has shown that the smile that results from successful mockery, caricature or satire is a consequence of a sense of superiority and triumph.[33] Indeed, the close relationship between the smile and the grimace, between the laugh and the snap or growl, was first demonstrated by Darwin who observed that we show our teeth when we smile or laugh in the same way that the lower animals indicate aggression.[34] In Sher's case, the aggression is turned primarily against the Jew and ultimately against himself.

Most significant in demonstrating Sher's attitude towards the condition of Jewishness is the way in which he treats not merely what he sees as the Jewish appearance but, more dramatically, what he defines as the Jewish mind. With few exceptions the Jews he portrays have defective mental capacity. Onkel Lazar, who is mentally unimpaired but ugly and mean, makes a telling comment that once again clearly reveals both his self-hatred and that of the author:

> Plungyan, Litva, it was all contaminated, the air was ... The lunatics never smashed in our heads, so what? They didn't need to. Our brains were damaged already. At birth. (p.357)

The belief that the Jew is mentally defective has antecedents in nineteenth and early twentieth century racist pseudo-biology. Gilman has shown how statistics quantifying the occurrence of mental illness in the Jewish population in European countries were frequently cited during this period to support the belief that Jews were more prone to psychopathology than the general population. Notwithstanding the categorisation of Jews as cunning and clever, this belief became a commonplace of European psychology, and had horrific results in the Nazi concentration camps where Jews and other 'defectives' were destroyed.[35]

Smous seems to be based on the image of the insane Jew with the damaged discourse, of popular belief. He is no wise or pious fool, like I.B. Singer's Gimpel or Shakespeare's Fool, nor is he simply a schlemiel, though the origins of the character may indeed lie in a perverted understanding of the schlemiel figure. Smous is virtually an idiot. Further, he has no language usable in Africa. The only English words he knows are 'good', 'no', 'yes', 'howare*you*?', 'bye-bye'. By creating a character who understands and communicates virtually nothing, while over his head people converse in their different languages, the author bypasses and marginalises him.

His situation is paralleled with that of the San woman, whose language is equally inexplicable. The bond between members of two out-groups – the despised and outcast black woman and the equally despised and outcast Jew – is emphasised throughout the text by their dependency on each other. This is an aspect that Sher has expressed:

> I suppose the Jewish and the gay thing, although still very kind of unformed, must have given me some sense of being an outsider myself and must have connected, even subconsciously, with knowing to some extent what the black and coloured people were experiencing. Knowing what it was like to be the disliked group, the disapproved of group. But purely subconsciously, in no logical way. (p.359)

It is impossible to over-stress the importance of personal names as potent markers of selfhood. Smous's real name, already problematic in Lithuania, is imploded by the author. Even in the sections of the text set in Lithuania, he is only signified by reference to a future and short-lived trade: that of smous. In Africa, with a language and name, he is most fundamentally alienated. The Viennese intellectual, Otto Weininger, a foremost Jewish self-hater of the turn of the century, attempted ultimately to destroy the Jewishness in himself by committing suicide. Perhaps a parallel may be found in Sher's treatment of Smous. Through the numerous narrative strategies whereby Sher marginalises him, he effects a devastating subversion of Smous's humanity, and in this way he assassinates his Jewish character.

That the catharsis Sher has attempted to achieve by writing the novel has been incomplete, is seen in the publication of his second novel, *The Indoor Boy*, in 1991. Once again the three stigmata are invoked. The chief character, Leon Lipschitz, is a bisexual South African expatriate Jew living in London. He echoes what Sher has himself stated in interviews: 'The three A's are at my heels, hey, but I'm still one step ahead. The three A's – Apartheid, Anti-Semitism and AIDS ... Well, maybe that's the reason why I keep escaping ...' (pp.32-33)

Lipschitz is almost as unsavoury as Smous. He is idle, addicted to drink and drugs, and involved in deviant sexual practices. The interest of the text, however, lies in the manner in which it confirms the tendencies of the previous novel. Once again the Jewish characters – Lipschitz, his father and his mother – are grotesques. Again, Jews are caricatured or mocked. Synagogue worshippers are

> a raggedy old crowd, scourged by strokes or booze. Purplish drowned faces, or yellowy with winter tans. The men are bald and have damp moustaches. The women wear wigs or hairdos like ice sculptures, with turquoise daubed round their eyes, and smudged carmine on their lips. Their necks and wrists are bound in platinum, ivory, bone and plastic; and huge rings bulge on knuckly fingers ... (pp.194-195)

Lipschitz's father interrupts the barmitzvah service after 'a scrum mills round [the barmitzvah boy]' (p.196):

> 'Moshe ... *spierdalaj stad* (fuck off)!' he growls in Polish. '*Kurwa!*' Turning to me he asks, 'You know what

this means, hahh – *kurwa*?'
'Yes,' I sigh '- cunt'...
'... *Chazzer*!' he snaps, changing to Yiddish,
'*Farkackteh dreykop* (shitty muddlehead)! Only good for
shitting out. Only good for the fowl sacrifice! ... *geyt
kacken ahfen yam*! (go shit in the sea)' ... The Torah is
going back to the Ark. A clamour of song and chattering
of prayers starts up, coming in waves, as people *daven*
(pray), rocking and swaying.
'Jub-jub-jub!' grunts Dad, catching their rhythm.
'Kak-kak-kak! Buzz-buzz-buzz!'... (pp.196-197)

The conflation of the discourses of the Jewish religion with
scatological and scurrilous references to obscenities and excrement,
and the deliberate introduction of the stigmatising Yiddish
expressions, recall the mockery of Louis Cohen in his fiction of the
diamond fields. As in *Middlepost*, Sher attacks language itself. The
sacred words of Hebrew prayers are deliberately derided, debased and
converted into meaningless or obscene syllables – 'Jub-jub-jub ...
Kak-kak-kak ... Buzz-buzz-buzz'.

Again, as in *Middlepost*, Sher shows a prurient interest in the
circumcised penis. Lipschitz stares at his sleeping father's penis:

On the eighth day after his birth, the men of his family
would've gathered round, uncovered him like now, and
looked down ... while the *mohel* took hold of it and sliced
some off. Who was in that circle of faces? Were any of
them moffies? ... And when the *mohel* bent right close,
like I am now, and sucked it clean, like I could now, did
any of them blush? (p.219)

Clearly paraded here are Sher's obsessions – his sense of himself as a
Jew and as a homosexual. The unfortunate effect of the working out of
private vulnerabilities is that his novels tend to reinforce existing
negative stereotypes and perpetuate the very anti-Semitic prejudice in
which they originated.

The three authors discussed in this chapter are all in one way or
another actively concerned with the struggle against inhumanity and

injustice.[36] They would doubtless deny that their work has anti-Semitic tendencies. But in attacking Jews as a special category, they are guilty not only of anti-Semitism, but of themselves contributing to an ongoing racist discourse.

JEWS AND BLACKS

In previous chapters it has been shown that the Jewish connection with black people is a recurring topic in South African fiction, but only after the 1970s, with the proliferation of writing by blacks (as distinct from coloureds), can a Jewish presence be traced in the work of 'African' authors.

Apart from Muslims and those who, with the Palestine Liberation Organisation (PLO), disparage the Jews as 'Zionists', most blacks do not distinguish between Jews and other whites. The distinction is more frequently made between Afrikaners (Boere) and others. Furthermore, exposure of blacks to Western literature, with its baggage of stereotypes, has been sparse, and references to Jews in the work of blacks are usually based on personal perception.

During the early years of Jewish immigration, there was brisk trade between Jews and blacks, especially in small country towns, or on the mines. At times they enjoyed friendship and mutual respect[1] and sometimes sexual relationships. More recently, because of their high profile in business, Jews are viewed by some with suspicion and hostility as part of an oppressive capitalist system.

While the colour bar restricted social encounters between urban Jews and blacks,[2] the actual or perceived involvement of the 'bolshevik Jew' and the 'natives' during the early part of the twentieth century, has been highlighted, in particular by the research of Riva Krut. The image of the kaffirboetie is also based on some actual relationships between Jews and blacks. In *The Autobiography of an Unknown South African* (1971), Naboth Mokgatle expresses his special sympathy with Jews:

[In 1932] *Bantu World* was bringing news which broke my heart, about the plight of the Jewish people in Germany. What I read there happening to them was my own story, the story of the African people in South Africa. When I read that they were deprived of freedom of movement in the land of their birth, that they were segregated, denied education, dismissed from their jobs, forced into concentration camps, some of them dying without their relatives' knowledge, hunted, persecuted, their intellectuals despised, barred from practising medicine, carrying cards to identify them as Jews, their dignity destroyed, their homes no longer their castles raided at any time of the day or night, that was a description of the Africans' life in the country of their birth. (p.190)

Mokgatle's emotional acknowledgment of the parallel between his experience of oppression and that of the Jews under Nazism, is very similar to the ideas expressed by Peter Abrahams, writing about the same period.

Mokgatle mentions a number of Jews who were influential in his life. Archie Levitan introduced him to the Communist movement (p.212), and he came in contact with other communists, such as Maurice [probably Hymie] Basner (p.213), Harry Bloom (p.242), and Joe Slovo (p.310). He refers to some trade unionists – among them the Jews – Solomon (Solly) Sachs, Maurice Kagan, Issy Wolfson, and Louis Joffe, who helped blacks organise in trade unions (pp.228-228). He attended a special adult school organised by the Communist Party, where many Jews were his teachers (p.241). Before the apartheid regime suppressed these and like schools, a number of Jews were involved in educational upliftment. This is fictionally recorded by Laurence Lerner, a white South African who emigrated to England. In his novel, *The Englishmen* (1959), the following exchange takes place between teachers in a charity night school for blacks:

'Hello, Ruth,' said Richard. 'Hello, Hannah.' 'Of course all my teachers are Jewish,' he remarked to Franklin …'I mean most Communists seem to be Jewish; and most Liberals too. Don't you think so?'

'I haven't yet got used to lumping Communists with Liberals,' replied Franklin. 'Do you mean that Jews stick up for the African as another downtrodden race?'

'No, not exactly that,' said Richard. Ruth Kaplan's father owned the largest shoe-store in Cape Town, and he had to persuade her not to come to night school in the family Packard. He could hardly think of her as down-trodden. (p.124)

On the other hand, Jews were by no means immune from bigotry and, like the white population as a whole, were guilty of prejudice against and prejudicial behaviour towards blacks, as well as connivance in apartheid. In a series of notorious incidents in 1943 and 1944, Jewish farmers in the Bethal district were implicated in the murder of black farm workers.[3]

The first recorded study of black attitudes to Jews was that of Melville Edelstein who surveyed the opinions of black pupils in Soweto in 1971. His research seemed to indicate that there was a considerable 'social distance' between the two groups. He noted that his correspondents had only the barest actual contact with Jews, and that there appeared to be a correlation between antipathy to Jews and membership of white-orientated churches. Edelstein suggested that anti-Jewish stereotypes had been transmitted by New Testament teachings.[4]

In 1988 Tzippi Hoffman and Alan Fischer published a number of interviews with South Africans, exploring group attitudes towards Jews. Curtis Nkondo, president of the Azanian People's Organisation, spoke positively. He praised Jewish 'expertise in medicine, law, and the economic spheres'. He did not believe that there was any anti-Semitic feeling among blacks. Highlighting Jewish involvement in the struggle, he said – 'you find more radicals amongst them ... Even in the business world you find the liberal element amongst them more than from anybody else'. He maintained that 'for a long time people who have worked for the Jews have respected them.'[5]

Aubrey Mokoena, a member of the National Executive Committee of the United Democratic Front felt differently. The Jews, he argued, 'fail to stand up to be counted. They screw our people in their shops, and they criticise through their liberal press the policies of the government, while they secretly pray for the restoration of the Afrikaners in power because they give them their security.' Zionism, he added 'is much like apartheid, a protection of minority interests.'[6]

Two recent studies suggest that anti-Semitism is generally increasing among blacks. In South Africa the Human Sciences Research Council in 1990 reported considerable antipathy of blacks towards Jews as opposed to very little in the white population.[7] This finding is paralleled in America where the Yankelovitch poll showed that during the last quarter-century anti-Semitism has declined among white Americans but has increased among blacks, especially those younger and better-educated.[8]

Images of the Jew in the Work of Black Writers

In the few works of black writers in which the Jew does make an appearance, he is a shopkeeper or bourgeois landlord, or sometimes a professional – a lawyer, journalist, teacher or social worker.

The most negative of the few references to Jews is found in Mtu-tuzeli Matshoba's story, 'Behind the Veil of Complacency' from his collection, *Call Me Not a Man* (1979). The story deals in a general way with prejudice and focuses on a shopkeeper who is, in fact, not identified as a Jew. However, the traditional markers of the negative Jewish stereotype appear:

> Of stature he was short, with a back that reminded the young man of a camel ... with a long nose ... He did not strike the united black souls in his shop as being anywhere near pleasant ...
>
> '*Wat* can I do for you?' asked a throaty voice without any ... mollifying tones ...
>
> '... Give me a packet of Rothmans Golden Milds,' [the customer] said, placing a fifty cent coin on the counter. [The shopkeeper] promptly snatched it.
>
> He put a packet of Peter Stuvesant in front of the young man ...
>
> [He] brought the right order but held it in his hand. 'What else?'...
>
> 'Matches' ...

Shylock brought it ...
The little hawk-like eyes moved [around]. For a split
second the two thought they had seen a flicker which
could only have been seen once before, in Shylock's eye
as Shakespeare first imagined him. (p.193)

The shopkeeper tries to cheat his black customers and grows angry:
'... [h]e was growling, and punctuating his venom with 'Kaffer!' ...
with the scream of a bird of hell. 'You *kaffer*! Go to Soweto, you *kaffer*
... *kaffer* ... !' (p.196). While the shopkeeper is portrayed as a racist, it
is suggested that his prejudice against the blacks is more an attribute
of belonging to the white group than one which is specifically Jewish.
Ironically, the black author's own prejudice towards the Jew is
stressed – physically by the Shylock association, and in the hint of a
foreign accent.

In some writings, physical stigmata are striking: In Dugmore
Boetie's *Familiarity is the Kingdom of the Lost* (1969), there is a brief
mention of an elderly Jewish woman. The narrator claims: 'I knew by
her hawklike features that she was Jewish' (p.44). The portrait of Mr
Friedland, a shopkeeper in Zoe Wicomb's *You Can't Get Lost in Cape
Town* (1987) is another instance. He has a 'large protruding stomach',
'glossy black plumage' and a 'corvine beak' (p.175).

On the other hand, in some fiction the fellow feeling of some blacks
for Jews is recorded. There is a brief reference to the affectionate
treatment of the Jew, who seems to be a social friend of the narrator, in
Mothobi Mutloatse's *Casey and Co. Selected Writings of 'Casey Kid'
Motsisi* (1978):

I rang up James Aronowitz, called him a bloody Jew and
asked him if he had a drink for one of God's children.
He said to come over ... James greeted me at the door
with his perpetual grin. Emily – his servant-come[*sic*]-
mistress – was there too ... (p.106)

Notable in this short exchange is the usually pejorative expression
'bloody Jew', used as a term of affection. There is also a suggestion
that the good relations between the Jew and the black extend to the
Jew's taking his (black) servant as a mistress.[9]

In Mongane Wally Serote's *To Every Birth Its Blood* (1981), a compassionate reporter, named David Horwitz, features briefly. He is only identifiable as a Jew by his name and in the statement of an Afrikaans police officer who warns the blacks about people like David: 'the liberals put all you Bantu into trouble, and then take a plane to London or Tel-Aviv' (p.156). There is a bond of friendship between Horwitz and a black girl who has sexual fantasies about him. Horwitz, a kaffirboetie, assists blacks by giving them lifts in his motor car to the township and to the border with Botswana, and tries to show that '[he] did not in any way feel that [he was] associated with the present regime' (p.233).

Modikwe Dikobe's *The Marabi Dance* (1973) is set in Johannesburg during the 1930s. Mr Tereplasky and his son, Lazar, are proprietors of a dairy. Only identified as Jews by a name that seems meant to be Jewish, they behave in an ambivalent way towards the blacks in their employ. Lazar is sometimes kindly: ' "You are my father's old boy,' he would say, patting him on the shoulders. "You shall never be out of work" ' (p.48). At other times he is impatient: ' "I have had enough of him – milk not fetched in time, bottles not properly washed, horses not fed on time and giving trouble. I have lost enough money through him ..." ' (p.48).

During the war, however, when Lazar Tereplasky and one of the employees, July Mabongo, are up north together, the Jew turns out to be a 'true comrade'. Mabongo tells his wife: ' "He sleeps with me in the same tent" ' (p.94). Mrs Tereplasky is a social worker, honorary secretary of an organisation concerned about forced removals of Africans to Orlando.[10] She tries to do all she can for Mabongo's daughter – ' "I shall undertake to see that her rent is paid for several years," ' (p.100) she says. A policeman comments: ' "You are a lucky girl to have a white person to pay your rent. These kaffirboeties spoil the kaffirs" ' (p.110).[11]

The short story, 'The Music of the Violin' from Njabulo Ndebele's collection *Fools and Other Stories* (1983), is more critical of Jews:

> Mrs Beatrice started. 'A white woman [Mrs Kaplinsky] came all the way from Emmarentia – high-class exclusive suburb, mind you – to address the meeting on Jewish recipes ... It was wonderful' ...

'Sometimes those South African Jews sicken me,' said
the other man reflectively.
'Why?' the two women asked.
'Well, they're hypocrites! I mean look, they say they
were killed left and right by the Germans, but here they
are, here, helping the Boers to sit on us.'
'How can you say such a thing?' asked his wife.
'People like Mrs Kaplinsky are very good friends of ours.
Some of her best friends are Africans.' (pp.128-129)

By reversing the out-group perception of Jews ('some of her best
friends ...'), Ndebele makes a satiric point against Jews, which
counters the image of the kaffirboetie.

An ambivalent treatment is found in Miriam Tlali's semi-autobiographical novel, *Muriel at Metropolitan* (1975). The text foregrounds a
Mr Bloch, a shopkeeper who uses many Yiddish expressions and is
'short and plumpy ... walk[ing] with his feet turned out, nearly like
Charlie Chaplin' (p.15). He is alternately kindly and exploitative.
The narrator observes: 'You could never know with the boss. He
could be very firm, even hard as granite, but he could also be very soft
and disgustingly lenient' (p.16). All the other Jewish characters, Mr
Bloch's relatives, are treated in a satirical manner, and while Mr Bloch
brings in his own physician to attend a sick black man, he is also guilty
of racism and usury: 'What's that? What? Who is it, a *soggen* (black)?
Oh well with a *soggen* you can go as high as you want to. Up to 37
percent you can charge ...' (p.63)

Criticism and neutral observation are, however, equally blended,
and while the novel certainly makes a political statement about the
treatment of blacks by whites, there is no evidence that the ill-
treatment is attributed to the Jews as a group, other than a statement
by an aggrieved Italian. He makes excuses to avoid hiring Muriel,
telling her that the government would require the provision of a
separate toilet for her. She answers:

'But I don't have a separate toilet here at Metro-
politan ... Mr Bloch has never been charged.'
'Ah, ah, but he is a Jew. These Jews they bribe the
Boers. So they can do what they like. But you don't know

what they do to us immigrants ... they want to get us out
of business ...' (p.94)

Ambivalent attitudes are also found in Richard Rive's work. Rive, a
coloured writer from Cape Town, refers to Jews several times, notably
in *'Buckingham Palace' District Six* (1986). In 1966, in terms of the
Group Areas Act, District Six was reserved for white occupation only.
The former inhabitants, mainly coloured, were forced to leave. Rive
documents this tragedy in a tale both poignant and humorous.

During the period of Jewish immigration at the turn of the twentieth
century, many Jews settled in District Six, and lived in close contact
with the coloured community. In constructing his Jewish characters,
Rive is therefore able to draw on personal experience. In his novel the
local Jewish shopkeeper, Mr Solomon Katzen, owns a row of five
cottages, known as 'Buckingham Palace', and at first seems to be a
negative stereotype – a miser and unsympathetic landlord.[12] When the
eviction orders arrive, however, he redeems himself and appears in a
different guise. He refuses to evict his tenants, declaring 'I will not give
in. I know how it was'. He tells the coloured people, 'I had to escape
from Germany with just the clothes I had on. That was just before the
war broke out ... So now I cannot do to your people what was done to
my people ... ' (p.135).

Like Peter Abrahams, Rive stresses the Jew's difficult history of
prejudice. Katzen remembers school where other children 'sometimes called us "dirty Jews" and "Christ killers". Yes ... it hurt me a
lot,' he says, 'but I had learnt early already not to show it, even when
they spat at me ...' (p.149). He also invokes the exclusion of Jews
from universities and professions, and their relegation to the status of
'*untermenschen* – sub-humans' (p.151).

As a result of his own experiences of prejudice and oppression,
Katzen identifies with the coloured people of District Six, and defiantly
refuses to sell his houses to the Department of Community Development for expropriation. In transforming Katzen into a kaffirboetie,
Rive conveys his own identification of the oppressed Jew and the
coloured person. However, in the construction of Mr Katzen's uncaring son, a 'big-time lawyer' from Johannesburg (p.174), the
familiar second generation, upwardly mobile type re-emerges. The
son refuses any identification with the coloured people and washes

his hands of them – ' "[l]ike Pontius Pilate," Oubaas said ...' (p.187).
He is exploitative and uncaring.

In a short story, 'Riva', from the collection *Advance Retreat* (1983),
Rive ambivalently constructs a Jewish woman whose friendly over-
tures are rebuffed by the narrator, a young coloured man. A possible
reason for the narrator's distrust of the Jewish woman is that she is
distinguished by her laugh – 'a short snort, followed by peals of loud,
uncontrolled laughter' (p.62) – which seems oddly out of keeping
with the idealised concept that the narrator has of persecuted Jews.

Shortly before he meets Riva he had been reading 'a novel about
the massacre in the ravines of Babi Yar, gripping and revolting ...'
(p.62) and, as a motif of persecution, particularly of the Jews, the
reference to Babi Yar is repeated in several places in the text. Riva's
overwhelming presence, however, and her big laugh cause the
narrator to dream of her 'striding with heavy, impatient boots and
stick-thin legs over mountains of dead bodies in the ravines of Babi
Yar. She was snorting and laughing while pushing bodies aside,
climbing upwards over dead arms and legs' (p.65). Thus, since Riva
does not conform to the stereotype of the Jew as victim, the narrator
fantasises that she represents the oppressor. In the disjunction between these two images – victim and oppressor – lies his inability to
cope with the idea of Riva.

The only Indian author to deal with the subject of the Jews of South
Africa is Ahmed Essop. He has twice explored the theme of their
divided loyalties – to Israel as well as South Africa – and is concerned
with what he believes to be a racist component of Zionism. In his story
'In Two Worlds' from *The Hajji and Other Stories* (1978), Harry Levin,
a kaffirboetie, has identified himself with the blacks of South Africa,
but is nevertheless moved to fight for Israel against the Arabs. The
narrator acknowledges the 'agony of his situation' (p.102), but the
Indian community judges him a racist: 'by identifying himself with a
national state, [he has] displayed the spirit of partiality for a racial
group ... he placed national loyalty above human loyalty' (pp.101-
102). The spectre of the 'clannish' Jew appears.

The theme is further developed in a subsequent story, 'The Metamorphosis', from *Noorjehan and Other Stories* (1990). Here Essop
constructs the character of an elderly Jewish woman who transcends
the barriers of class, nationality, religion and colour, to become truly

compassionate and liberated. She is an ideal, in contrast to Harry Levin, whose support for Zionism, it is suggested, has impeded his true liberation. Naomi Rosenberg had come to South Africa as a young woman in order to escape the Nazi regime. The Holocaust involvement once again signals the black author's identification with the Jew when he or she is the object of persecution. Naomi has three upwardly mobile children whom she has brought up as 'part of the larger patrician white class ...' (p.27). One is 'Alexander ... [who] was on the board of directors of a gold-mining company ... [and has] now inherited the mantle of the legendary mining magnates who had once presided over the financial world of the city' (p.23). Alexander and his wife live in Houghton, own a Jaguar and '[a] chauffeur-driven silver Rolls-Royce' (p.23). His wife is the familiar materialistic, luxury-loving Jewish woman, in fact a kugel – 'her body an object for dress designers, her hair and face for cosmeticians' (p.27). A son-in-law is an advocate. Her son is an architect, but he is also 'a member of the Communist Party ... and was satisfied to live in an old house [near] Mayfair' (p.23).

Through reading newspaper articles, Naomi becomes concerned about the sufferings of blacks and joins the 'Pharos' society, a group of women involved in protests. Naomi is shocked by reports of Israeli atrocities against Arabs in the 'occupied territories', and appalled at the growing military links between Israel and South Africa. Essop suggests that she is the exceptional Jew, one who is able to transcend family and community. Having progressed 'beyond the threshold of national loyalty' (p.37), she proclaims her outrage and thereby angers her own community. A Jewish delegation voices the defence of the Israelis:

> 'Our people ... have been persecuted through the centuries. We have our homeland now ... Ours is the sacred promised land ... We Jews have suffered much. We can never oppress others ... The greatest single factor in the history of humanity is our identity and survival ...' (pp.37-38)

In Naomi's reply Essop presents a counter-argument, and makes the case for those who believe that Zionism may be equated with racism. She tells the delegation:

'That borders on dangerous self-love ... if everyone started claiming what belonged to their ancestors there would be chaos throughout the world ... Tell me, is fanatical nationalism very different from religious bigotry or belief in Herrenvolk supremacy?' (p.38)

Here Essop reiterates the orthodox ideology of those Muslims who, as Dr Nasser (Nasser Amkidwa), Representative of the Palestine Liberation Organisation at the United Nations, has said, 'cannot differentiate between the apartheid regime in South Africa and Zionism in general. They have very similar ideological bases'. He believes that the parallel between Zionism and apartheid is discrimination. 'Zionism is also based on extreme fundamental religious views', he said.[13]

Naomi's attitude, which presumably represents the author's, is that of many blacks, not only Muslims but Christians as well. Archbishop Desmond Tutu, Nobel Peace Laureate and Archbishop of Cape Town, is on record as affirming the perceived similarity between Zionism and racism:

[Zionism is] a policy that to me looks like it has very many parallels with racism. The effect is the same, whether you want to call it that or not I think is in a sense irrelevant. The point is that it's our perception and that it is the perception in the end that matters.[14]

Essop's story ends with Naomi's martyrdom, her imprisonment under Section 10 of the Internal Security Act. While the story is strongly anti-Zionist, Naomi herself is a positive stereotype, a variation, although a powerful one, of the kaffirboetie.

Jews and Blacks in the Work of White Writers

Christopher Hope's story, 'On the Frontier', from *Private Parts* (1982) and republished in *Learning to Fly* (1990), is one of the few instances, apart from his story 'The Kugel', of an extended treatment by a white Gentile author of the relationship between a Jew and a black man.

The main character is a Jewish chemist, Maxie Meyerson, son of eastern European immigrants. Maxie struggles to pay off a mortgage on a chemist shop in a small town. A black man, an albino, asks him for a job. Despite his sympathetic feeling – he makes the connection between the black and the Jew – 'it was bad being neither one thing nor the other, despised by every colour in the country, worse even than being a Peruvian' (p.88), Maxie refuses to give the albino a job. The man reproves him, claiming: 'You of all people should see that you could have done me a good turn. You're a Jew. You must know what it's like to be out there on your own ... People like us should stick together' (pp.91-92). This is an ironic reversal of the trope of good relations between blacks and Jews. Eventually, Maxie's woman assistant takes pity on the albino. After a humiliating incident where he is used to demonstrate the chemist's suntanning lotion, she is deeply moved and runs away with him. Like many of Dan Jacobson's characters, Maxie feels guilty and remorseful:

> Meyerson presided in his shop in the suburb which had a quiet, settled, established look to it ... He became famous in the suburbs after the albino business. He prospered. And every penny he made was a knife in his heart. (p.100)

The change from 'Maxie' to 'Meyerson' signals the authorial distance from the character and indicates that his fame is hollow. Hope criticises the Jew, member of an out-group, for his inhumanity towards the albino, a doubly stigmatised person, rejected even by his own black group because of his lack of pigmentation. The Jew's prosperity, it is suggested, is achieved at the expense of the black man – a suggestion which he made glancingly in his story 'The Kugel' and which was first made in Dan Jacobson's 'The Zulu and the Zeide'(1958).

Recently some Jewish authors have sought to emphasise the parallel between the situation of the Jew and that of the black.

Gillian Slovo, daughter of two well-known Jewish communists, Joe Slovo and Ruth First, was born in South Africa. In 1964 her family was forced into exile and settled in London. Slovo remains committed to what she termed the blacks' 'struggle for freedom' in South Africa.[15] Her novel, *Ties of Blood* (1989), greatly develops the theme first treated over sixty years earlier by Sarah Gertrude Millin.

In 'The Zulu and the Zeide' Dan Jacobson hinted at the parallel between the Jewish experience of immigrating from Lithuania and that of the blacks who come to the city from rural areas. Slovo expands this theme. She suggests that Jewish commitment to the struggle of the blacks against apartheid flows precisely from the Jews' own experience of discrimination and oppression. The novel documents the intertwining lives of several generations of two families – one Jewish, the descendants of Riva and Zelig Cyn who emigrated from Lithuania in 1902; the other black, the family and descendants of Nathaniel and Evelyn Bopape. Nathaniel, the son of a chief, has left the ancestral home in protest against the poll tax, and his sense of the blacks as a 'beaten people' (p.22). Throughout the novel, the similarity between Jewish experience of marginalisation and oppression and the suffering of blacks under a brutal apartheid regime is emphasised:

> Zelig had nothing but contempt for whites who regarded contact with blacks as polluting. After all he still remembered how he was once an outcast in the land of his birth: considered less than human because he had been born a Jew. (p.41)

> [Zelig] identified in Nathaniel's face the same pain that he daily struggled to suppress ... He offered Nathaniel an arm.
> 'I'm sorry,' he muttered. 'I understand.' (pp.46-47)

Slovo's novel is a didactic illustration of a thesis. There is minimal characterisation; throughout nearly 800 pages she indicts the apartheid regime and highlights the parallel between Jew and black. In discussing a strike with Zelig's son-in-law, Nathaniel makes the point: 'Can you not see the parallel?' he asked. 'Weren't you the one who told me how the tsar's police let the peasants arm themselves against the Jews?' (pp.99-100)

In some respects the plot seems to be based on the known circumstances of the lives of Slovo's parents, but in sketching the Jewish characters, many of the predictable and typical situations of previous South African fiction are replicated. Yiddish expressions are used frequently. The descendants of the Cyns and their spouses are either upwardly mobile professionals or businessmen, or more frequently communists. Riva's daughter and her husband, who is simultaneously a wealthy accountant and a communist, move to 'a new house in Yeoville ... the latest in fashions' (p.131), and the wealthy Jewish woman wears high-heeled shoes and a foxskin. Their daughter, Riva's granddaughter, chooses to go to 'Christian assembly' (p.186), representing the assimilationist tendencies documented by earlier writers.

Several of the typical situations occur: there is sexual attraction between a black man and a Jewish woman, reference to the Greyshirts and the *Ossewa Brandwag* and meetings on the City Hall steps. In being blown up by a car bomb, after a lifetime of working for the cause of the blacks, Jacob Swiece, a character based both on Albie Sachs, injured by a car bomb and on Ruth First, killed by a letter bomb, becomes a Jew-martyr. The novel transforms the bolshevik stereotype into a means of affirming the Jew's commitment to the struggle against apartheid.

Rose Zwi's prize-winning novella, *Under the Umbrella Tree* (1990), set shortly after the Soweto uprising of 16 June 1976, also seeks to stress the parallels between the experience of blacks and Jews. One of the central characters – an old woman, Freda, an emigrant from Russia – tells a group of elderly blacks: 'We were the blacks of Europe ... like you are the Jews of Africa' (p.61). Freda and her daughter-in-law are visiting the family of their maid. Parallels between the two families are highlighted. The blacks apologise for speaking broken English. Freda replies: 'My English isn't so good either ...[a]fter nearly fifty years in Africa, I've still got a Russian accent and I still count in Yiddish' (p.20). The elderly blacks relate how, in order to avoid starvation, they had to leave the rural areas to go to town. Using the expression found so often in South African philo-Semitic texts, Freda replies, 'I understand,' and goes on to draw the parallel between the migration of the blacks and that of her family:

> 'I understand ... When we were small children in Russia, my father didn't have work, so he went to Africa, to look for gold. He didn't find any, and it took seven years before he could save enough money to bring us to Africa. My mother had a hard time in the

old country. She had five children to feed. She got up at four o'clock every morning to bake yeast buns and bread for a bakery ... You're thinking how can white people be so poor? You should have seen the ghettoes and the villages where the Jews lived in Eastern Europe. Some of them looked even worse than Alexandra township.' (pp.60-61)

The blacks are sympathetic: 'Hau! Wragtig! Shame! [they] exclaimed as Freda described her childhood in a Lithuanian village' (p.64). Although they cannot understand the language, they feel an emotional response to Freda's songs in Yiddish and Hebrew: 'That song,' [Freda] said, wiping her eyes, 'was about workers who till the soil but own no land, who sew for the rich but themselves wear rags, who build palaces but live in hovels. You see what I mean about the similarities?' (p.95)

Freda's son, Tony, is a Jewish leftist. He marries an Afrikaans girl whose father accuses him of being a 'Jew! Communist! Seducer!' (p.59) Tony is sent to jail for twenty years for his work in support of the blacks. 'Soon he will be liberated, together with all the other oppressed people' (p.59), Freda tells them. Thus, once again, as Gillian Slovo did in her novel of the previous year, Zwi underscores the suffering of the Jew in support of the black cause.

Other, more hackneyed situations are introduced: before his arrest, Tony takes a coloured mistress; a Jewish woman is introduced who 'wore heavy jewellery' (p.83); her husband is a psychoanalyst – '[w]hat else should a bright Jewish boy from Vienna become[?]' (p.83), his wife comments. A radical black man thinks that Freda is 'fat and ugly' (p.35). He muses about other Jewish women who live in hotels in Hillbrow: '[they] ordered more than [they] could eat, mutilated it with a blunt hotel knife, then left the mess of half-masticated food on [the] plate. While black children were dying of hunger ...' (pp.34-35). Freda, however, like Essop's Naomi Rosenberg, is the exception.

Despite the use of stereotypes and stereoptypical situations, marked in Zwi's earlier work, the novella, with its tight narrative structure, parallelism and irony, makes a powerful statement about suffering, responsibility and guilt.

A critical treatment of Jewish relationships with blacks can be found in Nadine Gordimer's story, 'The Visit', published in the *Jewish Chronicle* (9 September 1966, p.39). The plot concerns two visits to David Levy when he returns home from synagogue on a Friday night. The first visit is made by two black men whom Levy, assuming they have come to rob him, angrily chases away. The second is from two members of the police who have come to search the room of his student son. Levy behaves subserviently towards them. After this Levy and his wife feel uncomfortable and emigrate to Israel. The epigraph to the story is: ' "On Friday evening two angels accompany each pious man from the synagogue ..." – From the Talmud.' The purpose of the story seems to be to show that David Levy, in his racist thinking, is not a 'pious man'. In his study of Gordimer, Stephen Clingman does not mention this story in his otherwise exhaustive list of Gordimer's fiction. It has never been republished.

Epilogue

This exploration has demonstrated that in South African English fiction there is a marked consistency in the appearance of three main Jewish prototypes. While the external details of the stereotypes may change with time and circumstance, and the intensity of the emotions underpinning them may diminish, their essence remains fairly constant. This finding differs from that of Bryan Cheyette, whose investigation of the Jew in British fiction convinces him that British writers actively construct images of 'the Jew' in relation to their own literary and political concerns, and do not passively draw on changeless archetypes.[1]

In South African constructions of Jews a characteristic feature – the grafting of local material on to a matrix inherited from European models – is notable in the work of both Jewish and Gentile authors. The early local figures of the IDB and the smous or shopkeeper, that alien Other who appeared to be insinuating his way into South African society and economy and threatening the livelihood of local inhabitants, laid the foundations for most later negative images. The threatening image was further fuelled by the legendary dimension of the successful Jewish parvenu, Barney Barnato. It was well suited to the purposes of colonial writing, being a useful shorthand, easily identifiable and appealing strongly to gut emotions and prejudices. In pandering to the individual's need to order a perception of society into categories of self and Other, it was able to reinforce existing presuppositions and prejudices. Throughout the twentieth century, writers both Jewish and Gentile, continued to construct their fictional Jews on this matrix.

As the second and third generation became predominantly English speaking and were socially assimilated, Jews in South African fiction were treated less often as exotic figures of superstition. Images reflecting this upward mobility and urbanisation of the community are frequently less negative. They may even be positive. Demythologised, the image remained entrenched as part of the fabric of society, appearing as the prosperous merchant and his wife, the 'kugel', the professional or the leftist. But the physical, and often the speech markers of difference remain.

After the middle of the century xenophobic attitudes towards Jews were somewhat ameliorated by a government supportive of the Jewish homeland, by the upward mobility of the Afrikaners and English themselves, by the need for 'white' unity, and to an extent by the consciousness of the Holocaust.

Some striking patterns can be traced throughout the period under discussion in the way Jewish writers through their construction of Jewish characters responded to the social and political climate. Some, scorning their own background, sought to exorcise their sense of inferiority and to ingratiate themselves with the dominant culture by using the very discourse of anti-Semitism in satirising Jewish figures. Others defiantly celebrate their ethnicity. Recently there has been some attempt on the part of a few Jewish authors to emulate those coloured authors who suggested a parallel between the experience of immigrant Jews, persecuted and discriminated against in Europe, and the plight of blacks suffering under apartheid laws.

This study ended when South Africa was undergoing perhaps the most fundamental political change of its history. While it has not been a time propitious for fiction, the years surrounding the change in government have been a time of celebrating heroes, of relating the secrets behind the dramatic events leading up to the elections of 1994, of gathering and assessing social history and of exposing the wrongs of the past and recommending reconciliation between black and white. Yet, several novels have been published, following the lead of the non-fictional writers.[2] In a country groping to formulate a new, inclusive national identity to replace its former principal divide, the portrayal of minorities like the Jews has fallen very much into the background. The emphasis on discovering a common humanity, the search for reconciliation and rapprochement, has turned writers away from both crude and nuanced portraits of the Other.

—•—

NOTES

INTRODUCTION

1. *The Great Hatred*, London: Gollancz, 1943, p.8.
2. See Dubb, A. 'Demographic Picture'. In Arkin, M. *South African Jewry. A Contemporary Survey*. Cape Town: Oxford University Press, 1984, pp.24-26.
3. In 1974 Allie Dubb estimated the average rate of 'out-marriage' at 4,8 per cent: '... approximately 20 per cent of households formed by children of heads of households surveyed in 1974 would have been mixed, had conversion of the non-Jewish partner not taken place ...' Dubb, A. op. cit, p.36. Following world-wide trends the number of 'out-marriages' had increased considerably by the 1990s. See Harris, J. 'SA Jewry The Facts', in *The South African Jewish Times*, 7 October 1994, p.4. Harris cites Dubb's 1991 sociodemographic survey of the Jewish population which shows that 15 per cent of Jews assimilate.
4. I do not here refer to the Halachic definition of a Jew. I note, however, that 'Judaism is not just a religious creed analogous to Christianity. It is the religious civilisation of one particular nation, it resides in the Jewish people and reflects its history.' Herman, S.N. *Jewish Identity*. London: Sage, 1977, p.36.
   I use the word 'Jew' to refer to both genders. For the sake of convenience I may use the male pronoun when discussing Jews generally.
5. My use of the term 'blacks' refers primarily to 'Africans', but also to people of mixed descent known in South Africa as coloureds, and to Indians. I use the word 'coloured' despite its racist overtones, as it has habitually been used in South Africa and is used by the writers themselves. The first significant image of a Jew in black fiction was in Peter Abrahams's *Dark Testament* (1942), hence I only refer to black authors who publish after this period.
6. E.D. Hirsch. *Validity in Interpretation*. New Haven and London: Yale University Press, 1967, p.180.
7. For example, the Victorian illustrated weeklies, the *Illustrated London News* and especially *Punch*, which were created in the tradition of political satire, constantly ridiculed and satirised Jews. Since the object of the magazine is to interest its reader, exaggeration is used as a more compelling device than realistic portrayal. See Lipman, V.D. 'The Victorian Jewish Background', in Cowen, A. and Cowen

R. *Victorian Jews through British Eyes*. Oxford: Oxford University Press, 1986, p.xix.

CHAPTER ONE

1. See Allport, G. *The Nature of Prejudice*. Cambridge Massachusetts: Addison-Wesley, 1954, Chapters 22-24.
2. Sherwood, R. *The Psychodynamics of Race*. New Jersey: Humanities Press, 1980, p.xii.
3. Gilman, S.L. *Difference and Pathology: Stereotypes of Sexuality, Race and Madness*. Ithaca, New York: Cornell University Press, 1985, p.17-18, 21.
4. For a clear and informative discussion of the whole issue of prejudice and stereotyping see Tajfel, H. *Human Groups and Social Categories*, Cambridge: Cambridge University Press, 1981.
5. Robert Wistrich observes that the term, 'Antisemitism', was first invented in the 1870s by the German journalist Wilhelm Marr to describe the hatred of Jews and Judaism which he and others like him advocated as a reaction to Jewish emancipation and their entry into non-Jewish society. See Wistrich, R.S. *Anti-Semitism. The Longest Hatred*. London: Thames Methuen, 1991.
6. For a fuller discussion of these and allied issues see Hellig, J. 'The Holocaust and the Theological Roots of Anti-Semitism'. *Jewish Affairs* 38(4), April 1983, pp.43-46; Hay, M. *Thy Brother's Blood: The Roots of Christian Anti-Semitism*. New York: Hart, 1975; and Bratton, F.G. *The Crime of Christendom. The Theological Source of Christian Anti-Semitism*. Boston: Beacon, 1969.
7. See Reuther, R.R 'Anti-Semitism and Christian Theology', in Fleischner, E. ed. *Auschwitz: Beginning of a New Era?* New York, KTAV, 1977, pp.79-92; Poliakov, L. *The History of Anti-Semitism*. London: Routledge and Kegan Paul, 1965-1973. I, Chapter 10; Wistrich, R. op cit, Introduction, pp.xv-xxvi.
8. See Parkes, R. *Anti-Semitism*. London: Valentine Mitchell, 1963, pp.48-56; Auerbach, F. 'The Protocols. Survival of an Evil Fiction'. South African Jewish Board of Deputies Pamphlet. Johannesburg: August 1988, pp.1-7.
9. See *Holocaust*. Jerusalem: Yad Vashem, 1991, pp.14-21.
10. Lewis, B. *The Jews of Islam*. Princeton University Press, 1984, p.188; Wistrich, R. op cit, pp.201-203; Lewis, B. 'The Arab World Discovers Anti-Semitism'. *Commentary* 81(5), May 1986, pp.30-34.
11. 'Zionism and Racism – The Slander'. Supplement to *Zionist Record*, 30 March 1984, p.3.
12. See 'Zionism Move Signals end of Third World Defiance'. *The Weekly Mail*, September 27 to October 3, 1991.
13. See Pogrebin, L.C. *Deborah, Golda and Me*, 1991; rpt. Doubleday, New York and London, 1991, p.212; Wistrich, R. *The Myth of Zionist Racism*. London: W.U.J.S. Publications, 1976, pp.12-28.
    Dan V. Segre suggests that the state of Israel – as a hybrid national and religious entity – challenges modern concepts of the national state. Since Zionism is

incompatible with the doctrines of proletarian internationalism, it has become unacceptable to those with leftist leanings. Segre, D. 'Is Anti-Zionism a New Form of Antisemitism?' in Curtis, M. ed. *Antisemitism in the Contemporary World.* Boulder and London: Westview, 1986, pp.146 -153. See also Wistrich, R. 'The "Jewish Question": Left-wing Anti-Zionism in Western Societies', in Curtis, M. ed. op cit, pp.51-57.

14. Allport, G. op.cit, p.217.

15. Schermerhorn, R.A. *Comparative Ethnic Relations: Framework for Theory and Research.* New York: Random House, 1970, p.6. Cited in Holmes, C. *Anti-Semitism in British Society, 1876-1939.* London: Edward Arnold, 1979, pp.231-232.

16. There were a number of crypto-Jews (marranos) from Spain and Portugal who lived in England after the expulsion of 1290 and there were at least ninety known Jews in the country at the time of Elizabeth I. See Wolf, L. 'Jews in Elizabethan England', Transactions of the Jewish Historical Society of England, II, (1928), pp.33-35. Cited in Glassman, B. *Anti-Semitic Stereotypes Without Jews: Images of the Jews in England 1290-1700.* Detroit: Wayne State University Press, 1975. For a full discussion of the medieval attitude towards Jews including topics such as the Spanish Inquisition which are peripheral to this study, see Wistrich, R. *Anti-Semitism: The Longest Hatred,* pp.29-42.

17. Gilman, S.L. *Difference and Pathology,* p.20.

18. See the case of the prosecution and execution in 1594 of Roderigo Lopez, the crypto-Jewish Portuguese physician accused of attempting to poison Queen Elizabeth I. Modder, M.F. *The Jew in the Literature of England to the End of the Nineteenth Century.* Philadelphia: The Jewish Publication Society, 1939, pp.4-25.

19. Cheyette, B. *Constructions of 'the Jew' in English Literature and Society. Racial Representations, 1875-1945.* Cambridge: Cambridge University Press, 1993, p.11.

20. p.51. Cited in Naman, A.A. *The Jew in the Victorian Novel.* New York: AMS Press, 1980, p.179. Ikey, *slang.* Familiar form of Ike, used typically for a Jew; hence a Jewish receiver or money-lender ... 1836.' Supplement to OED.

21. Holmes, C. *Anti-Semitism in British Society,1876-1939.* London: Edward Arnold, 1979, p.227.

22. Ibid, pp.5, 9.

23. Cheyette, B. op cit, p.67f.

24. For a full discussion of the Wandering Jew see Rosenberg, E. *From Shylock to Svengali: Jewish Stereotypes in English Fiction.* Stanford: Stanford University Press, 1960, Chapters 8-10.

25. Smouse 1705 (Du *smous* Jew, usurer, corresp. to G. *shums* talk, patter – Yiddish *shmuess* ... tales, news, the reference being to the persuasive talk of Jewish pedlars. *The Shorter Oxford English Dictionary.*

26. See Edelstein, A. *An Unacknowledged Harmony. Philo-Semitism and the Survival of European Jewry.* Westport Connecticut and London England: Greenwood, 1982, pp.10-19, Chapters 5 and 6. Although only a specific group of Jews may be identified, such as those Jews who have suffered during the Holocaust, philo-Semitism includes at the least a tolerant attitude toward other groups of Jews.

27. See Rosenberg, E. op cit, pp.39-49, Landa, M.J. *The Jew in Drama*. London: P.S. King, 1926, p.133.

28. Cohen-Steiner, O. 'Jews and Jewesses in Victorian Fiction: From Religious Stereotype to Ethnic Hazard'. In *Patterns of Prejudice*, 21(2), Summer 1987, pp.25-34. Note, however, that Shylock's daughter, Jessica is a very early example of the figure of the beautiful Jewish woman who renounces Judaism and marries a Christian.

29. Herrman, L. 'Cape Jewry before 1870', in Saron, G. and Hotz, L. eds. *The Jews in South Africa. A History*. Johannesburg and Cape Town: South African Jewish Board of Deputies, 1935, pp.1-5.

30. Quoted in Herrman, L. *A History of the Jews in South Africa. A Social Psychological Study based upon the Attitudes of a Group of South African Jewish Students*. Cape Town: South African Jewish Board of Deputies, 1935, p.199.

31. Krut, R. 'The Making of a South African Jewish Community in Johannesburg, 1886-1914', in Bozzoli, B. ed. *Class, Community and Conflict. South African Perspectives*. Johannesburg: Ravan, 1987, p.135.

32. Conscription of Jews was introduced in the Russian Empire by Tsar Nicholas I in 1827, in a campaign to de-Judaise Jews. Each Jewish community was required to supply a quota of boys between the ages of twelve and eighteen. When insufficient teenagers could be found, children as young as six years old were taken to make up the levy. Frequently children were captured and pressed into service which was fixed at twenty-five years. Few households were exempt from this system which persisted until 1917. See Dubnow, S.M. *History of the Jews in Russia and Poland. From the Earliest Times until the Present Day*. Trans. from the Russian by I. Friedlander, 2, Philadelphia: The Jewish Publication Society of America, 1918, pp.14-44.

33. *Zuid Afrikaansche Zeitung*, 3 June 1881. Quoted in Shain, M. *Jewry and Cape Society*, Cape Town: Historical Publication Society, 1983. p.6.

34. Farmer, H. 'What is wrong with South Africa'. Quoted in the *South African Jewish Chronicle*, 30 November 1908. Cited in Shain, M. *The Roots of Antisemitism in South Africa*. United States of America: The University Press of Virginia and Johannesburg: Witwatersrand University Press, 1994, p.51. Note the 'red' hair and 'greasy' coat which corresponds with Dickens's description of Fagin:

> standing over ... [the fire] ... was a very old shrivelled Jew, whose villainous-looking and repulsive face was obscured by a quantity of matted red hair. He was dressed in a greasy flannel gown ... Dickens, C. *Oliver Twist* 1837-1839; rpt. London: Thomas Nelson, 1945, p.60.

Almost all Jews emigrating from eastern Europe passed through the Jewish shelter in London. See Newman A.'Why Did our Lithuanian Grandparents Come to South Africa?', *Jewish Affairs* 49(2), Winter 1994, pp.9-12.

35. *Johannesburg Times*, 1.4.1896. Cited in Shain M. *The Roots of Antisemitism*, p.27.

36. Saron, G. 'Jewish Immigration, 1880-1913'. In Saron, G. and Hotz, L. (eds.), *The Jews in South Africa: A History*. London: Oxford University Press, 1955, p.89.

37. *Census of the Transvaal Colony and Swaziland – 1904*, Transvaal Archives Depot. Quoted in Shain, M. *The Roots of Antisemitism*, p.52.

Stuart Cumberland referred to 'Jewhannesburg' in *What I think of South Africa*. London: 1896, p.93. Cited in Krut, R. 'The Making of a South African Jewish Community', p.136.

38. Brandford, J. *A Dictionary of South African English*. Cape Town: Oxford University Press, 1980, p.216. See Shain, M. *The Roots of Antisemitism*, note 32 pp.163-164. Shain suggests that the term might refer to immigrants who had sojourned in Argentina under Baron de Hirsch's settlement scheme before coming to South Africa.

39. Cartoon in the *Owl* 6.5.1904 'The Coming of the Scum', reproduced in Shain, M. *The Roots of Antisemitism*, p.77.

40. Van Onselen, C. *New Babylon: Studies in the Social and Economic History of the Witwatersrand 1886-1914*, I. Johannesburg: Ravan Press, 1982, pp.67-87.

41. Ibid, pp.109-111 and Chapter Three *passim*.

42. The history of the Indian community in South Africa can in certain respects be compared to that of the Jewish community. Workers emigrated to South Africa as a result of poverty and difficult conditions in India. The Cape Colony and Natal encouraged this as the Indians provided a cheap labour force. These labourers were indentured for five years, and were thereafter entitled to land ownership rights but not in the Transvaal or Orange Free State. Many Indian immigrants turned to store-keeping in remote country districts and, like the Jews, were subject to anti-Alien agitation. After 1895 Indians were faced with a series of anti-Alien Acts similar to those enacted against Jews. Unlike the Jews they were also subjected to compulsory registration and identification by means of finger prints, and had to carry passes. By 1908 they were prohibited from moving between the areas that would become the future provinces of the Union, and in 1913 an Act excluded all immigration of Asians to South Africa apart from wives and minor children of those already present. Meer, F. *Portrait of Indian South Africans*. Durban: Avon House, 1969, pp.44-47.

43. Shimoni, G. *Jews and Zionism: The South African Experience 1910-1969*. Cape Town: Oxford University Press, 1980, pp.15-16.

44. Ibid, p.103.
For a brief but trenchant discussion of this phenomenon see Coetzee, J.M. 'Farm Novel and Plaasroman' in *White Writing. On the Culture of Letters in South Africa*. Sandton: Century Hutchinson; New Haven and London: Yale University Press, 1988, p.78.

45. See McCormick, K. 'Yiddish in District Six', *Jewish Affairs*, 48 (3), Spring 1993, pp.29-38.

46. Remarks made by a member of the Commission of Enquiry into Labour in the Cape Colony 1893. Cited in Shain, M. *The Roots of Antisemitism*, p.23.

47. Shain has shown that the concept of 'Hoggenheimer' originated with the English playwright, Owen Hall, who created a Jewish millionaire, Max Hoggenheimer of Park Lane, in his West End musical comedy, *The Girl from Kays*, which played at the Apollo Theatre, London, in November 1902 and was brought to South Africa in the following year. See Shain, M. *The Roots of Antisemitism*, pp.58-64.

48. *Encyclopaedia Judaica*, 3, pp.118-122.

49. Shimoni, G. op cit, p.78.
50. Shain, M. *The Roots of Antisemitism*, p.78.
51. Dramatising prevailing perceptions, Riva Krut wrote a fictionalised version of a Report of a Benoni meeting, 20 April 1919, given by Detective Whitlow to Sub-Inspector Loftus, forwarded to the Commissioner of Transvaal Police:

    If you ask me, those Jewish traders were just a little too quick to start things ... they were running around the countryside causing all kinds of trouble with the natives ... They came to South Africa full of ideas about the Russian revolution and Bolshevism, and they went around promoting propaganda and distributing pamphlets to the natives.

    'Confidential: Bolshevism on the Rand', South African Department of Justice files, Pretoria, South Africa, 1914-1928. *National Film Board Microfilm* (6 reels), 1975. Quoted in Krut, R. 'The History Seminar: Lumpens and *Luftmenschen* in the South African Jewish Community', pp.11-12.

    The tour of two Russian Jews, I. Sosnovic and L. Lapinsky, who in 1919 came to South Africa to lecture on the Russian Revolution exacerbated the identification of Jews with Bolshevism.
52. Mantzaris, E.A. 'Radical Community: The Yiddish-speaking Branch of the International Socialist League, 1918-1920', in Bozzoli, B. *Class, Community and Conflict. South African Perspectives.* Johannesburg: Ravan, 1987, p.170; Shimoni, G. op. cit, pp.53, 88-89, 162, 173-175; Adler, T. 'Lithuania's Diaspora: The Johannesburg Jewish Workers Club, 1928-1984'. *Journal of Southern African Studies*, 6 (1), October, 1979, pp.70-92.
53. Based on samples of university student population, MacCrone found that 'the Jewish group shows the least intolerance of any group and the widest range of tolerance'. MacCrone, I.D. *Race Attitudes in South Africa*. London: Oxford University Press, 1937, p.208. Cited in Shimoni, G. op cit, p.162.
54. For example, the South African Jewish Board of Deputies, despite its resistance to anti-Alien legislation, pursued a policy of non-intervention in political affairs. See Lazerson, J.N. *Against the Tide. Whites in the Struggle Against Apartheid.* Belville: University of the Western Cape, Mayibuye Books, 1994, pp.90-91, 98; Hyman, A. 'The Apolitical role of the South African Jewish Board of Deputies', *Jewish Affairs*. 49 (4), Summer 1994, pp.67-68.
55. The *Star*, 16 March 1922; the *Natal Advertiser*, 16 March 1922; the *Cape Times*, 18 March 1922. Quoted in Shimoni, G. op cit, pp.89-90.
56. *Rand Daily Mail* 28.11.1925. Cited in Shain, M. *The Roots of Antisemitism*, p.121.
57. Shimoni, G. op.cit, p.104.
58. The Commission reported that 'often traders, foreigners who came to South Africa to fill their pockets, took unfair advantage of existing conditions and undoubtedly made use of cunning means. The influence of Jews engaged in commerce was often pernicious. Calm, sensible people in all parts of the country repeatedly bear this out.' *Carnegie Commission of Investigation on the Poor White Question in South Africa.* Stellenbosch: Pro Ecclesia Press 1932, 1, pp.115-116. Cited in Shimoni, G. op cit, p.104.
59. Shimoni, G. op cit, pp.97-107.

60. SAIRR Records, Conradie to Rheinallt-Jones, 25 June 1934. Cited in Furlong, P.J. *Between Crown and Swastika. The Impact of the Radical Right on the Afrikaner Nationalist Movement in the Fascist Era*. Johannesburg: Witwatersrand University Press, 1991, p.37. For a full discussion of the 'shirt' movements see Furlong, P.J. op. cit, pp.16-45.

61. Greyshirt propaganda quoted by Shimoni, G. op. cit, pp.113-114. For a full discussion of the propaganda activities carried out by the Nazis in South Africa see 'It *Did* Happen Here. How the Nazis conducted propaganda in South Africa'. *Common Sense*, January 1940: 'Continuing: It *Did* Happen Here'. *Common Sense* February 1940, pp.8-11; 'Continuing: It *Did* Happen Here'. *Common Sense*, March 1940, pp.8-11.

62. Furlong, P.J. op. cit, pp.25-26.

63. In Cape Committee Reports to Meeting of Deputies, 12 November 1939, p.2. Cited by Furlong, P. J. op cit, p.68.

64. Furlong, P.J. op cit, pp.48, 63.

65. Shimoni, G. op cit, p.130. See 'The Anti-Jewish Movement in South Africa: The Need for Action', Jewish Board of Deputies Report, Hofmeyr Papers. A1/DH , Manuscript Collection, University of the Witwatersrand Library, pp.6, 17.

66. Shimoni, G., op cit, pp.141-144; Krut, R. 'The Making of a South African Jewish Community in Johannesburg', p.139.
A statistical survey of the Johannesburg Jewish population conducted in 1935 revealed that 39,43 per cent of all males over 15 years of age were engaged in commercial, financial and insurance occupations. Tradesmen constituted 10 per cent of the gainfully employed: plumbers, mechanics, blacksmiths and similar occupations 2,45 per cent; tailors and shoemakers 5,62 per cent and workers in wood and furniture 2,76 per cent. Only 8,39 per cent were professionals, but it was already obvious that their numbers would grow rapidly. Sonnabend, H. *Statistical Survey of Johannesburg Jewish Population* [typescript 1935] and Sonnabend, H. 'The Social Role of the Jew in South Africa'. *Jewish Affairs*, 31 (1), January 1948, pp.14-19. Cited in Shimoni, G. op. cit, p.162.

67. Furlong, P.J. op cit, p.63.

68. Shimoni, G. op cit, p.127.

69. See, for example, Morris Hoffman's 'Lost her Head', published in 1939.

70. For a fuller discussion of the origins and development of this society see Braude, S. 'Combating Anti-Jewish Propaganda. The South African Society of Jews and Christians', in *Jewish Affairs*, 46 (3), October/November 1991, pp.31-36.

71. Anti-Semitism was further fuelled by the exposure in 1947 of the fraud of Milne and Erleigh, two prominent Jewish financiers in Johannesburg. See Paton, A. *Hofmeyr*. London: Oxford University Press, 1964, p.464. The family of Erleigh had long since converted to Christianity – probably more of an outrage to Christian sensibilities.

72. See 'Anti-Semitic Writings'. *Jewish Affairs*, 13 (3), March 1958, p.43; 'Vandals Enter Johannesburg Synagogue'. *Zionist Record*, 27 June 1952; 'Incidents of an Anti-Semitic Nature Reported 1961-1964'. Jewish Board of Deputies Pamphlet, 25 August 1964, 308 (3), pp.1-3.

In *The Family Reunion* (1973), a novel set outside South Africa, Rose Moss treats Jewish immigration, and uses historical and political fact, largely untransmuted by literary imagination, which functions as a summary of some of the key issues in Jewish social history of this time:

> Rubin ... had chosen ... South Africa, where tales had it the streets were paved with gold ... [soon he experienced] new anti-Semitism for old. The Nationalists ... admired Hitler ... Still they were too busy with kaffirs, Coloureds, Indians, Chinese and English to spare much virulence for the Jews. For the moment they were satisfied with occasional baitings, synagogue and grave desecrations, and warnings that they were not unmindful of the support given by Jews to the opposition, the liberals, the Elders of the Protocols of Zion [*sic*], Communists ... They denied that they were anti-Semitic. On the contrary, they professed admiration for the kindred and successful nationalism that had founded and defended the State of Israel. They sanctioned Zionism in their own country, and encouraged all Jews to go to the country where they belonged. (pp.13-14)

73. Shimoni, G. op cit, pp.214-234, 355-357.
74. Interview with Denis Goldberg, London, 3 February 1987. Quoted in Lazerson, J.N. op cit, p.82.
75. In 1991, Letty Cottin Pogrebin cited the Harris and Yankelovich public opinion polls which have found anti-Semitic feeling present in one-third of Americans. See Pogrebin, L.C. op cit, p.210. There is no reason to believe that anti-Semitic opinion is less in South Africa.
76. See *Anti-Semitism in South Africa*. South African Jewish Board of Deputies Pamphlet. Johannesburg, 1988, pp.1-2.
77. Dubb, A. 'Demographic Picture', in Arkin, M. *South African Jewry: A Contemporary Survey*, p.38.
78. Dubb, A. 'Little Decrease in SA Jewish Population'. *Jewish Voice*. 2 (4). June 1991, p.4.

CHAPTER TWO

1. Results of Census, *Colony of the Cape of Good Hope 1875*. Cited in Shain, M. *The Roots of Antisemitism*, p.11.
2. There were 1400 Jews at the diggings at this time, 600 males directly involved with the diggings. See Haberfeld, C.B. 'Diamond City and its Jews', in *World of South African Jewry*, 2, ed. M. Dorfan, Johannesburg: R and J Publications, October 1988, pp.27-29.
3. Donker, A. 'English-Language Publishing in South Africa', in Gardner, S. ed. *Publisher-Writer-Reader: Sociology of Southern African Literature*. Johannesburg: Witwatersrand University Press, 1986, p.19. There was an enormous increase in South African writing, as part of the literature of imperialism. See Mendellsohn, M. *Mendellsohn's South African Bibliography*, Kegan Paul, 1910, vol. 1.
4. JanMahomed, A.R., 'The Economy of Manichean Allegory: The Function of

Racial Difference in Colonialist Literature'. *Critical Inquiry*, 12, Autumn 1985, pp.63-72.

5. Spurr, D. *The Rhetoric of Empire. Colonial Discourse in Journalism, Travel Writing, and Imperial Administration*. Durham and London: Duke University Press, 1993, pp.10-11.

6. Hofmeyr, C.I. 'Mining, Social Change and Literature. An Analysis of South African Literature with Particular Reference to the Mining Novel 1870-1920'. Unpublished Masters dissertation. University of the Witwatersrand, 1981, pp.17, 22.

7. See JanMahomed, A.R. 'The Economy of Manichean Allegory'. *Critical Inquiry*, 12, Autumn 1985, pp.63, 67.

8. Rosenthal, E. 'On the Diamond Fields', in Saron, G. and Hotz, L. eds. op cit, pp.105-107.

9. 'Leaves from a South African Journal: The Diamond Fields', in *Short Stories on Great Subjects*, 4, London: Longmans Green, 1874, p.535. A version of this text cited in Shain, M. *The Roots of Antisemitism*, p.11.

10. For information on the career of Barney Barnato see Jackson, S. *The Great Barnato*. London: Heinemann, 1971.

11. Hofmeyr, C.I. op. cit, pp.21, 77.

12. Gilman, S.L. *Jewish Self-Hatred: Anti-Semitism and the Hidden Language of the Jews*, Baltimore and London: Johns Hopkins, 1990, pp.6-7.

13. Gilman, S.L. *Difference and Pathology*, pp.34-35.

14. Ragussis, M., 'Repression, Conversion, and Literary Form: *Harrington* and the Novel of Jewish Identity'. *Critical Inquiry*, 16, Autumn 1989, op. cit, p.114.

15. Gilman, S.L. *Jewish Self-Hatred*, p.292.
The frequent reference in South African fiction to relationships between Jewish men and Gentile women is based on actual perceptions. Jewish immigration to the diamond fields consisted mainly of single men, who, being without women of their own religion, sometimes made alliances with Gentile women. This became commonplace in South African fiction long before it made an appearance in American fiction. See Fisch, H. *The Dual Image: A Study of the Jew in English and American Literature*. London: World Jewish Library, 1971, pp.126-127, for a discussion of the psychological determinants of the attraction between the Jewish man and the Gentile woman.

16. Compare a character in Westrup's novel, *The Debt*, 'Mr Greenway' (né Liknavitsky), a prosperous tailor in Johannesburg, who is treated with some authorial sympathy but who nevertheless displays 'Jewish' characteristics such as rubbing his hands together. (p.86)'.
Another early novel in which Jews feature briefly is L. Vescelius-Sheldon's *An I.D.B. in South Africa* (1888). See also two ambivalently portrayed Jews in *Jack Harkaway in the Transvaal: or, Fighting for the Flag* by S.B. Hemyng (1841-1901), 1902.

17. Ngugi Wa Thiong'o. *Decolonising the Mind. The Politics of Language in African Literature*. London: 1986; rpt. James Currey and Heinemann, 1991, p.13.

18. Gilman. S.L., *Jewish Self-Hatred*, pp.17, 24, 76, 258.

19. Landa, M.J. op cit, pp.172-173.
20. Gross, J. *Shylock. Four Hundred Years in the Life of a Legend.* London: Chatto and Windus, 1992, p.116.
21. A cartoon with the caption 'Britannia Rulth the Wavth ma thear' in *Daily News* 1 April 1904, cited in Holmes, C. op. cit, p.31, is a reference to alleged Jewish influence in international affairs, and the powerful Jewish representation in merchant banking, which thrived on personal Jewish international connections.
See also a cartoon by Egersdörfer in the *Owl* 18 March 1904, portraying a Jewish taskmaster in conversation with Milner, entitled 'Milner, Moses and the Mongols' in which the Jew, arguing that Chinese labour is necessary and Jews support it, says: 'Vy yeth, of courth they do.' Cited in Shain, M. *The Roots of Antisemitism*, op cit, p.60.
22. It has been impossible to ascertain the date of this novel. It appears to have been published at the beginning of the twentieth century.
A similar positive image can be found in a reference to a local shopkeeper in Cornell, F. C. *The Glamour of Prospecting. Wanderings of a South African Prospector in Search of Copper, Gold, Emeralds, and Diamonds.* London: T. Fisher Unwin, 1920. He 'was a Jew, and had all the curiosity and enterprise of his extraordinary race' (p.60).
23. See Shain, M. '"Vant to Puy a Vaatch": The Smous and Pioneer Trader in South African Jewish Historiography'. *Jewish Affairs* 42(9), September 1987, pp.111-128.
24. See Eric Rosenthal's Introduction to the facsimile reprint of Cohen's *Reminiscences of Johannesburg and London* 1924; rpt. 1976, Africana Book Society, for biographical information on Cohen.
25. In 1911 he was successfully sued and nearly destroyed by J.B. Robinson in a libel case when his *Reminiscences of Kimberley*, first published in serialised form in a London paper, *The Winning Post*, appeared as a book. This suggests that at least some of what purported to be factual reminiscences were mere inventions. In these reminiscences, using the familiar anti-Jewish terminology, he contemptuously refers to the Jews as 'the scum of Germany and Whitechapel' (p.25). Stephen Black used the term 'scum' in *The Golden Calf* (1925) and both Black and Cohen possibly echoed its frequent use in anti-Jewish satiric cartoons such as 'The Coming of the Scum' published in the *Owl*, 6 May 1904. There, however, the scathingly pejorative term 'scum' refers to the eastern European Jews arriving at the end of the nineteenth century who had through their foreignness and destitution acquired this negative label. Cohen, and Black following him, project the connotation of 'scum' on to the Anglo-German Jews as well. Cohen describes the Jews of Kimberley:

> [T]hey have crystallised into "magnates" since ... [they] stole from their simple-minded victims by intrigue and (theft) *guile* their claims and ground, and then, when they were in full possession, if anyone touched a glittering gem belonging to them, they howled like dervishes. They took good care no drastic laws were made until they (did the same themselves) *invented the pastime*, the lot of them, and "bought" the very foundations of their wealth with the

money amassed by their initial thefts from the original claim-holders ...
(certain South African "financiers" are really the greatest rascals that
Nature ever spawned, and who would sell their souls if a purchaser could
be found for such vile trash.) (p.37)
Passages in brackets represent those omitted by Cohen in a revision of the manuscript. Passages in italics show passages inserted in substitution in the revised
manuscript which Cohen worked on but never published. The changes alert the
reader to the fact that in what he proffered as factual reminiscences, Cohen either
exaggerated or lied about the role played by the Jews on the diamond fields. The
way in which Cohen's revisions softened the impact of 'theft' to 'guile', for example, suggests that he is not a trustworthy witness. It also further suggests a definite
animus against the Jews, which is evident in his fictional work. The manuscript,
containing the revisions, is in the Louis Cohen papers, A1538. Manuscript
Collection, University of the Witwatersrand Library.
Cohen also wrote *Reminiscences of Johannesburg and London*, 1924. Facsimile
reprint 1976 Africana Book Society. Intro. by E. Rosenthal, and produced a play
in 1878, *The Land of Diamonds*, never published. See Rosenthal, E. Introduction,
p.xvii.
26. For a comprehensive and definitive discussion of the topic see Gilman, S.L.
Jewish Self-Hatred, pp.301-303, 393, 437.

CHAPTER THREE

1. 'In the *Grahamstown Journal* on 4 May 1832 a correspondent signing himself
"Zekiel Homespun", obviously a Jewish *nom de plume*, writes of the arrival of a
smous from the northern districts to the market at Grahamstown.' Kaplan, M.
assisted by Robertson, M. *Jewish Roots in the South African Economy*. Cape Town:
Struik, 1986, p.35.
2. See, for example, the life of Sammy Marks, who started as a smous and went on
to make a fortune on the diamond fields and several other fortunes as a coal and
steel industrialist. Mendelsohn, R. *Sammy Marks*. *'The Uncrowned King of the
Transvaal'*. Cape Town: David Philip, Athens Ohio: Ohio University Press. In
association with Jewish Publications – SA, 1991.
3. See I. Herrman, L. 'Cape Jewry before 1870', in Saron, G. and Hotz, L. eds. *The
Jews in South Africa. A History*. Johannesburg and Cape Town: South African
Jewish Board of Deputies, 1935, pp.1-5.
See Abrahams, I. 'Western Province Jewry, 1870-1902'; G. Aschman, 'Oudtshoorn in the Early Days'. Aschman points out that '*my Joodjie*' was the affection-
ate term applied by the Boers to the smous. p.136.
4. Romm, I.C. *South African Jewish Times*, September 1985, pp.44-45.
5. Shain. M. *The Roots of Antisemitism*, pp.13-16, 22-26.
For information on Jewish involvement with the ostrich feather industry, see
Feldman, L. *Oudtshoorn: Jerusalem of Africa*. Ed. with an introductory essay by J.
Sherman. Johannesburg: University of the Witwatersrand. Friends of the Library,

1989. See also Aschman, G. 'Oudtshoorn in the Early Days', in Saron, G. and Hotz, L. eds. *op. cit*, pp.121-137.

6. Boon, M.J. *The History of the Orange Free State*. London: 1885, p.54. Quoted in Shain, M. *The Roots of Antisemitism in South Africa*, p.15.

7. *Cape Punch* 4 July 1888. Quoted in Shain, M. *The Roots of Antisemitism in South Africa*, p.16.

8. Shain, M. *The Roots of Antisemitism*, pp.23-24.

9. As J. Higham points out '[s]tereotypes ... may blend affection and contempt ... [or] mingle pity and censure.' Higham, J. 'Anti-Semitism in the Gilded Age: A Reinterpretation'. *Mississippi Historical Review*, 43, 1956-7, p.563. Cited in Holmes, C. op. cit, p.41.

10. A resumé of this novel is given in Weinstock, D.J. The Boer War in the Novel in English 1884-1966: A Descriptive and Critical Bibliography. Unpublished Doctoral thesis. University Of California, Los Angeles, 1968. Facsimile Reproduced by microfilm, 521-528. Weinstock lists 29 novels of the Anglo-Boer War in which reference is made to Jews or in which Jewish characters appear.

11. It appears from Schreiner's diary that the section of the novel concerning 'the Jew' was written during 1883. See Diary Entry, London, September 1883. Schreiner, S.C. 'A Note on the Genesis of the Book', in Rive, R. ed. *Olive Schreiner Letters, 1871-1899*. Cape Town: David Philip, 1987, p.484.

12.   [Fagin] stepped gently to the door, which he fastened. He then drew forth ... a small box, which he placed carefully on the table. His eyes glistened as he raised the lid and looked in. Dragging an old chair to the table, he sat down, and took from it a magnificent gold watch, sparkling with jewels ... Having replaced [the watch] the Jew took out [a trinket] so small that it lay in the palm of his hand ... [he] pored over it long and earnestly ...
Dickens, C. *Oliver Twist*, op. cit, pp.62-63.

13. In the chapter 'Prostitutes and Proletarians, 1886-1914' in *New Babylon*, Charles van Onselen documents the activities of the Jewish pimps and professional gangsters who were involved in Johannesburg's prostitution business by the mid-1890s.

14. 'The men whom [Bertie] comes into contact with, from the first who seduces her to the last who leaves her in London streets, are none of them depraved, they are more or less all of them "good fellows" in different ways – the only misfortune is that they look upon a woman as a creature created entirely for their benefit.' Letter to Karl Pearson, July 1886. Rive, R. op. cit, p.91.

15. 'The Psychology of the Boer'. In *Thoughts on South Africa*. London: T. Fisher Unwin, 1923, p.275.

16. Letter to Betty Molteno, October 1898. In Rive, R. op. cit, p.336.

17. 'The Problem of Slavery'. In *Thoughts on South Africa*, p.138.

18. 'A Letter on the Jew'. Cape Town: H. Liberman. Paper read at the Jewish Territorial Organisation meeting, 1 July 1906. Published in *Cape Times*, 2 July 1906. Reproduced in *Jewish Affairs* 31(8), August 1976, pp.6-11.

19. Rosenberg. E. op. cit, Chapter 3 *passim*.

20. Smith, P. *A.B.* ' ... *a minor marginal note*'. London: Jonathan Cape, 1933. p.62.

21. *Cape Times*, 18 March 1904. Quoted in Shain M. *The Roots of Antisemitism*, p.56.
22. Smith, P. South African Diary, 17 August 1913- 23 May 1914, Section 2, pp.153-154. Pauline Smith Papers, A1353. Manuscript Collection, University of the Witwatersrand Library. Photographic copy. Original in Jagger Library, University of Cape Town.
23. Ibid, Section 16, pp.3-4.
24. For example 'Triton' in the *Cape Times* Special, 17 December 1900, refers to property 'all mortgaged to the Jewish *smous*'. Cited in Shain, M. *Jewry and Cape Society*, p.13.
    H. I. E. Dhlomo, in a short story, 'Farmer and Servant' in Visser, N. and Couzens, T. (eds.) *Collected Works*, 1985, p.448, writing of the 1940s and 1950s, states: 'Some farmers had bonded their land to money-lenders, many of whom were Jews.'
25. In her diary she refers to the 'Herring' case:
    > All the town [Oudtshoorn] is in a seethe over this ... it is something like this. A farmer agreed to let a farm to a Jew or Jew syndicate, and the lease was drawn up in Jacobson's office for this Jew (or company of Jews), and the farmer signed as he thought this lease which was read to him by the Jew. Later the signed lease was produced and a clause was discovered in it binding the farmer to *sell* his land to this Jew within a certain time if the Jew wished to purchase. This clause had never been read to the farmer at all and was not in the lease drawn by Jacobson but *was* in the 2nd lease which the farmer thinking he was signing Jacobson's [*sic*] had signed. It seems they had the two leases back to back and so done the Boer. The man Herring (the Jew tool) was arrested ... (April 17, 1914). South African Diary, Section 14, p.44.
26. Rooke, D. 'A Note on Pauline Smith'. In Driver D. (ed.), *Pauline Smith*. Johannesburg: McGraw-Hill, 1983, p.79.
27. South African Diary, Section 15, p.3.
28. Ibid, Section 15, p.11.
29. Coetzee, J.M. *White Writing: On the Culture of Letters in South Africa*. Sandton: Century Hutchinson; New Haven and London: Yale University Press, 1988, pp.78-79.
    See also the discussion of Jewish stereotypes in Van der Merwe, C.N. *Breaking Barriers: Stereotypes and Changing of Values in Afrikaans Writing 1875-1990*. Amsterdam/Atlanta, 1994, pp.18-22.
30. Coetzee, J.M. 'Blood, Taint, Flaw, Degeneration: The Novels of Sarah Gertrude Millin'. *English Studies in Africa* 23(1), 1980, pp.41-58.
31. Braun, L. 'Not Gobineau but Heine – Not Racial Theory but Biblical Theme: The Case of Sarah Gertrude Millin'. *English Studies in Africa* 34(1), 1991, pp.27-38.
    Braun cites Pienaar, M. 'An Evaluation of the Novels of Sarah Gertrude Millin'. Master's Dissertation, University of South Africa, 1979, p.147.
32. Braun, L. op. cit, pp.28, 29.
33. Unpaginated notes. S.G. Millin Papers, A539/9, Manuscript Collection, University of the Witwatersrand Library. Quoted by Braun, L. op. cit, p.29.

34. Millin, S.G. *The Night is Long*. London: Faber, 1941, p.148.
35. Ibid, p.176.
36. Ibid, p.174.
37. Ibid.
38. The use of the word 'Kaffir' for a black man is not significant here since in 1928, the date of publication of the novel, the word had not assumed the derogatory sense which it was to do some years later. The earliest recorded reference to the change of usage is in the OED Supplement quoting the *New Statesman* (1959): 'Kaffir has become a term of abuse.'
39. S.G. Millin Papers, MS 188, Box 29, The Brenthurst Library, pp.6a-7.
40. Ibid, pp.3, 21.
41. S.G. Millin Papers, A539/ M2, Manuscript Collection, University of the Witwatersrand Library, pp.4, 7.
42. Ibid, pp.1-2.
43. Ibid, pp.2-3.
44. Millin, S.G. *The Night is Long*, pp.309, 310.
45. See Rubin, M. *Sarah Gertrude Millin: A South African Life*. Johannesburg: Ad. Donker, 1977. See also Bernstein, E. 'Sarah Gertrude Millin, The Writer and The Jewess', *Jewish Affairs*, 23 (7), 1968, pp. 14-18.

CHAPTER FOUR

1. 'Margaret's Piece'. In *You'd Prefer me not to Mention it ... The Lives of Four Jewish Daughters of Refugees*. [London]: Jewish Women's History Group, 1983.
   Compare Wolfe Miller's novel *Man in the Background* (1958) which also details childhood experience of anti-Semitism in a country town in the Transvaal between the Wars:
   > He wagged his finger threateningly. 'You a Jew-boy?'
   > Martin shook his head.
   > 'Then why you got a shop?' ... 'Siss, you're playing with a Jew-boy! Ya-ya, you're playing with a Jew-boy!' ...
   > Tommy's brother, Hybie [*sic*] set off in pursuit of the tormentor ...
   > 'You bloody fool, I'll kill you! I'll smash your face in! You big bully!'
   > 'Do it! cried Hybie, losing his temper too. 'You just try it you dirty little Afrikaner-Boer, *I'll* kill *you*!' (pp.29-33)
2. Lazerson, J.N. op. cit, pp.97-98.
3. See 'Vandals Enter Johannesburg Synagogue'. *Zionist Record*, 27 June 1952; 'Concern over Synagogue Raids'. *Cape Times*, 17 March 1958; 'Predikant tells his flock: "Don't vote for Jew"'. *Sunday Express*, 10 November 1957.
4. Meyer, M.A. *Jewish Identity in the Modern World*. Seattle and London: University of Washington Press, 1990. p.33.
5. Memmi, A. *The Liberation of the Jew*. New York: Orion, 1966, pp.116-119.
6. Interview with Phillip Stein. In Stein, P. and Jacobson, R. (eds.), *Sophiatown Speaks*. Johannesburg: Junction Avenue Press, 1986, p.63. The situation Stein

describes is the subject of the Junction Avenue Theatre Company's extremely successful play, *Sophiatown* (1986).

7. Gershater, C. 'From Lithuania to South Africa'. In Saron, G. and Hotz, L. (eds.), op. cit, p.75.

8. See Sherman, J. (ed.), *From a Land Far Off*, Introduction, p.11.
   In a group of 'stories' based on accounts which he heard in the course of his duties as rabbi in country communities, [Rabbi] J. Newman records 'the struggles of the early Jewish settlers in country places'. *With Ink in the Book: Stories.* Johannesburg: L. Rubin, 1958, p.x. In the story, 'Out of his Place', Rabbi Newman records how he was told by the chairman of a congregation:
   "In the course of time I learned a few things about the life of ... a Jewish hermit ... He was the only Jew in the place, and there were very few Europeans there with whom he hardly associated ... He had his servants, and there were also young children about. Some were dark-skinned, with European features, and one or two more, much lighter in colour, resembled the Spanish and Oriental races ... I became convinced that they were his children and the offspring of one woman among several who lived around him ." (p.12)
   It is further revealed that the mother of the children is herself the daughter of a previous union between a black woman and a Jew who had subsequently returned to Russia.

9. Compare the expression of this sentiment from the Jewish point of view: '... the other gentile boys did not have to bear the burden of guilt and sympathy towards the blacks which we bore as part of our Jewishness.' Jacobson, D. 'An Apprenticeship'. In *Beggar my Neighbour*. London: Weidenfeld and Nicolson, 1958, p.77.

10. Rive, R. Introduction, *The Path of Thunder*. Cape Town and Johannesburg: David Philip, 1984, p.7.

11. Compare how, in literary stereotypes of the coloured, the same dichotomy is found between the older generation – 'docile, acquiescent, compliant and long-suffering' – and the 'rebellious' younger generation. February, V.A. *Mind Your Colour. The Coloured Stereotype in South African Literature.* London: Routledge and Kegan Paul, 1981, p.56.

12. Perhaps this novel was also a direct response to the series of discriminatory Acts passed after 1948 – the Prohibition of Mixed Marriages Act of 1949, the Population Registration Act of 1950, and the Group Areas Act of 1950.

13. Rappaport, S. *Jew and Gentile: The Philo-Semitic Aspect.* New York: Philosophical Library, 1980, p.4.

14. Rosenberg, E. op. cit, p.40.

15. Sachs, B. *Personalities and Places.* (Second Series) Johannesburg: Dial, 1965, p.50.
   In an article published in 1947, the writer Herman Charles Bosman maintained that the anti-Jewish orientation on the part of many Afrikaners was due not to anti-Semitism or to Nazi propaganda, but to anti-British feeling. He argued further that the Jews had highly exaggerated its importance. He castigated 'pseudo-apologists' for the Jews, as being the very ones who 'put the Jew in the dock' in the first place. *The South African Jewish Times*, September 1947, pp.27, 38.

CHAPTER FIVE

1. Trans. by J. Sherman. In Sherman, J. (ed.), *From a Land Far Off*, pp.33-49.
2. For example Mendel Kaplan's books, *From Shtetl to Steelworks* (1979); *Jewish Roots in the South African Economy* (1986); *Founders and Followers: Johannesburg Jewry 1887-1915* (1991).
3. For a list of Jewish writers who deal with black experience see Bibliography. For a list of Jewish authors of this period who write on other themes see Bernstein, E. *My Judaism, My Jews*. Johannesburg: Exclusive Books, 1962, pp.137-152.
4. 'Some Early Reminiscences of South African Jewish Life'. *Jewish Affairs* 11(4), April 1956. p.22.
5. Ibid, p.25.
6. 'In the Days of my Youth'. *South African Rosh Hashona Annual and Jewish Year Book, 1932*. Johannesburg: n.p. 1932, p.2.
7. *South African Odyssey*, p.8.
8. Ibid, p.250.
9. This text forms a vivid contrast to Sarah Shaban's memoir, *The Golden Corn* (1970), which stresses the Jewish aspects of Shaban's own life in a Lithuanian town prior to emigrating to South Africa. However, after happening to be in Israel during the 1972 War, Misheiker wrote and had privately published a moving account of her experiences – *Days of October* – South Africa (n.d.).
10. Prell, R.E. 'Why the Jewish Princess Doesn't Sweat: Desire and Consumption in Postwar American Jewish Culture', in Eilberg-Schwartz, H. ed. *People of the Body: Jews and Judaism from an Embodied Perspective*. Albany: State University of New York Press, 1992, p.338.
11. Other stories – 'Rejected and Admitted' and 'Subjects of the Czar' – also record the emigration of refugees from Russia to South Africa.

CHAPTER SIX

1. Jacobson, D. 'A White Liberal Trapped by his Prejudices'. *Commentary*, 15, May 1953, p.456.
2. Dan Jacobson, 'Interview with Ian Hamilton'. *New Review*, 4, October 1977, p.26.
3. Roberts, S. op. cit; Christie, S., Hutchings, G., and Maclennan, D. *Perspectives on South African Fiction*. Johannesburg: Ad. Donker, 1980.
4. Jacobson, D. 'Apartheid and South African Jewry'. An Exchange. *Commentary*, 21, November 1957, p.459.
5. From *A Long Way from London*. London: Weidenfeld and Nicolson, 1958. This story was first published as 'Dutchman, Jew, Piccanin', in *Commentary*, 16, September 1953, pp.219-223. The original title demonstrates Jacobson's open intention to interrogate stereotypes.
6. In *Time and Time Again*. London: Andre Deutsch, 1985, Jacobson's collection of autobiographical stories, he describes an incident in which his father throws a

'Greyshirt' off the back of a truck from which the Jew-hater is trying to address a crowd. (p.27).

7. '[O]ther groups in the social environment constitute the frame of reference for evaluating the own group's prestige. The ingroup's prestige depends on the outcome of comparisons between ingroup and relevant outgroups.' Turner, J. and Brown, R. 'Social Status, Cognitive Alternatives, Intergroup Relations'. In Tajfel, H. (ed.), *Differentiation between Social Groups*, London, New York: Academic Press, 1978, p.204.

8. In *A Long way from London* (1958).

9. Compare with a similar situation depicted in *The Beginners*, Chapters 1-3.

10. In *Beggar my Neighbour*. London: Weidenfeld and Nicolson, 1964. The stories in this collection were published earlier in journals.

11. Wisse, R.R. *The Schlemiel as Modern Hero*, 1971; rpt. Chicago and London: The University of Chicago Press, 1980. pp.71-75.
    The Little Man is the title of a novel by the Yiddish author Mendele Mocher Sforim. Examples of fiction in English dealing with the schlemiel are Saul Bellow ed. *Great Jewish Short Stories* (1963) containing ten schlemiel tales; Saul Bellow's *Herzog* (1964), Bernard Malamud's *Idiots First* (1964) and *Pictures of Fidelman* (1969); Philip Roth's *Portnoy's Complaint* (1969) and Norman Podhoretz's *Making It* (1967).
    Sander Gilman discusses the emergence of the figure in non-Yiddish writing during the Enlightenment and particularly in the satiric dramatic writings of the first generation of emancipated Jews in Berlin after the Enlightenment. The schlemiel figure was there used to exorcise the current negative image of the Jew. On to this image the writers could project the self-doubt and insecurity which they felt as outsiders in a hostile culture. See *Jewish Self-Hatred*, pp.107-113.

12. See Mower White, C.J. *Consistency in Cognitive Social Behaviour. An Introduction to Social Psychology*. London: Routledge and Kegan Paul, 1987, p.157.
    See also Sully, J. *An Essay on Laughter*, London: n.p., 1907 cited in Greig, J.Y.T. *The Psychology of Laughter and Comedy*. London: George Allan and Unwin, 1923, p.192.

13. Sartre, J-P. *Anti-Semite and Jew*. 1946; trans. from the French by G.J. Becker. New York: Schocken Books, 1965, p.97.

14. '[Charlie Chaplin] defends himself as best he can with a sleight of hand and a pirouette, but reveals at the same time his sharply painful marginality, his bewilderment and the brutality of the world.' Memmi, A. *The Liberation of the Jew*; trans. from the French by J. Huyn, New York: Orion, 1966, pp.48.

15. Roberts, S. 'At a Distance: Dan Jacobson's South African Fiction'. In Chapman, M., Gardner, C. and Mphahlele E. (eds.), *Perspectives on South African Literature*. Johannesburg: Ad. Donker, 1992, p.219.

16. In *Beggar my Neighbour* (1964).

17. In *Through the Wilderness and other Stories*. New York: Macmillan, 1973. Most of the stories in this collection were published earlier in journals.

18. In *A Long way from London* (1958).
    In his novel, *The Utmost Sail* (1955), Bernard Sachs describes a character, Simon

Sender, who is self-consciously aware that, as a Jew, he is one of those who 'are the product of the criminality of this age ... displaced persons – *luftmenschen*.' (p.95)

19. In *Beggar my Neighbour* (1964).
20. Memmi, A. *The Liberation of the Jew*, p.50.
    There are many theories of what constitutes a 'Jewish joke'. Gilman, for example, maintains that the 'Jewish joke' told either by Jews or by Gentiles, is a means of diffusing anxiety and of presenting in 'softened and refined tones what the mobs in the street are shouting about the Jews.' Gilman, S.L. *Jewish Self-Hatred*. p.259. See essays in Chapman, A.J. and Foot, H.C. (eds.), *It's A Funny Thing, Humour*. Oxford: Pergamon, 1977.
21. Renee Winegarten has stated that *The Beginners* is the first novel in world literature to 'express with exceptional sensibility the impact of Israel on Jews in the Diaspora'. 'The Novels of Dan Jacobson'. *Midstream* 12(5), May 1966, p.72.
22. Jacobson, D. 'A White Liberal Trapped by his Prejudices', p.456.

CHAPTER SEVEN

1. Compare another historical novel written at a similar time – *Westward the Sun* (1942) by Brigid Knight (Mrs Kathleen Henrietta Nash-Webber Sinclair) which is set between 1877 and 1896. Solomon Gluckman – an ambivalent portrait – is a Jewish pedlar, later a Johannesburg financier.
2. Ashmore, R.D. and Del Boca, F.K. 'Conceptual Approaches to Stereotypes and Stereotyping', in Hamilton, D.L. ed. *Cognitive Processes in Stereotyping and Intergroup Behaviour*. New Jersey: Lawrence Erinbaum, 1981, p.21.
3. Like Meninsky, Sir Lionel Phillips was born in London and has been described as 'vivacious and charming; small of stature'. Fraser, M. (ed.), *Some Reminiscences of Lionel Phillips*. Johannesburg: Ad. Donker, 1986 [Original version published 1924] Introduction, p.11. Phillips was well aware of the odium in which the Randlords were held as a result of the 'absence of a generous public spirit on the part of ... a few men, among whom there have been individuals of poor repute [who] have amassed large fortunes ...' (p.143), and he strenuously attempted to counteract this image. Introduction, pp.24-25.
4. An Afrikaans novel – Etienne Le Roux's *Sewe Dae by die Silbersteins* (1962), translated into English as *Seven Days at the Silbersteins* in 1964 – is set in the home of rich Jews, the Silbersteins, who are shown as cultured and intellectual but also wealthy and ostentatious, thereby combining positive and negative stereotypes.
5. A second story, 'Fate and Aunt Rachel', refers to more specific South African issues. It concerns David Smilenski's brother, Benjamin Smiles, who 'changed his name when he came to South Africa, years ago ... Smiles bought a concession in the territory'(p.172). His Aunt Rachel speaks with a 'guttural accent' (p.174).
6. In Herman Charles Bosman's *Willemsdorp* (written in 1951) a chemist is named Hirschberg. In Gerald Gordon's *The Crooked Rain* (1954) a Jewish lawyer is

named Barney Klein. More recent images may be found in Sheila Roberts's *The Weekenders* (1980) where a compassionate doctor is named Dr Steinberg. In Christopher Hope's novel *A Separate Development* (1980) Ralph Swirsky is a chemist and a commercial traveller is named Epstein. In Alison Stewart's novel, *Born into the Country* (1988), Stan Ahrenson is a leftist lawyer. He is 'apparently dedicated to the liberation of people whose equality would severely jeopardize [his] own living standards' (p.53). Although, in this respect, he would seem to represent the positive image, some negativity remains – he is 'a tiny, rotund man with a high voice full of nasal inflections', and he 'lived in the city's affluent white fringe ... [and drove] a shiny beige Mercedes Benz. Last time, he had one of those Italian cars, dark green but whatever its colour, expensive' (p.53). In Caroline Slaughter's *The Innocents* (1986), Abe Greenberg is another highly regarded and clever leftist lawyer who defends blacks accused of terrorism.

7. Pogrebin, L.C. op cit, p.259.
8. Prell, R.E. op cit, p.340.
9. All page references are to the version published in *Learning to Fly*.
10. Soweto slang, used with a measure of irony, for fashionable attire is 'Jewish'. Barron, C. 'A Flock of Pidgins', *Sunday Times*, 29 January 1995, p.8.
11. Pogrebin, L.C. op cit, p.233.
12. Fisch, H. *The Dual Image* (1971), p.131.
13. For a discussion of this sub-genre of Jewish-American literature which depicts the immigration of a family to America, the investment of hopes in the children and relationships within a family undergoing stress and conflict, see Sherman, B. *The Invention of the Jew*. New York and London: Thomas Yoseloff, 1969, pp.22-30.

CHAPTER EIGHT

1. Herman, S.N. *Jewish Identity*. London: Sage, 1977, p.183.
2. 'A Writer in South Africa: Nadine Gordimer'. *London Magazine*, May 1965, p.23.
3. Wagner, K. *Rereading Nadine Gordimer. Text and Subtext in the Novels*. South Africa: Maskew Miller Longman, Witwatersrand University Press in conjunction with Indiana Press, 1994, p.36.
4. Gordimer N. 'A South African Childhood'. The *New Yorker*, 16 October 1954, pp.111-116.
5. Stein, P. and Purkey, M. 'So *Nu*? What's Jewish? Sophiatown meets the Jewish Girl'. *Jewish Affairs* 46(2), September 1991, p.77.
6. 'On Freedom, Communism and Judaism. A Conversation between Nadine Gordimer and Natan Sharansky'. *The Jerusalem Report*, 24 October 1991, pp.5-7.
   An early story,'The Watcher of the Dead', first published in *Jewish Affairs* in 1948, was publicised as 'her first story with a Jewish theme'(p.31). It is a sketch of a young girl's reaction to the employment, according to Jewish custom, of a *wacher* to watch over the corpse of her recently deceased grandmother. The story was reprinted in The *New Yorker* (1951) and subsequently in *The Soft Voice of the Serpent* (1953) where acknowledgments are made to The *New Yorker* but significantly, not to *Jewish*

Affairs. For the international and largely non-Jewish market some detail of the story have been changed. The Jewish aspects have been distanced from the narrator who is a version of the narrators of *The Lying Days* and 'The Defeated'. The narrator claims: 'If Mother had ever known any Jewish customs – and I doubt it – she had forgotten them long before we were born ... being Jewish had simply meant that we had a free half hour while the other children at our convent school went to catechism' (p.57). This chimes with the statements Gordimer has made about her own upbringing.

7. Newman, J. *Nadine Gordimer*. London and New York: Routledge, 1988, p.14. 'Gordimer calls herself Jewish in an early interview, though it was her father (and not her mother) who was a Latvian or Lithuanian Jew, and despite the fact that she says she was not given a Jewish education.' Wagner, K. op cit, note 61, p.241.

8. Wagner, K. op cit, p.36.

9. *The Jerusalem Report*, 24 October 1991, p.7.

10. The child is fascinated by the 'native' shop. In a parallel passage in 'The Defeated', the narrator similarly reports: 'I would saunter along the shopwindows amongst them, and for me there was a quickening of glamour about the place ...'(p.195). The transfiguring word 'glamour' is crucial in projecting the narrator's, and the author's, idealisation of black experience – as sharp contrast to the demotion of Jewish experience.

11. Clingman, S. *The Novels of Nadine Gordimer: History from the Inside*. Johannesburg: Ravan, 1986, p.222.

12. Goffman, E. *Stigma: Notes on the Management of Spoiled Identity*. 1973; rpt. Harmondsworth: Penguin, 1979.

13. Sartre, J-P. *Anti-Semite and Jew*. 1948; trans. Becker, G.J., rpt. New York: Schocken Books, 1974. [First published as *Reflexions sur la Question Juive*. Paris: Paul Morihen, 1946], p.91.

14. See Rock P. *The Making of Symbolic Interactionism*. London and Basingstoke: Macmillan, 1979, pp.129-132; Jones E.E. et al. eds. *Social Stigma The Psychology of Marked Relationships*. New York: W.H. Freeman, 1984. pp.32-36; Tajfel, H. *Human Groups and Social Categories*, pp.254-256. Shibutani, T. *Society and Personality*. New Jersey: Prentice-Hall, 1961. p.436; Katz, J. *Jewish Emancipation and Self Emancipation*. Philadelphia, New York, Jerusalem: The Jewish Publication Society, 1986, p.131; Katz, J. *Out of the Ghetto. The Social Background of Jewish Emancipation 1770-1870*. Cambridge Massachusetts: Harvard University Press, 1973, p.6. Philip Roth's novel of Jewish-American identity conflict, *The Counterlife* (London: 1987, rpt. Harmondsworth: Penguin Books, 1988), has a graphic description of the symptoms of *Jewish* 'spoiled identity' as: 'Jewish cringing, deference, diplomacy, apprehension, alienation, self-pity, self-satire, self-mistrust, depression, clowning, bitterness, nervousness, inwardness, hypercriticalness, hypertouchiness, social anxiety, social assimilation ... in short ... all the Jewish "abnormalities," those peculiarities of self-division whose traces remain imprinted in just about every ... Jew ...' (p.124).

15. The notion of slippage between in- and out-groups is, of course, not confined to the differences between Jews and Gentiles. It is well documented in the study of

American Negroes who certainly until the black power movement of the 1960s, and arguably thereafter, suffered from a communal sense of stigma, and have striven to approximate the social norm of 'white' in their appearance, values and aspirations. Pickwoad, S. 'Black People's Adaptive Behaviour and Self-Hate', in *Patterns of Prejudice* 9(2), March-April 1975. pp.1-19.

16. Clingman has noted with what he describes as 'some surprise' a racialistic passage in an unfinished and unpublished novel, written in 1946. The story focuses on stereotypical material: one character is a Jew, at one time a concession store-keeper who has become a wealthy director of companies. A group of coloured people is described as a 'squalid, degenerate meeting-place of black and white blood; the common ground of commercial sex which is the only level upon which the ancient taboos are swept aside and the two bloods may meet' (p.25). Clingman comments on the lack of irony in the passage and identifies the dis-course of a 'paranoid-blood consciousness'. Clingman finds this baffling since the passage occurs shortly after a reference in the story to the Holocaust. He is forced to the conclusion that the extract shows the degree to which the young Gordimer was held within the dominant patterns of white ideology in South Africa. He calls it 'an extraordinary reference point – Gordimer's curiously unconscious low-water mark'. Clingman, S., op cit, pp.25-26.

17. *The Jerusalem Report*, p.5.

18. Pogrebin, L.C. op cit, pp.228-231.

19. See subtitle of Clingman, S. *The Novels of Nadine Gordimer. History from the Inside*. op cit.

20. The early fiction is remarkable for the number of stereotypes and stereotypical sit-uations used. In *The Lying Days*, she repeats the situation of the sentimental or sexual relationship between the Gentile and the Jew when describing the affection that develops between Helen and the young Joel. In 'The Defeated' Miriam Saiyetowitz, daughter of the concession storekeeper, is a kugel. She 'had married a doctor ... [and lived] ... in one of the more expensive suburbs ...' (p.211). Her appearance is predictable. She has a 'large, dark-featured face' (p.207), and 'beau-tiful breasts' (p.206). A photograph shows her to be 'carefully made-up and framed in a good hairdresser's version of her dark hair ... [with] a smooth hand, wearing large, plain, expensive diamond rings. Her bosom was proud and rounded now – a little too heavy, a little overripe in the climate of ease.' (p.211) The obses-sive reference to diamonds – stock reference of the negative image – recurs in the story. The narrator suggests that the 'poor' Mr. Saiyetowitz is not a typical conces-sion storekeeper: 'Storekeepers with this quality of peasant craft made money all about Mr. Saiyetowitz, bought houses and motorcars and banded their wives' retired hands with diamonds ... ' (p.207).

Despite the fact that the characters she delineates most frequently in her writing belong to the liberal or radical left in Johannesburg in which Jews have always been prominent, Gordimer hardly touched on the subject of the Jews between the 1950s and 1980s, at a period when other Jewish authors also remained signifi-cantly silent. Some Jewish characters are Boaz Davis in *Occasion for Loving* (1963); a refugee and a commercial traveller in the short stories, 'Son-in-law' and

'Through Time and Distance' respectively in her collection *Not for Publication* (1965); in her later fiction a lawyer, Metkin, who features briefly in *My Son's Story* (1990).

21. Wade, M. 'Gordimer's Rainbow'. Rev. of Clingman, S. *The Novels of Nadine Gordimer: History from the Inside* and N. Gordimer, *A Sport of Nature. Southern African Review of Books*, July 1987, pp.13-14.

22. Other sketches of Jews appear in Becker's work, in her second novel, *The Union* (1971) and 'The Real Princess', first published in *The Purple Renoster*, Winter 1968. In these texts there is no particular animus against Jews.

23. *The Guardian*, 2 September 1988.

24. See, for example, Peter Conrad, *The Observer*, 11 September 1988.

25. '*Middlepost*: Antony Sher', *Business Day*, 14 November 1988.

26. In an article, 'South Africa's Chosen People'. *The Guardian*, 2 September 1988.

27. Bernstein, H. op cit, pp.359-361.

28. See 'The New Israelite Hospital in Hamburg' (1842) where Heine writes about the thousand-year-old family complaint ...
Incurable, profound suffering! No help can be looked for from steam-baths, shower-baths, or all the impediments
of surgery, or all the medicines which this house offers its sick inmates ...
In the translation from S.S. Prawer in *Heine's Jewish Comedy*. Oxford: Clarendon Press, 1983, p.433.

29. Gilman, S.L. *Difference and Pathology*, pp.20, 27.

30. Jack Tinker quoting Sher in *The Star*, 27 July 1990.

31. 'Whoever detests the Jewish character, detests it first of all in himself ... Hatred, like love, is a projected phenomenon: you hate that person who you feel reminds you unpleasantly of yourself.' Weininger, O. *Geschlecht und Charakter*. Vienna: W. Braumuller, 1920. Cited in Meyer, M.A. *Jewish Identity in the Modern World*. Seattle and London: University of Washington Press, 1990, p.42.

32. Sartre, J-P. op. cit, pp.106-107.

33. Ludovici, A.M. *The Secret of Laughter*. London: Constable, 1932, pp.5, 82-87.

34. Darwin, C. *The Expression of the Emotions in Animals*. London: 1904, [n.p.] Cited in Greig, J.Y.T. *The Psychology of Laughter and Comedy*. London: George Allen and Unwin, 1923, p.120.

35. Gilman, S.L. *Jewish Self-Hatred*, pp.286-289, 361-362.

36. Gordimer's radical involvement is well known; Becker has written extensively condemning terrorism, especially that of the PLO; Sher returned to South Africa only after the change to democratic government and expressed the intention of working for the upliftment of non-racial theatre.

CHAPTER NINE

1. See for example a transcript of a tape recording with Chaim Schultz. Trading among black tribesmen in the 1920s near Pretoria, he has trouble with a boycott of his store in protest against a price increase. '[T]he chief invited me to a

friendly meeting in his kraal' (p.38), he says. The boycott is lifted. A 1984/B11.17, Kaplan-Kushlik Foundation.
In the context of trade, Jews were referred to as 'ma Juta'. See Sol T. Plaatje to Chief Silas Molema, 31 August 1917. Plaatje Papers, A979 Da 44. Manuscript Collection, University of the Witwatersrand Library.

2. In his autobiography, *Blame me on History* (1963), Bloke Modisane describes how the first whites to befriend him were Phil[l]ip Stein, Ellen Hellmann and Dr 'Bodo' Koch. Although Modisane does not say so, they are all Jews.

3. See Basner M. *Am I an African? The Political Memoirs of H M Basner.* Johannesburg: Witwatersrand University Press, 1993, p.179.
In 1988 Issy Pinshaw reported that '[t]he shift of the Jewish community from the PFP to the National Party is discernable from elections over the past two and a half years. 'I believe the white community ... of which the Jewish community forms a part, is closing ranks in the country ...' he observed. Hoffman T. and Fischer, A. (eds.), *The Jews of South Africa. What Future?* South Africa: Southern Books, 1988, p.298. There have been numerous Jewish members of the National Party. Note, also, the common usage among Jews of pejorative Yiddish words like 'shwartzer', 'soggen', and 'shocherdike' to refer to a black person.

4. Edelstein, M.E. *What do Young Africans Think?* Johannesburg: Institute of Race Relations, 1972. Cited in Shimoni, G. op. cit, pp.362, 412.

5. Hoffman T. and Fischer, A. eds., op cit, pp.28-30.

6. Ibid, pp.33-34.

7. 'The Attitude of White and Black Elites towards Black Anti-Semitism' Opinion Surveys Research for a New South Africa, Pretoria 8-14 August 1990, cited in Dubb, A. and Shain M. 'South Africa' in American Jewish Year Book 1992, ed. Singer, D. Philadelphia, 1992, cited in Shain, M. *The Roots of Antisemitism*, p.153.

8. Cited in Pogrebin, L.C. op.cit, pp.275-276.

9. Compare Ray Kaynich in Sipho Sepamla's *The Root is One* (1979). This character may be constructed as a Jew, but the name is not conclusive and no reference is made to his being a Jew. He is sexually attracted to a black woman, and when warned about 'the law' replies 'I'll quit for Europe!' (p.7).

10. Compare similar treatments of Jewish women with a social conscience in the work of some white writers. There is, for example, the sentimental treatment of the Jewish social worker in Stephen Gray's *Caltrop's Desire* who visits Caltrop in hospital:

> 'Mrs Feinstein, I'm sorry about your people. I mean, during the last war, the gas chambers and everything.'
>
> 'Oh,' she replied, 'that. Well, yes, it's terrible, you know, but we're used to it, you know. My husband, he lost his sister and his two little nieces' ...
>
> When she had gone I ... burst into a sob. I shall say a kaddish for her in-laws when I'm on the other side ... (p.97)

See also the figure of Miss Bentwisch, half-Jewish daughter of a Jewish mining magnate who gives large sums of money to African and 'coloured' charities in Dan Jacobson's *The Evidence of Love* (1959).

11. Other fleeting and neutral references to Jews with stereotypical occupations are the shopkeepers in Ezekiel's Mphahlele's autobiographical work, *Down Second Avenue* (1959), where he refers to 'Goldstein's general store' (p.22) and a 'Jewish millinery shop' (p.176); and the professional, the psychiatrist a 'Swiss-German Jew' (p.41) in Lewis Nkosi's novel, *Mating Birds* (1987).

12. Compare the treatment of Solly, the Jewish owner of the fish and chips shop in District Six in Rive's story, 'Rain'. In an earlier version, published in 1977 (Rive, R. *Selected Writings*), Solly is identified as a Jew, and some animosity between the Jew and his 'coloured' customers is suggested:

> 'You blooming Jews are always making coloured people out [sic].'
> 'Go to hell!' Solly dismissed the attack on his race ... (p.12).

However, in the later version of the story in *Advance Retreat. Selected Short Stories* (1983), this passage has been omitted, possibly in an effort to remove any suggestion of animus towards Jews, both on the part of the character and on that of the author.

A fleeting ambivalent image of an Jew features in Alex La Guma's 'A Walk in the Night' from *A Walk in the Night and Other Stories*. 'Mister Ike' serves in a pub. 'He greeted every customer with a phlegmatic geniality' which yet ambivalently inspired among his coloured customers 'a sort of servile familiarity'. (p.13)

13. In Hoffman, T. and Fischer, A., op. cit, pp.104-105.

14. Ibid, p.15.

15. Expression used in the blurb of her novel, *Ties of Blood* (1989).

EPILOGUE

1. Cheyette, B. op cit, pp 1-12.

2. What few Jews there are in South African fiction since 1992 have hardly been noteworthy as Jews. The principal character of Christopher Hope's *The Love Songs of Nathan J. Swirsky* (1993) is a sympathetically drawn Jewish pharmacist, though his Jewishness is hardly important. In Nadine Gordimer's *None to Accompany Me* (1994) a Jewish lawyer, Lazar Feldman, plays a tiny part. In a recent article Todd Pitock has exposed Gordimer's treatment of Feldman, arguing that he is shown as a 'posturing liberal'. 'After volunteering to accompany Vera Stark, the protagonist, to the funeral of a Black activist, he comes up with "the perfect alibi... the flu virus"'. Pitock highlights a curious episode in the novel where Vera's 'virile' lover, at first thought to be a Jew, is literally the son of a Nazi. Pitock, T. 'Unloved Back Home' ('Nadine Gordimer and the Perils of Political Fiction'). *Tikkun*, 10 (3), 1995, p.78.

———•———

BIBLIOGRAPHY

A: PRIMARY MATERIAL
(South African Fiction which features Jewish characters)

Abrahams, L. 'The Messiah'. In *The Celibacy of Felix Greenspan*. Johannesburg: Bateleur, 1977, pp.27-30.

Abrahams, P. 'Brother Jew'. In *Dark Testament*. London: George Allen and Unwin, 1942, pp.17-21.

———— 'Hatred'. In *Dark Testament*, pp.77-92.

———— 'Jewish Sister'. In *Dark Testament*, pp.27-33

———— *The Path of Thunder*. New York: Harper, 1948.

———— *This Island Now*. London: Faber, 1966.

Barwin, V. 'A Convent Jewess'. In *Millionaires and Tatterdemalions: Stories of Jewish Life in South Africa*. London: Edgar Goldston, 1952, pp.81-97.

———— 'Gold from Ophir'. In *Millionaires and Tatterdemalions*, pp.35-67.

———— 'Rejected and Admitted'. In *Millionaires and Tatterdemalions*, pp.71-78.

———— 'Subjects of the Czar'. In *Millionaires and Tatterdemalions*, pp.115-153.

———— 'The Call'. In *Millionaires and Tatterdemalions*, pp.101-111.

———— 'The Emigrant Ship'. In *Millionaires and Tatterdemalions*, pp.9-32.

Becker, J. *The Keep*. London: Chatto and Windus, 1967.

———— 'The Real Princess'. In Ricci, D. (ed.) *Reef of Time*. Johannesburg: Ad. Donker, 1986, pp.156-168. First published in *The Purple Renoster*, Winter 1968.

———— *The Union*. London: Chatto and Windus, 1971.

Black, S. *The Dorp*. London: Andrew Melrose, 1920.

———— *The Golden Calf. A Story of the Diamond Fields*. London: T. Werner Laurie, 1925.

Blore, H. *An Imperial Light Horseman*. London: C. Arthur Pearson, 1900.

Boetie, D. *Familiarity is the Kingdom of the Lost*. London: Cresset, 1969.

Bosman, H.C. *Willemsdorp*. Uncompleted in 1951; 6th ed. Cape Town: Human and Rousseau, 1976.

Brett Young, F. *The City of Gold*. 1939; rpt. London: Mayfair Books, 1966.

Brown, J.A. *The White Locusts*. Johannesburg: Jonathan Ball, 1983.

Cloete, S. *Turning Wheels*. 1937; rpt. London: Collins, 1974.

Davidson, M. *Jewish Merry Go Round*. Johannesburg: The Free Press, 1959.
_____ *My Jewish Clients*. Johannesburg: Eagle, 1953.
Dhlomo, H I E. 'Farmer and Servant'. In Visser, N. and Couzens, T. (eds), *Collected Works*. Johannesburg: Ravan, 1985, pp444-466.
Dikobe, M. *The Marabi Dance*. London: Heinemann, 1973.
Eady, W.T. *IDB or the Adventures of Solomon Davis*. London: Chapman and Hall, 1887.
Essop, A. 'The Metamorphosis'. In *Noorjehan and Other Stories*. Johannesburg: Ravan, 1990, pp.23-41.
_____ 'Two Worlds'. In *The Hajji and Other Stories*. Johannesburg: Ravan, 1978, pp.98-102.
Fraser, C. *Saartje*. London: Arthur H. Stockwell, n.d.
Freed, L. *Home Ground*. 1986; rpt. Harmondsworth: Penguin Books, 1988.
Gordimer, N. *A Sport of Nature*. Cape Town: David Philip, 1987.
_____ 'A Watcher of the Dead'. *Jewish Affairs* 3(4), April 1948, pp.31-35. Rpt. in *The Soft Voice of the Serpent*, London: Victor Gollancz, 1953, pp.56-67.
_____ 'My Father's Story'. In *Jump and other Stories*. Cape Town: David Philip, 1991, pp.57-66.
_____ *My Son's Story*. Cape Town: David Philip and Johannesburg: Taurus, 1990.
_____ *None to Accompany Me*. Great Britain: Bloomsbury, 1994.
_____ 'Son-in-Law'. In *Not for Publication*. London: Victor Gollancz, 1965, pp.22-30.
_____ 'The Defeated'. In *The Soft Voice of the Serpent*, pp.194-212.
_____ *The Lying Days*. London: Victor Gollancz, 1953.
_____ 'The Visit'. In *Jewish Chronicle*, 9 September 1966, p.39.
_____ 'Through Time and Distance'. In *Not for Publication*, pp.48-57.
Gordon, G. *The Crooked Rain*. London: Macdonald, 1954.
Goudvis, B. *Little Eden*. Cape Town: CNA, 1949.
_____ 'Mousha'. In *The Mistress of Mooiplaas and Other Stories*. Cape Town: CNA, 1956, pp.38-53.
Gray, S. *Caltrop's Desire*. London: Rex Collings, 1981.
Griffith, G.[C.] 'A Run to Freetown'. In *Knaves of Diamonds: Being Tales of Mine and Veld*. London: C. Arthur Pearson, 1899, pp.23-54.
_____ 'The Diamond Dog'. In *Knaves of Diamonds*, pp.1-22.
_____ 'The King's Rose Diamond'. In *Knaves of Diamonds*, pp.58-85.
Hemyng S.B. *Jack Harkaway in the Transvaal: or, Fighting for the Flag*. London: E.J. Brett, 1902.
Hirson, D. *The House Next Door to Africa*. Cape Town: David Philip, 1986.
Hoffman, M. 'Lost her Head'. In Sherman, J. (ed.), *From a Land Far Off: South African Yiddish Stories in English Translation*. Cape Town: Jewish Publications – South Africa, 1987, pp.33-49.
Hope, C. *A Separate Development*. Johannesburg: Ravan, 1980.
_____ 'On the Frontier'. In *Private Parts and Other Tales*. Johannesburg: Bateleur, 1981, pp.156-174, and *Learning to Fly*. London: Minerva, 1990, pp.84-100.
_____ 'The Kugel'. In *Private Parts and Other Tales*, pp.139-155, and *Learning to Fly*, pp.110-124.

_____ *The Love Songs of Nathan J. Swirsky*. London: Macmillan, 1993.

Jacobi, C. 'A Real Kavalsky'. In *A Real Kavalsky and Other Stories*. Cape Town, Pretoria: HAUM, 1972, pp.7-72. First published in Holland in Dutch in 1966. Trans. by author.

Jacobson. D. 'A Day in the Country'. In *A Long Way from London*. London: Weidenfeld and Nicolson, 1958, pp.19-30.

_____ 'An Apprenticeship'. In *Beggar my Neighbour*. London: Weidenfeld and Nicolson, 1964, pp.74-84.

_____ 'Droit de Seigneur'. In *Beggar my Neighbour*, pp.7-21.

_____ *The Beginners*. London: Weidenfeld and Nicolson, 1966.

_____ *The Evidence of Love*. 1959; rpt. London: Weidenfeld and Nicolson, 1960.

_____ 'The Example of Lipi Lippmann'. In *Beggar my Neighbour*, pp.62-73.

_____ *The Price of Diamonds*. London: Weidenfeld and Nicolson, 1957.

_____ 'The Promised Land'. In *A Long Way from London*. London: Weidenfeld and Nicolson, 1958, pp.172-190.

_____ 'The Zulu and the Zeide'. In *A Long Way from London*, pp.102-121.

_____ 'Through the Wilderness'. In *Through the Wilderness and other Stories*. New York: Macmillan, 1973, pp.1-38.

Knight, Brigid (Mrs Kathleen Henrietta Nash-Webber). *Westward the Sun*. New York: Crowell, 1942. In England *The Sun climbs Slowly*. London: Cassell, 1942.

La Guma, A. *A Walk in the Night and Other Stories*. 1962, rpt. Cape Town: David Philip, Africasouth Paperbacks 1991.

Lerner, L. *The Englishmen*. London: Hamish Hamilton, 1959.

Leroux, E. *Seven Days at the Silbersteins*. Trans. C. Eglington, South Africa: CNA, 1964. First published in Afrikaans by Human and Rousseau, 1962.

Levinson, B. 'A Doornfontein Memory'. *Jewish Affairs* 30(4), April 1975, pp.29-32.

Ludman, B. *The Day of the Kugel*. Cape Town : Maskew Miller Longman, 1989.

Manion, S. *The Greater Hunger*. Ilfracombe: Arthur H. Stockwell, 1964.

Markowitz A. *Facing North*. Johannesburg: Paul te Dera, 1949.

_____ *Market Street*. Johannesburg: Fieldhall, 1959.

Matshoba, M. 'Behind the Veil of Complacency'. In *Call me not a Man*. Johannesburg: Ravan, 1979, pp.188-198.

Metrowich, F.C. *Scotty Smith: South Africa's Robin Hood*. Cape Town: Books of Africa, 1962.

Miller, W. *Man in the Background*. London: Jonathan Cape, 1958.

Millin, S.G. *The Coming of the Lord*. London: Constable, 1928.

Misheiker, B. *Strange Odyssey*. London: Harrap, 1952.

Modisane, B. *Blame me on History*. 1963; rpt. Johannesburg, Ad. Donker, 1986.

Moss R. *The Family Reunion*. New York: Scribners, 1973.

Motluatse, M. (ed.), *Casey and Co. Selected Writings of Casey 'Kid' Motsisi*. Johannesburg: Ravan, 1983.

Murray, A.A. *Anybody's Spring*. London: Andre Deutsch, 1959.

Nash, T.E. *The Geyer Brood*. London: Cassel, 1946.

Ndebele, N. 'The Music of the Violin'. In *Fools and Other Stories*. Johannesburg: Ravan, 1983, pp.124-151.

Newman, J. *With Ink in the Book.* Johannesburg: L. Rubin, 1958.

Nkosi, L. *Mating Birds.* Johannesburg: Ravan, 1987.

'Old Diamond Field Days: The Pioneer Talks', *Owl*, 5 (23), 8 June 1900, p.324.

Parker, G. *The Judgement House.* London: Methuen, 1913.

Paton, A. *Too Late the Phalarope.* Cape Town: Frederick L. Cannon/Jonathan Cape, 1953.

Rive, R. *'Buckingham Palace', District Six.* Cape Town: David Philip, 1986.

_____ 'Rain'. In *Advance, Retreat. Selected Short Stories.* Cape Town: David Philip, 1983. pp.10-19. Also published in Rive, R. *Selected Writings: Stories, Essays, Plays.* Johannesburg: Ad. Donker, 1977, pp.11-19.

_____ 'Riva'. In *Advance, Retreat,* pp.59-72.

Roberts, S. *The Weekenders.* Johannesburg: Bateleur, 1980.

Rooke, D. *Diamond Jo.* London: Victor Gollancz, 1965.

Sachs, B. *The Utmost Sail.* Johannesburg: Kayor, 1955.

Schreiner, O. *From Man to Man.* London: T. Fisher Unwin, 1926; rpt. London: Virago Press, 1982.

_____ *Undine.* London: Ernest Benn, 1929.

Scully, W.C. *Between Sun and Sand. A Tale of an African Desert.* Cape Town: Juta, 1898.

_____ *The Harrow. (South Africa 1900-1902): A Novel.* Cape Town: Nasionale Pers, 1921.

Segal A. *Johannesburg Friday.* London: Geoffrey Bles, 1954.

Serote, M. *To Every Birth its Blood.* Johannesburg: Ravan, 1981.

Shaban, S. *The Golden Corn.* London: Grosvenor, 1970.

Sher, A. *Middlepost.* London: Chatto and Windus, 1988.

_____ *The Indoor Boy.* London: Chatto and Windus, 1991.

Simon, B. 'Our War'. In *Jo'burg Sis!.* Johannesburg: Bateleur, 1974, pp.165-180.

Slaughter C. *The Innocents.* Harmondsworth: Penguin, 1986.

Slovo, G. *Ties of Blood,* 1989; rpt. London: Headline, 1990.

Smith, P. 'Anna's Marriage'. In *The Little Karoo.* 1925; rpt. Cape Town: A.A. Balkema, 1981, pp.54-63.

_____ *The Beadle.* New York: Vanguard, 1927.

_____ 'The Miller'. In *The Little Karoo.* 1925; rpt. Cape Town: A.A. Balkema, 1981, pp.31-40.

Smith. W. *The Sound of Thunder.* 1966. rpt. London: Pan Books, 1973.

Sowden, L. *Kop of Gold.* Johannesburg, APB, 1955.

_____ *The Crooked Bluegum.* London: The Bodley Head, 1955.

Stewart, A. *Born into the Country.* Johannesburg: Justified, 1988.

'Stories of Strange People' No 5. 'Sam Saulinski'. *Owl*, 6 November 1892.

Tlali, M. *Muriel at Metropolitan.* Johannesburg, Ravan, 1975.

Vescelius-Sheldon, L. *An I.D.B. in South Africa.* New York: John W. Lovell, 1888.

Walker, O. *Wanton City.* London: Werner Laurie, 1949.

Westrup, W. *The Debt.* London: Aston Rivers, 1912.

_____ *The Toll.* London: Hurst and Blackett, 1914.

Wicht, H. 'Fate and Aunt Rachel'. In *The Mountain*. Cape Town: Howard Timmins, 1966, pp.171-178.

_____ 'The Wanderer's Coin'. In *The Mountain*, pp.15-21.

Wicomb, Z. *You Can't Get Lost in Cape Town*. London: Virago, 1987.

Wilhelm, P. 'Dolphins'. In *LM and other stories*. Johannesburg: Ravan, 1975, pp.43-53.

Zwi, R. *Another Year in Africa*. Johannesburg: Bateleur, 1980.

_____ *Exiles*. Johannesburg: Ad. Donker, 1984.

_____ *The Inverted Pyramid*. Johannesburg: Ravan, 1981.

_____ *The Umbrella Tree*. Australia: Penguin Books Australia, 1990.

B: AUTOBIOGRAPHICAL AND SEMI-AUTOBIOGRAPHICAL TEXTS

Basner, M. *Am I an African?*. The Political Memoirs of H M Basner. Johannesburg: Witwatersrand University Press, 1993.

Boon, M.J. *Jottings by the Way or Boon's Madness on the Road. Being a Philosophical View of Life, Past, Present and to Come, in the Orange Free State, Natal and Cape Colony*. London: George Standring, 1884.

Cohen, L. *Reminiscences of Kimberley*. London: Century, 1911.

_____ *Reminiscences of Johannesburg and London*. London: Robert Holden, 1924; rpt. Johannesburg: African Book Society, 1976. Foreword by Eric Rosenthal.

Frack, I. *Every Man must Play a Part*. Cape Town, Purnell, 1970.

Froude, J.A. 'Leaves from a South African Journal: – The Diamond Fields'. In Short Stories on Great Subjects, IV, London: Longmans Green, 1874, pp.531-543.

Goldblatt, L. *It was but Yesterday: The Story of a Lithuanian Village*. Johannesburg, Kayor, 1951.

Goudvis, B. 'In the Days of my Youth'. *South African Rosh Hashona Annual and Jewish Year Book*, Johannesburg: n.p., 1932, pp.5-7. [Photocopy].

_____ *South African Odyssey*. [196?] Unpublished typescript.

_____ 'Some Early Reminiscences of South African Jewish life'. *Jewish Affairs* 11(4), April 1956, pp.20-25.

Green, L.G. *Full Many a Glorious Morning; a Recent Journey by Rail and Road in Four Countries of Southern Africa*. Cape Town: Howard Timmins, 1968.

Henochberg, A.J. *An Old Stager's Memoirs*. South Africa: CNA, 1933.

Jacobson, D. *Time and Time Again*. London: Andre Deutsch, 1985.

Kentridge, M. *I Recall*. Johannesburg: The Free Press, 1959.

Levin, M. *From Vilna to Johannesburg*. Johannesburg: Beacon, 1965.

Levinson, I. *The Untold Story*. Johannesburg: Kruger, 1958.

Leviseur, S. *Memories*. Ed. by K. Schoeman, Cape Town and Johannesburg: Human and Rousseau, 1982.

_____ *Ouma Looks Back*. Cape Town: Unie-volkspers, 1944.

Lewin, H. *Bandiet*. London: Barrie and Jenkins Ltd., 1974; rpt. London: Heinemann, 1981.

'Margaret's Piece'. In *You'd Prefer me not to mention it ... The Lives of Four Jewish Daughters of Refugees*. London: Jewish Women's History Group, 1983.

Misheiker, B. *Days of October*. Johannesburg (n.d. 1973?)

Mphahlele, E. *Down Second Avenue*. London: Faber, 1959.

Millin, S.G. *The Night is Long*. London: Faber, 1941.

Modisane, B. *Blame Me on History*. 1963; rpt. Johannesburg: Ad. Donker, 1986.

Mokgatle, N. *The Autobiography of an Unknown South African*. Berkeley and Los Angeles: University of California Press, 1971.

Payton, C.A. ('Sarcelle of "The Field"'), *The Diamond Diggings of South Africa. A Personal and Practical Account*. London: Horace Cox, 1872.

Sachs, B. *A Multitude of Dreams. A Semi-Autobiographical Study*. Johannesburg: Kayor, 1949.

_____ *Mist of Memory. An Autobiography*. London: Vallentine, Mitchell, 1973.

Slosberg, B. *Pagan Tapestry*. London: Rich and Cowan, 1940.

Searelle, L. (pseud. I Israels) *Tales of the Transvaal*. London: T. Fisher Unwin, [1896].

Smith. P. *A.B. '... a minor marginal note'*. London: Jonathan Cape, 1933.

_____ *South African Diary*. 17 August 1913 – 23 May 1914. Pauline Smith Papers, A1353. Manuscript Collection, University of the Witwatersrand Library. Photographic copy. Original in Jagger Library, University of Cape Town.

Solomon, B. *Time Remembered*. Cape Town: Howard Timmins, 1968.

Sonnenberg, M. *The Way I Saw It*. Cape Town: Howard Timmins, 1957.

C: WORKS OF ENGLISH OR AMERICAN WRITERS

Dickens, C. *Great Expectations* 1861; rpt. Ed. with an introduction by James Gibson, London: Macmillan. 1982.

_____ *Oliver Twist*. 1837-1839; rpt. London: Thomas Nelson and Sons, 1945.

Du Maurier, George. *Trilby* 1894; rpt. Alexander, P. ed. *Svengali. George du Maurier's Trilby*. London: W.H. Allen, 1980.

Eliot, G. *Daniel Deronda*. 1876; rpt. Harmondsworth: Penguin, 1986.

Roth, P. *The Counterlife*. London: 1987; rpt. Harmondsworth: Penguin, 1988.

D: NOVELS BY JEWISH WRITERS DEALING WITH BLACK EXPERIENCE

Altman, P. *Law of the Vultures*. London: Jonathan Cape, 1952.

Bloom, H. *Episode in the Transvaal*. London: Collins, 1956.

Byron, R. (pseud.) *Hamilton Avenue*. London: Constable, 1957.

Gordon, G. *Four People: A Novel of South Africa*. Cape Town and Johannesburg: Purnell, 1964.

_____ *Let the Day Perish*. London: Methuen, 1952.

Hendriks, K. (M. Goldman). *Duiker Bay*. Cape Town: Ark, 1956.

_____ *The Bend in the Road.* Cape Town: Howard Timmins, 1953.

May, H.J. (H.J. Schlosberg) and Williams, G. *I am Black: The Story of Shabala.* London: Cassel, 1936.

Sand, F. *My Son Africa.* Los Angeles: Sherbourne, 1965.

Stein, S. *Second Class Taxi.* 1958; rpt. Cape Town: David Philip, 1983.

E: OTHER REFERENCES CITED OR CONSULTED

Abel, E.C. *The Roots of Anti-Semitism.* London: Associated University Presses, 1975.

Ackerman, N. W. and Ackerman, J. M. *Anti-Semitism and Emotional Disorder: A Psychoanalytic Interpretation.* New York: Harper, 1950.

Adey, D. *Companion to South African English Literature.* Johannesburg: Ad. Donker, 1986.

Adler, T. 'A History of the Jewish Workers Club'. In Papers presented at the African Studies Seminar, University of the Witwatersrand. University of the Witwatersrand, Johannesburg: African Studies Institute, 1977.

_____ 'Lithuania's Diaspora: The Johannesburg Jewish Workers Club, 1928-1984'. *Journal of Southern African Studies* 6 (1), October, 1979, pp.70-92.

Adorno, T.W. et al. *The Authoritarian Personality.* New York: Harper, 1950.

Ainley, S.C., Becker, G. and Coleman, L.M. *The Dilemma of Difference: A Multidisciplinary View of Stigma.* New York: Plenum, 1986.

Allport, G. *The Nature of Prejudice.* Cambridge Massachusetts: Addison-Wesley, 1954.

Al-Raheb, H. *The Zionist Character in the English Novel.* London: Zed Books, 1985.

Alter, R. 'Emancipation, Enlightenment and All That'. *Commentary* 53(2), February 1972, pp.62-68.

Angove, J. *In the Early Days. Pioneer Life on the South African Diamond Fields.* Kimberley and London: Handel House, 1910.

'Anti-Semitism in South Africa'. Jewish Board of Deputies Pamphlet, August 1988, pp.1-4.

'Anti-Semitic Writings'. From the Board's Report to the Annual Congress. *Jewish Affairs* 13(3), March 1958, p.43.

Arkin, M. 'Re-evaluating South African Zionism'. *Jewish Affairs* 46(4), December 1991, pp.23-27.

_____ ed. *South African Jewry: A Contemporary Survey.* Cape Town: Oxford University Press, 1984.

Aschman, G. 'Oudtshoorn in the Early Days', in Saron, G. and Hotz, L. eds. op. cit., pp.121-137.

Ashmore, R.D. and Del Boca, F.K. 'Conceptual Approaches to Stereotypes and Stereotyping' in Hamilton, D.L. ed. *Cognitive Processes in Stereotyping and Intergroup Behaviour.* New Jersey: Lawrence Erinbaum, 1981.

Auerbach, F. *The Protocols: Survival of an Evil Fiction.* South African Jewish Board of Deputies Pamphlet, Johannesburg: 1991, pp.1-7.

Baron, S.W. 'Newer Approaches to Jewish Emancipation'. *Diogenes* 29, Spring 1960, pp.56-81.

Barron, C. 'A Flock of Pidgins', *Sunday Times*, 29 January 1995, pp.8-9.

Barthes, R. *Mythologies*. 1957; trans. from French by A. Levers, 1972; rpt. St. Albans: Paladin, 1976.

Bauer, Y. ed. *Present-Day Antisemitism*. Proceedings of the Eighth International Seminar of the Study Circle on World Jewry. Jerusalem: The Vidal Sassoon International Center for the Study of Antisemitism, 1988.

Beaumont, K.J. 'Dan Jacobson's Early Short Novels: A Case Study of the Defeat of a Liberal-Humanist Novelistic Discourse in South Africa in the 1950s'. Unpublished Master's Dissertation, University of Natal, 1990.

Beeton, D.R. *A Pilot Bibliography of South African English Literature (from the beginnings to 1971)*. Pretoria: University of South Africa, 1976.

Beinash, J. *Books and Pamphlets by South African Jewish Writers 1940-1962*. Johannesburg: University of the Witwatersrand Librarianship Department, 1965.

Bekker, J. 'Trapped Identity in the Novels of Dan Jacobson'. Unpublished Master's Dissertation, Rhodes University, 1981.

Bell, D. 'Reflections on Jewish Identity'. *Commentary* 31(6), June 1961, pp.471-478.

Belsey, C. *Critical Practice*. London and New York: Methuen, 1980.

Berelowitz, I. 'Recollections of my Father and of District Six'. *The Herald Times*, 12 December 1986.

Berger, D. ed. *History and Hate. The Dimensions of Anti-Semitism*. Philadelphia, New York, Jerusalem: The Jewish Publication Society, 1986.

Berger, N. *Chapters from South African History Jewish and General. Book One: Johannesburg*. Johannesburg: Kayor, 1982.

_____ *In those Days, In these Times. (1929-1979): Spotlighting Events in Jewry – South African and General*. Johannesburg: Kayor, 1979.

_____ *Jewish Trails through Southern Africa. A Documentary*. Johannesburg: Kayor, 1976.

Bernstein, E. 'Jews and Communism'. *Jewish Affairs* 3(3), March 1948, pp.20-23.

_____ *My Judaism, My Jews*. Johannesburg: Exclusive Books, 1962.

_____ 'Sarah Gertrude Millin, The Writer and the Jewess'. *Jewish Affairs*, 23 (7), 1968, pp. 14-18.

_____ 'South Africa's First Great Writer (Olive Schreiner)'. *Jewish Affairs* 10(4), April 1955, pp.15-18.

Bernstein, H. *The Rift. The Exile Experience of South Africans*. London: Jonathan Cape, 1994.

Bettelheim, B. and Janowitz, M. *Social Change and Prejudice*. London: Collier-Macmillan, 1964.

Billington, M. 'Antony Sher, the Protean Outsider'. *The Guardian*; rpt. *The Weekly Mail*, 10-17 August 1990, p.11.

Black, E.C. *The Social Politics of Anglo-Jewry 1880-1920*. Oxford and New York: Basil Blackwell, 1988.

Black, S. 'Helena's Hope, Ltd.' (1912), in Gray, S. ed. *Stephen Black. Three Plays*. Johannesburg: Ad. Donker, 1984, pp.127-182.

'Boerejode Saamtrek Forges Old Ties'. *Cape Times*, 30 September 1989.

Boon, M.J. *A History of the Orange Free State*. London: William Reeves, 1885.

Bosman, H.C. 'The Goodwill Propaganda Hoax'. *The South African Jewish Times*. September 1947, pp.27, 38.

Bozzoli, B. ed. *Class, Community and Conflict: South African Perspectives*. Johannesburg: Ravan, 1987.

Bradford, J. *A Dictionary of South African English*. 1978; rpt. New Revised Edition, Cape Town: Oxford University Press, 1980.

Bratton, F.G. *The Crimes of Christendom: The Theological Source of Christian Anti-Semitism*. Boston: Beacon, 1969.

Braude, C. 'The Left, the Right and Jews'. *The Jewish Voice* 2(4), June 1991, pp.2, 4.

Braun, L. 'Not Gobineau but Heine – Not Racial Theory but Biblical Theme: The Case of Sarah Gertrude Millin'. *English Studies in Africa* 34(1), 1991, pp.27-38.

Casper, B.M. *Judaism Today and Yesterday*. New York and London: Thomas Yosseloff, 1965.

Chapman, A.J. and Ford, H.C. *It's a Funny Thing, Humour*. Oxford: Pergamon, 1977.

Cheyette, B. *Constructions of 'the Jew' in English Literature and Society. Racial Representations, 1875-1945*. Cambridge: Cambridge University Press, 1993.

_____ 'Hillaire Belloc and the "Marconi Scandal" 1900-1914: A Reassessment of the Interactionist Model of Racial Hatred'. *Immigrants and Minorities* 8(1) and 2 March 1989, pp.131-142.

_____ 'The Other Self: Anglo-Jewish Fiction and the Representation of Jews in England, 1875-1905', in Cesarani, D. ed. *The Making of Modern Anglo-Jewry*. Oxford: Basil Blackwell, 1990, pp.97-111.

Chilvers, H.A. *The Story of De Beers*. London: Cassel, 1940.

Christie, S., Hutchings. G., and Maclennan, D. *Perspectives on South African Fiction*. Johannesburg: A. Donker, 1980.

Clayton, C. ed. *Olive Schreiner*. Johannesburg: McGraw-Hill, 1983.

_____ ed. *Women and Writing in South Africa*. Marshalltown: Heinemann, 1989.

Clingman, S. *The Novels of Nadine Gordimer: History from the Inside*. Johannesburg: Ravan, 1986.

Coetzee, J.M. 'Blood, Taint, Flaw, Degeneration: The Novels of Sarah Gertrude Millin'. *English Studies in Africa* 23(1), 1980, pp.41-58.

_____ *White Writing: On the Culture of Letters in South Africa*. Sandton: Century Hutchinson; New Haven and London: Yale University Press, 1988.

Cohen, L. (pseud. 'Majude'). *Gay Young Creatures*. Kimberley: Angove and Repton, 1880.

Louis Cohen Papers. A1538 and A22. Manuscript Collection, University of the Witwatersrand Library.

Cohen-Steiner, O. 'Jews and Jewesses in Victorian Fiction: From Religious Stereotype to Ethnic Hazard', in *Patterns of Prejudice* 21(2), Summer 1987, pp.25-34.

Cooke, J.W. *The Novels of Nadine Gordimer*. Evaton: Northwestern and Illinois University, 1976.

'Concern over Synagogue Raids'. *Cape Times*, 17 March 1958.

Conrad, P. Rev. of *Middlepost* by A. Sher. *The Observer*, 11 September 1988.

'Continuing: It Did Happen Here'. *Common Sense*, February 1940, pp.8-11.

'Continuing: It Did Happen Here'. *Common Sense*, March 1940, pp.8-11.

Cooper, B. 'New Criteria for an "Abnormal Mutation"? An Evaluation of Gordimer's *A Sport of Nature*', in Trump, M. ed. *Rendering Things Visible*. Johannesburg, Raván Press, 1990, pp.69-93.

Cornell, F.C. *The Glamour of Prospecting. Wanderings of a South African Prospector in Search of Copper, Gold, Emeralds, and Diamonds*. London: T. Fisher Unwin, 1920.

'Country Communities. "Die Mense van die Boek", "Ons Boere-Jode"'. Hannah and Friedel Abt Museum, 800.1, September 1985.

Cowen, A. and Cowen R. (eds), *Victorian Jews through British Eyes*. Oxford: Oxford University Press, 1986. Curtis, M. (ed.), *Antisemitism in the Contemporary World*. Boulder and London: Westview, 1986.

Donker, A. 'English-Language Publishing in South Africa'. In Gardner, S. (ed.), *Publisher – Writer – Reader: Sociology of Southern African Literature*. Proc. of a Colloquium at the University of the Witwatersrand, Johannesburg, 30 September – 2 October 1982. Johannesburg: Witwatersrand University Press, 1986, pp.17-24.

Driver, D. (ed.), *Pauline Smith*. Johannesburg: McGraw-Hill, 1983.

Dubb, A. 'Demographic Picture'. In Arkin, M. *South African Jewry: A Contemporary Survey*, pp.23-44.

_____ *Jewish South Africans: A Sociological View of the Johannesburg Community*. Grahamstown: Institute of Social and Economic Research, Rhodes University, 1977.

_____ 'Little Decrease in South African Jewish Population'. *Jewish Voice* 2(4). June 1991.

Dubnow, S.M. *History of the Jews in Russia and Poland. From the Earliest Times Until the Present Day*. Trans. from the Russian by I. Friedlander, 2, Philadelphia: The Jewish Publication Society of America, 1918.

Edelstein, A. *An Unacknowledged Harmony: Philo-Semitism and the Survival of European Jewry*. Westport Connecticut and London: Greenwood, 1982.

Edelstein, M.E. *What do Young Africans Think?* Johannesburg: Institute of Race Relations, 1972.

Emden, P.H. *Jews of Britain*. London: Sampson Low Marston, 1943.

_____ *Randlords*. London: Hodder and Stoughton, 1935.

Encyclopaedia Judaica. Jerusalem: Keter, 1971, Vols. 3, 5, 9, 15, 16.

Endelman, T. Rev. of *A History of the Jews*, by Paul Johnson. *Times Literary Supplement*, 26 June 1987.

Erb, R. 'Die Wahrnehmung der Physiognomie der Juden: Die Nase'. In Pleticha, H. (ed.), *Das Bild des Juden in der Volks- und Jugendliteratur vom 19. Jahrhundert bis 1945*. Wurzburg: Konighausen & Neumann, 1985, pp.107-126.

Fackenheim, E.L. *What is Judaism? An Interpretation for the Present Age*. New York: Summit, 1987.

Fanon, F. *Black Skins, White Masks*. New York: Grove Press, 1967.

February, V.A. *Mind Your Colour. The Coloured Stereotype in South African Literature*. London: Routledge and Kegan Paul, 1981.

Feldman, L. *Oudtshoorn Jerusalem of Africa*. Ed. J. Sherman. Johannesburg: Friends of the Library, University of the Witwatersrand, 1989.

Fiedler, L. *Love and Death in the American Novel*. 1960; rpt. London: Jonathan Cape, 1967.

Fisch, H. *The Dual Image: A Study of the Jew in English Literature*. London: Lincolns-Prager, 1959.

_____ *The Dual Image: A Study of the Jew in English and American Literature*. London: World Jewish Library, 1971.

Fleischner, E. (ed.), *Auschwitz: Beginning of a New Era*. New York: KTAV, 1977.

Frankenthal, S. and Shain, M. 'An Introduction to the South African Jewish Community'. *Zionist Record*, 1 February 1985.

_____ 'The Open Ghetto: Growing up Jewish in South Africa'. In Burman, S. and Reynolds, P. (eds.), *Growing up in a Divided Society. The Contexts of Childhood in South Africa*. Johannesburg: Ravan, 1986, pp.208-225.

Fraser, M. (ed.), *Some Reminiscences of Lionel Phillips*. Johannesburg: Ad. Donker, 1986. [First published in its original version London: Hutchinson, 1924.]

Frazer, J. 'A Much-feted Trespasser [Antony Sher]'. *Jewish Chronicle*, 5 October 1990, p.21.

Freud, S. *Jokes and Their Relation to the Unconscious*. 1916; rpt. New York: James Strachey, 1960.

Furlong, P.J. *Between Crown and Swastika. The Impact of the Radical Right on the Afrikaner Nationalist Movement in the Fascist Era*. Johannesburg: Witwatersrand University Press, 1991.

Gardiner, M. 'Critical Responses and the Fiction of Pauline Smith'. AUETSA Papers, 1982, [unpublished typescript], pp.1-18.

Gelber, M.H. 'What is Literary Antisemitism?'. *Jewish Social Studies* 47(1), Winter 1985, pp.1-20.

Gershater, C. 'From Lithuania to South Africa'. In Saron, G. and Hotz, L. (eds.), *The Jews in South Africa. A History*. Cape Town and London: Oxford University Press, 1955, pp.59-84.

Gilbert, M. 'The Holocaust in Retrospect: After 40 Years'. Lecture given 26 April 1984. University of Cape Town: Kaplan Centre, 1984.

Gilman, S.L. *Difference and Pathology: Stereotypes of Sexuality, Race and Madness*. Ithaca, New York: Cornell University Press, 1985.

_____ *Jewish Self-Hatred: Anti-Semitism and the Hidden Language of the Jews*. Baltimore and London: Johns Hopkins, 1990.

Gitlin, M. *The Vision Amazing: The Story of South African Zionism*. Johannesburg: Menorah, 1950.

Gittleman, S. *From Shtetl to Suburbia: The Family in Jewish Literary Imagination*. Boston: Beacon, 1978.

Glassman, B. *Anti-Semitic Stereotypes Without Jews: Images of the Jews in England 1290-1770*. Detroit: Wayne State University Press, 1975.

Glock, C.Y. and Stark, R. *Christian Beliefs and Anti-Semitism*. New York and London: Harper, 1966.

Goffman, E. *Stigma: Notes on the Management of Spoiled Identity*. 1973; rpt. Harmondsworth: Penguin Books, 1979.

Goldberg, A. '*Jewish Affairs*: Half a Century in Perspective'. *Jewish Affairs* 46(4), December 1991, pp.7-10.

Goldman, A. 'Of Van der Merwes, Smiths and Cohens'. *World of South African Jewry*. II, ed. M. Dorfan, Johannesburg: R and J Publications, October 1988, pp.7-8.

Goodman, L. 'The Tales of Hyman Polsky, a Pioneer Yiddish Writer'. *Jewish Affairs* 30(4), April 1975, pp.41-47.

Gordimer, N. 'A South African Childhood'. *New Yorker*, 16 October 1954, pp.111-114.

_____ 'A Writer in South Africa: Nadine Gordimer'. *London Magazine*, May 1965, p.23.

_____ 'In Search of a Way to Live'. Interview with Anthony Sampson, *The Observer*; rpt. *The Sunday Star*, 5 April 1987.

_____ 'On Freedom, Communism and Judaism. A Conversation between Nadine Gordimer and Natan Sharansky'. *The Jerusalem Report*, 24 October 1991, pp.5-7.

Gray, J.L. 'The Jew in the Economic Life of South Africa', Publication No 5. The Society of Jews and Christians, n.d.

Gray, S. 'Stephen Black. Some Introductory Notes'. *English in Africa*, September 1981, 8(2), pp.65-94.

Grayzel, S. *A History of the Jews*. 1947; rpt. Philadelphia: The Jewish Publication Society of America, 1968.

Greig, J.Y.T. *The Psychology of Laughter and Comedy*. London: George Allen and Unwin, 1923.

Greig, R. '*Middlepost*: Antony Sher'. Rev. in *Business Day*, 14 November 1988.

Gross, J. *Shylock. Four Hundred Years in the Life of a Legend*. London: Chatto and Windus, 1992.

Grossman, M.P. 'A Study in the Trends and Tendencies of Hebrew and Yiddish Writings in South Africa. Since the Beginning of the Early Nineties of the Last Century to 1930'. 3 Vols. Unpublished Doctoral Thesis. University of the Witwatersrand, 1973.

Hamilton, D.L. (ed.), *Cognitive Processes in Stereotyping and Intergroup Behaviour*. New Jersey: Lawrence Erinbaum, 1981.

Haresnape, G. *Pauline Smith*. New York: Twayne, 1969.

Harrap, L. *The Image of the Jew in American Literature*. Philadelphia: The Jewish Publication Society of America, 1974.

Harris, J. 'SA Jewry The Facts', in *The South African Jewish Times*, 7 October 1994, p.4.

Hay, M. *My Brother's Blood. The Roots of Christian Anti-Semitism*. New York: Hart, 1975.

Hellig, J. 'Judaism and Islam: Some Aspects of their Interrelationship'. *Jewish Affairs* 40(9), September 1985, pp.89-94.

_____ 'The Doctrine of Chosenness: Its Relation to Anti-Semitism'. In Musiker, R. and Sherman, J. (eds.), *Waters out of the Well*. Johannesburg: The Library. University of the Witwatersrand, 1988.

_____ 'The Holocaust and the Theological Roots of Anti-Semitism'. *Jewish Affairs* 38(4), April 1983, pp.43-46.

Herman, S.N. *Jewish Identity*. London: Sage, 1977.

_____ *The Reaction of Jews to Anti-Semitism*. Johannesburg, Witwatersrand University Press, 1945.

Herrman, L. *A History of the Jews in South Africa from the Earliest times to 1895*. Cape Town: South African Jewish Board of Deputies, 1935.

Hersch, M.D. 'Through the Eyes of a Litvak, 1893', Part II, *Jewish Affairs* 11(12), December 1956, pp.23-29.

Higham, J. 'Anti-Semitism in the Gilded Age. A Reinterpretation'. *Mississippi Historical Review*, 43, 1956-7, p.563.

Hilberg, R. *The Destruction of the European Jews*, 1, New York and London: Holmes and Meier, 1985.

Hillegas, H.C. *Oom Paul's People*. New York: Appleton, 1899.

Hirsch, E.D. Jr. *The Aims of Interpretation*. Chicago and London: The University of Chicago Press, 1976.

_____ *Validity in Interpretation*. New Haven and London: Yale University Press, 1967.

Hoberfeld, C.B. 'Diamond City and its Jews'. *World of South African Jewry*, 2, ed. M. Dorfan, Johannesburg: October 1988, pp.27-29.

Hoffman T. and Fischer, A. (eds.), *The Jews of South Africa. What Future?* South Africa: Southern Books, 1988.

Hofmeyr, C.I. 'Mining, Social Change and Literature. An Analysis of South African Literature with Particular Reference to the Mining Novel 1870-1920'. Unpublished Master's Dissertation. University of the Witwatersrand, 1981.

Holmes, C. *Anti-Semitism in British Society, 1876-1939*. London: Edward Arnold, 1979.

Holocaust. [n.e.] Jerusalem: Yad Vashem, 1991.

Horowitz, P. *The Jews, the War and After*. London: Lloyd Cole, 194[3].

Hyman, A. 'The Apolitical role of the South African Jewish Board of Deputies', *Jewish Affairs* 49(4), Summer 1994, pp.67-68.

'Incidents of Anti-Semitic Nature Reported 1961-1964'. Jewish Board of Deputies Pamphlet, 25 August 1964, 308.3, pp.1-3.

Innes, D. 'The Exercise of Control in the Diamond Industry of South Africa – Some Preliminary Notes', in Adler, T. (ed.), *Perspectives on South Africa. A Collection of Working Papers*. Johannesburg: African Studies Institute, University of the Witwatersrand, 1977, pp.195-241.

'It did Happen Here. How the Nazis Conducted Propaganda in South Africa'. *Common Sense*, January 1940, pp.8-10.

Jackson, S. *The Great Barnato*, London: Heinemann, 1971.

Jacobson, D. 'Apartheid and South African Jewry'. An Exchange. *Commentary* 24(5), November 1957, pp.424-431.

_____ 'A White Liberal trapped by his Prejudices'. *Commentary*, [n. vol.], 15 May 1953, pp.454-459.

_____ Interview with Ian Hamilton, *New Review*, 4, October 1977, pp.25-29.

_____ 'The Jews of South Africa: Portrait of a Flourishing Community'. *Commentary* 23(1), January 1957. pp.39-45.

_____ 'Yiddish Fiction in South Africa'. In *Adult Pleasures*. London: Andre Deutsch, 1988, pp.129-135.

JanMahomed, A.R. *Manichean Aesthetics: The Politics of Literature in Colonial Africa.* Amhurst Massachusetts: University of Massachusetts Press, 1983.

_____ 'The Economy of Manichean Allegory: The Function of Racial Difference in Colonialist Literature'. *Critical Inquiry*, 12 Autumn 1985, pp.59-84.

Jefferson, A. and Robey, D. (eds.), *Modern Literary Theory*. 1982; rpt. London: Batsford, 1983.

Johnson, P. *A History of the Jews*. London: Weidenfeld and Nicolson, 1987.

Jones, E.E. *et al.* (eds). *Social Stigma. The Psychology of Marked Relationships*. New York: W.H. Freeman, 1984.

Jonker, A.H. *The Scapegoat of History*. South Africa: CNA, 1941.

Kaplan, M. and Robertson, M. (eds.), *Founders and Followers. Johannesburg Jewry 1887-1915*. Cape Town: Vlaeberg, 1991.

_____ *From Shtetl to Steelworks*. Cape Town: Kaplan Kushlick Foundation, 1979.

_____ Assisted by Robertson, M. *Jewish Roots in the South African Economy*. Cape Town: Struik, 1986.

Katz, J. *Emancipation and Self-Emancipation*. Philadelphia, New York, Jerusalem: The Jewish Publication Society, 1986.

_____ *From Prejudice to Destruction. Anti-Semitism 1700-1933*. Cambridge Massachusetts: Harvard University Press, 1980.

_____ *Out of the Ghetto: The Social Background of Jewish Emancipation. 1770-1870*. Cambridge Massachusetts: Harvard University Press, 1973.

Kennedy, B. *A Tale of Two Mining Cities: Johannesburg and Broken Hill 1885-1925*. Johannesburg: Ad. Donker, 1984.

King, M.A. 'A Study of the Development of the Structures and Themes in the Short Stories of Nadine Gordimer'. Unpublished Master's Dissertation. University of Cape Town, 1984.

Klevansky, I.H. *The Kugel Book*. Johannesburg: Jonathan Ball, 1982.

Kosmin, B.A. *Majuta: A History of the Jewish Community in Zimbabwe*. Gwelo: Membo, 1981.

Kramer, J.R. and Leventman, S. *Children of the Gilded Ghetto: Conflict Resolutions of Three Generations of American Jews*. New Haven and London: Yale University Press, 1961.

Krauthammer, C. 'Judging Israel'. *Time Magazine*, 26 February 1990.

Kropman, M. 'The Contribution of Pioneer Traders to the Ciskei'. Unpublished Master's Dissertation. University of Cape Town, 1977.

Krut, R.M. 'Building a Home and a Community. Jews in Johannesburg 1886-1914'. Unpublished Doctoral Thesis. University of London, 1985.

_____ 'The History Seminar: Lumpens and Luftmenschen in the South African Jewish Community'. Halifax: Dalhousie University, November 1982.

_____ 'The Making of a South African Jewish Community in Johannesburg 1886-1914'. In Bozzoli, (ed.), *Class, Community and Conflict. South African Perspectives*. Johannesburg: Ravan, 1987, pp.135-159.

Landa, M.J. *The Jew in Drama*. London: P.S. King, 1926.

Lazar, C. 'Spotlight Falls on South African Jews'. Rev. of *The Jews of South Africa – What Future?* by T. Hoffman and A. Fischer. *Sunday Star*, 5 February 1989.

Lazar, K.R. 'The Personal and the Political in some of Nadine Gordimer's Short Stories'. Unpublished Master's Dissertation. University of the Witwatersrand, 1988.

Lazerson, J.N. *Against the Tide. Whites in the Struggle Against Apartheid*. Belville: University of the Western Cape, Mayibuye Books, 1994.

Lester, M. (pseud. of M. Clouts) 'Dan Jacobson's New Short Stories'. Rev. in *Jewish Affairs* 20(3), March 1965, pp.41-42.

Leveson, M. 'Bertha Goudvis: Time Memory and Freedom'. In Clayton, C. (ed.), *Women and Writing in South Africa. A Critical Anthology*. Marshalltown: Heinemann, 1989.

_____ 'Power and Prejudice: Dan Jacobson's "Jewish" Fiction of the Fifties'. *English Studies in Africa* 34(2), 1991, pp.115-131.

_____ 'The Jewish Stereotype in Some South African English Fiction: A Preliminary Investigation'. In Musiker, R. and Sherman, J. *Waters out of the Well*. Johannesburg: The Library, University of the Witwatersrand, 1988.

Lewin, K. 'Self-Hatred among Jews'. In *Resolving Social Conflicts*. New York: Harper, 1948, pp.186-200.

Lewis, A.E. *Reminiscences of South Africa*. London: Fleetway, 1926.

Lewis, B. 'The Arab World discovers Anti-Semitism'. *Commentary* 81(5), May 1986, pp.30-34.

_____ *The Jews of Islam*. Princeton: Princeton University Press, 1984.

Lewsen, P. 'Olive Schreiner's Political Theories and Pamphlets'. In Clayton, C. (ed.), *Olive Schreiner*. Johannesburg: McGraw-Hill, 1983, pp.212-220.

Loercher, D. 'South Africa's Nadine Gordimer: Novelist with a Conscience'. In Bazin, D.T. and Seymour, M.D. *Conversations with Nadine Gordimer*. Jackson and London: University Press of Mississipi, 1990, pp.96-100.

Litvinoff, B. *The Burning Bush: Anti-Semitism and World History*. London: Collins, 1988.

Ludovici, A.M. *The Secret of Laughter*. London: Constable, 1932.

Lyons, J. 'Prejudice in Social Science'. *Midstream* 12(5), May 1966, pp.21-34.

Maccoby, H. *Judas Iscariot and the Myth of Jewish Evil*. London: Peter Halban, 1992.

_____ 'The Figure of Shylock'. *Midstream* 16(2), February, 1970, pp.56-69.

_____ 'Theologian of the Holocaust'. *Commentary* 74(6), December 1982, pp.33-37.

MacCrone, I.D. *Race Attitudes in South Africa*. London:Oxford University Press, 1937.

MacDonald, W. *Pioneers of the Golden Rand*. Johannesburg: Radford Adlington for author, 193[2].

Macdonall, D. *Theories of Discourse: An Introduction*. Oxford: Basil Blackwell, 1986.

Malan, C. (ed.), *Race and Literature. Ras en Literatuur*. Pinetown: Owen Burgess, 1987.

Mantzaris, E.A. 'Radical Community: The Yiddish-speaking Branch of the International Socialist League, 1918-1920'. In Bozzoli, B. *Class, Community and Conflict. South African Perspectives*. Johannesburg: Ravan, 1987, pp.160-177.

Markowitz, A. 'Spotlight on the Jews of the Dorps'. *Jewish Affairs* 36(11), November 1981, pp.69-72.

Marquard, J. (ed.), *A Century of South African Short Stories*. Johannesburg: Ad. Donker, 1978.

_____ 'A Neglected Pioneer in South African Literature – W.C. Scully'. Unpublished Doctoral Thesis. University of the Witwatersrand, 1984.

_____ (ed.), Introduction to *Transkei Stories*. Cape Town: David Philip, 1984.

_____ 'Scully's Desert Books'. Unpublished paper delivered at AUETSA Conference, July 1983, [typescript], pp.1-26, 1-5 [notes].

_____ 'Some Racial Stereotypes in South African Writing'. Unpublished paper delivered at conference at York University 1981, [typescript], pp.1-14.

Marrus, M. 'European Jewry and the Politics of Assimilation: Assessment and Reassessment'. *The Journal of Modern History* 49(1), March 1977, pp.89-109.

_____ 'The Theory and Practice of Anti-Semitism'. *Commentary* 72(2), August 1982, pp.38-42.

Mason, D. 'The Concept of Minority and Intergroup Conflict in Africa'. *Patterns of Prejudice* 18(4), October 1984, pp.3-15.

McCormick, K. 'Yiddish in District Six', *Jewish Affairs* 48(3), Spring 1993, pp.29-38.

Meer, F. *Portrait of Indian South Africans*. Durban: Avon House, 1969.

Memmi, A. *The Liberation of the Jew*. Trans. from the French by J. Hyun, New York: Orion, 1966.

Mendelsohn, R. *Sammy Marks. 'The Uncrowned King of the Transvaal'*. Cape Town: David Philip, Athens Ohio: Ohio University Press. In association with Jewish Publications – SA, 1991.

Mendelssohn, S. *Mendelssohn's South African Bibliography*. London: Kegan Paul, 1910. 2 vols.

Mendes-Flohr, R. and Reinharz, J. *The Jew in the Modern World. A Documentary History*. Oxford and New York: Oxford University Press, 1980.

Meyer, M.A. *Jewish Identity in the Modern World*. Seattle and London: University of Washington Press, 1990.

Millin, S.G. [S.G. Liebson] 'The Jew in English Literature'. *The Zionist Record*, 15 September 1911, pp.1-7.

S.G. Millin Papers, A539/M2. Manuscript Collection, University of the Witwatersrand Library.

_____ 'The Right to be Ugly', 1933. Unpublished article, pp.1-7. S.G. Millin Papers, A539/M2. Manuscript Collection, University of the Witwatersrand Library.

_____ Unpaginated notes. S.G. Millin Papers. A539/9. Manuscript Collection, University of the Witwatersrand Library.

Modder, M.F. *The Jew in the Literature of England to the End of the Nineteenth Century*. Philadelphia: The Jewish Publication Society, 1939.

Mosse, G.L. *Towards the Final Solution*. A History of European Racism. Madison: The University of Wisconsin Press, 1985.

Mower White, C.J. *Consistency in Cognitive Social Behaviour: An Introduction to Social Psychology*. London: Routledge and Kegan Paul, 1987.

Musiker, R. and Sherman, J. *Waters out of the Well. Essays in Jewish Studies*. Johannesburg: The Library. University of the Witwatersrand, 1988.

Naman, A.A. *The Jew in the Victorian Novel*. New York: AMS Press, 1980.

'Nazi-like Thugs Terrorize Jews'. *Sunday Tribune*, 30 November 1961.

'Never Forgetting. Anti-Semitism in Poland'. *The Economist*, 9 November 1991.

Newman A. 'Why Did our Lithuanian Grandparents Come to South Africa?', *Jewish Affairs* 49(2), Winter 1994, pp.9-12.

Newman, J. *Nadine Gordimer*. London and New York: Routledge, 1988.

Ngugi Wa Thiong'o. *Decolonising the Mind: The Politics of Language in African Literature*. 1986; rpt. London: James Currey and Heinemann, 1991.

O'Meara, D. *Volkskapitalisme: Class, Capital and Ideology in the Development of Afrikaner Nationalism 1934-1948*. Johannesburg: Ravan, 1983.

'On the Edge of Disquiet: South Africa's Jews and the ANC'. *Financial Mail* 118(8), November 1990, pp.24-25.

Parker, K. (ed.), *The South African Novel in English: Essays in Criticism and Society*. New York: Africana, 1978.

Parkes, J. *AntiSemitism*. London: Vallentine Mitchell, 1963.

Partridge, A.C. 'The Novel of Social Purpose in South Africa'. *SA PEN Yearbook 1956-1957*. Cape Town: Howard Timmins, 1956-7, pp.59-64.

Patai, R. *The Jewish Mind*. New York: Scribners, 1977.

Paton, A. *Hofmeyr*. London: Oxford University Press, 1964.

Pheiffer, R. 'The Jew in Afrikaans Literature'. *Patterns of Prejudice* 11(1), January-February 1977, pp.23-27.

Pickwoad, S. 'Black People's Adaptive Behaviour and Self-hate'. *Patterns of Prejudice* 9(2), March-April, 1975. pp.1-19.

Pienaar, M.E. 'An Evaluation of the Novels of Sarah Gertrude Millin'. Unpublished Master's Dissertation. University of South Africa, 1980.

Pinsker, S. *The Schlemiel as Metaphor: Studies in the Yiddish and American Jewish Novel*. Carbondale and Edwardsville: Southern Illinois University Press, 1971.

Pitock T. 'Unloved Back Home' ('Nadine Gordimer and the Perils of Political Fiction') *Tikkun* 10(3), 1995, pp.76-79.

Sol T. Plaatje Papers, A979 Da 44. Manuscript Collection, University of the Witwatersrand Library.

Pogrebin, L.C. *Deborah, Golda and Me: Being Female and Jewish in America*. 1991; rpt. New York and London: Doubleday, 1991.

Poliakov, L. *The History of Anti-Semitism*. London: Routledge and Kegan Paul, 1965-1973. Vols. 1-3.

'Predikant tells his flock: "Don't vote for Jew"'. *Sunday Express*, 10 November 1957. Rpt. in Jewish Board of Deputies Pamphlet, 308.3. [n. p., n.d.]

Prawer, S.S. *Heine's Jewish Comedy, A study of his Portraits of Jews and Judaism*. Oxford: Oxford University Press, 1983.

Prell, R.E. 'Why the Jewish Princess Doesn't Sweat: Desire and Consumption in Postwar American Jewish Culture'. in Eilberg-Schwartz, H. ed. *People of the Body: Jews and Judaism from an Embodied Perspective*. Albany: State University of New York Press, 1992, pp.329-359.

Pulzer, P.G.J. *The Rise of Political Anti-Semitism in Germany and Austria*. New York, London: John Wiley, 1964.

'Racism's Back,' *The Economist*, 16 November 1991.

Ragussis, M. 'Repression, Conversion, and Literary Form: *Harrington* and the Novel of Jewish Identity'. *Critical Inquiry*, 16, Autumn 1989, pp.113-143.

Rappaport, S. *Jew and Gentile: The Philo-Semitic Aspect*. New York: Philosophical Library, 1980.

Reuther, R.R. 'Anti-Semitism and Christian Theology', in Fleischner, E. (ed.), *Auschwitz: Beginning of a New Era?* New York, KTAV, 1977, pp.79-92.

Ricci, D. (compl. and ed.), *Reef of Time: Johannesburg in Writing*. Johannesburg: Ad Donker, 1986.

Richards;, I.A. *Principles of Literary Criticism*. London: Kegan Paul, Trench, Trubner & Co. Ltd., 1938.

Rive, R. Introduction to *The Path of Thunder* by P. Abrahams. Cape Town and Johannesburg: David Philip, 1984, pp.5-8.

_____ (ed.), *Olive Schreiner Letters, 1871-1899*. Cape Town: David Philip, 1987.

Roberts, B. *Kimberley Turbulent City*. Cape Town: David Philip in association with the Historical Society, 1976.

_____ *The Diamond Magnates*. London: Hamish Hamilton, 1972.

Roberts, S. 'At a Distance: Dan Jacobson's South African Fiction'. In Chapman, M., Gardner, C. and Mphahlele E. (eds.) *Perspectives on South African Literature*. Johannesburg, Ad. Donker, 1992, pp.213-220.

_____ *Dan Jacobson*, Boston: Twayne, 1984.

Robertson, M. *Diamond Fever: South African Diamond History from Primary Sources*. Cape Town: Oxford University Press, 1974.

Rochlin, S.A. 'The Jew in South African Literature'. *The South African Jewish Year Book*. Johannesburg: The South African Jewish Historical Society, 1929, pp.237-247.

Rock, T. *The Making of Symbolic Interactionism*. London and Basingstoke: Macmillan, 1979.

Rogow, A.A. *The Jew in a Gentile World*. New York: Macmillan, 1961.

Romm, I.C. 'What is a Smous?' *South African Jewish Times*, September 1985, pp.44-45.

Ronge, B. 'If the Kugel's still with us – we're fine'. *The Star Tonight*, November 25, 1994.

Rosenberg, E. *From Shylock to Svengali: Jewish Stereotypes in English Fiction*. Stanford: Stanford University Press, 1960.

Rosenthal, E. *Gold! Gold! Gold!. The Johannesburg Gold Rush*. Johannesburg: Ad. Donker, 1970.

Roth, C. *A History of the Jews in England*. 1970; rpt. New York: Schocken Books, 1974.

_____ (ed.), *Essays in Jewish History*. London: JHSE, 1934.

Roth, P. 'Writing about Jews'. *Commentary* 36(6), December 1963, pp.446-452.

Rubin, M. *Sarah Gertrude Millin, A South African Life*. Johannesburg: Ad. Donker, 1977.

Ruether, R.R. 'Anti-Semitism and Christian Theology'. In Fleischner, E. ed. *Auschwitz: Beginning of a New Era?* New York: KTAV 1977, pp.79-91.

_____ *Faith and Fratricide: The Theological Roots of Anti-Semitism*. New York: Seabury, 1974.

Ruthven, K.K. *Critical Assumptions*. Cambridge: Cambridge University Press, 1979.

Rylance, R. ed. *Debating Texts. A Reader in Twentieth-Century Literary Theory and Method*. Milton Keynes: Open University Press, 1987.

Sachar, H.M. *Diaspora: An Inquiry into the Contemporary Jewish World*. New York: Harper, 1985.

Sachs, B. *Personalities and Places*. (Second Series). Johannesburg: Dial, 1965.

_____ *The Road to Sharpeville*. Johannesburg: Dial, 1961.

Samuel, M. *The Great Hatred*. London: Victor Gollancz, 1943.

Saron, G. 'From Immigrants to South Africans'. *Jewish Affairs* 31(11), November 1976, pp.20-29.

_____ 'The Making of South African Jewry'. I Feldberg, L. (ed.), *South African Jewry*. Johannesburg: Fieldhill Publishing Co. Ltd., 1965.

_____ and Hotz, L. (eds.), *The Jews in South Africa: A History*. London: Oxford University Press, 1955.

Sartre J-P. *Anti-Semite and Jew*. 1948; trans. Becker, G.J. rpt. New York: Schocken Books, 1974. [First published as *Reflexions sur la Question Juive*. Paris: Paul Morihen, 1946].

Schreiner, O. 'A Letter on the Jew'. Cape Town: H. Liberman. Paper read at the Jewish Territorial Organization meeting, 1 July 1906. Published in the *Cape Times* 2 July 1906; rpt. in *Jewish Affairs* 31(8), August 1976, pp.6-11.

_____ *Closer Union*. Cape Town: Constitutional Reform Association, 1960. [First published as *Letter on the South African Union and the Principles of Government. The Transvaal Leader*. Johannesburg, 22 December 1908].

_____ *Thoughts on South Africa*. London: T. Fisher Unwin, 1923.

Schultz, C. Transcript of a tape recordings. Kaplan Kushlik Foundation, University of Cape Town, A1984/B11.17.

Sears, D.O., Freedman, J.L., Peplau, L.A. eds. *Social Psychology*. 1970; rpt. New Jersey: Prentice-Hall, 1985.

Select List of South African Jewish Authors. Pamphlet 15C/A. Johannesburg: Library of the South African Jewish Board of Deputies. n.d.

Shain, M. 'Diamonds, Pogroms and Undesirables – Anti-Alienism and Legislation in the Cape Colony, 1890-1906.' *South African Historical Journal*, 12, 1980, pp.13-28.

_____ 'From Pariah to Parvenu: the Anti-Jewish Stereotype in South Africa to 1910'. *Jewish Journal of Sociology* 26(2), December 1984, pp.111-127.

_____ 'Hoggenheimer – the Making of a Myth'. *Jewish Affairs* 36(9), September 1981, pp.112-116.

_____ 'Images of the Jew in Johannesburg 1887-1915'. In Kaplan, M. and Robertson, M. (eds.), *Founders and Followers. Johannesburg Jewry 1887-1915*. Cape Town: Vlaeberg, 1991, pp.152-161, 274-276.

_____ *Jewry and Cape Society*. Cape Town: Historical Publication Society, 1983.

_____ *The Roots of Antisemitism in South Africa*. Johannesburg: Witwatersrand University Press, 1994.

_____ 'The Jewish Population and Politics in the Cape Colony 1898-1910'. Unpublished Master's Dissertation. University of South Africa, 1978.

_____ '"Vant to Puy a Vaatch": The Smous and Pioneer Trader in South African Jewish Historiography'. *Jewish Affairs* 42(9), September 1987, pp.111-128.

Shatzmiller, J. *Shylock Reconsidered: Jews, Moneylenders, and Mediaeval Society*. Berkeley, Los Angeles, Oxford: University of California Press, 1990.

Sher, A. 'South Africa's Chosen People'. *The Guardian*, 2 September, 1988.

Sherman B. *The Invention of the Jew*. New York and London: Thomas Yasoloff, 1969.

Sherman, J. (ed). *From a Land far Off: A Selection of South African Yiddish Stories*. Cape Town: Jewish Publications – South Africa, 1987.

Sherwood, R. *The Psychodynamics of Race*. New Jersey: Humanities Press, 1980.

Shibutani, T. *Society and Personality*. New Jersey: Prentice Hall, 1961.

Shimoni, G. *Jews and Zionism: The South African Experience 1910-1969*. Cape Town: Oxford University Press, 1980.

Simonowitz, G. 'The Background to Jewish Immigration to South Africa and the Development of the Jewish Community in the South African Republic between 1890 and 1902'. Unpublished Honours Dissertation, University of the Witwatersrand, 1960.

Simpson, G.E. and Yinger, J.M. *Racial and Cultural Minorities*. New York: Harper, 1965.

Sonnabend, H. 'The Social Role of the Jew in South Africa'. *Jewish Affairs* 3(1), January 1948, pp.14-19.

Sontag, J. (ed.), *Jewish Perspectives: Twenty-five years of Jewish Writing*. London: Secker and Warburg, 1980.

Sontag, S. *Against Interpretation and other Essays*. 1961; rpt. New York: Dell, 1966.

'South Africa's Chosen People'. Unsigned rev. of *Middlepost* by Antony Sher. *The Guardian*, 22 September 1988.

Spurr, D. *The Rhetoric of Empire*. Colonial Discourse in Journalism, Travel Writing, and Imperial Administration. Durham and London: Duke University Press, 1993.

Stanbrook, A. 'How Funny is Charlie Chaplin?' *Business Day*, 17 March 1989.

Stein, P. Interview in P. Stein and R. Jacobson (eds), *Sophiatown Speaks*. Johannesburg: Junction Avenue, 1986, pp.61-63.

Stein, P. and Purkey, M. 'So *Nu*? What's Jewish? Sophiatown Meets the Jewish Girl'. *Jewish Affairs* 46(2), September 1991, pp.77-78.

Steiner, G. *Language and Silence.* 1966. Rpt.in *George Steiner. A Reader.* Harmondsworth: Penguin, 1984.

_____ 'Our Homeland, the Text'. *Salmagundi,* 66, Winter-Spring 1985, pp.4-25.

Stember, C. H. *et al. Jews in the Mind of America.* New York and London: Basic Books, 1966.

Stern, M.J. 'A Bibliography of South African Jewish Biography. 1900-1966'. Unpublished Master's Dissertation. University of Cape Town, 1967.

Szur, M. 'The Jewish Joke'. *Jewish Affairs* 31(1), January 1948, pp.23-27.

Tajfel, H. ed. *Differentiation between Social Groups.* London, New York: Academic Press, 1978.

_____ *Human Groups and Social Categories: Studies in Social Psychology.* Cambridge: Cambridge University Press, 1981.

_____ and Fraser, C. (eds.), *Introducing Social Psychology* 1978, rpt., Harmondsworth, Penguin, 1986.

'The Anti-Jewish Movement in South Africa: The Need for Action', Jewish Board of Deputies Report, Hofmeyr Papers. A1/DH , Manuscript Collection, University of the Witwatersrand Library. '

The Big Lie – The United Nations Votes on Zionism'. *Bnai Brith International,* 13 November 1975, pp.5-6.

Tinker, J. 'On Antony Sher'. *The Star,* 27 July 1990.

Trachtenberg, J. *The Devil and the Jews: A Mediaeval Conception of the Jew and Its Relation to Modern Anti-Semitism.* 1943; rpt. Philadelphia: Jewish Publication Society, 1983.

Trilling, L. 'The Changing Myth of the Jew'. *Commentary* 66(2), August, 1978, pp.24-34.

Turrell, R.V. *Capital and Labour on the Kimberley Diamond Fields 1871-1890.* Cambridge: Cambridge University Press, 1987.

'Vandals Enter Johannesburg Synagogue'. *Zionist Record,* 27 June 1952, p.3.

Van der Merwe, C.N. *Breaking Barriers: Stereotypes and Changing of Values in Afrikaans Writing 1875-1990.* Amsterdam/Atlanta, 1994.

Van Onselen, C. *New Babylon: Studies in the Social and Economic History of the Witwatersrand 1886-1914,* I. Johannesburg: Ravan Press, 1982.

_____ *New Nineveh: Studies in the Social and Economic History of the Witwatersrand 1886-1914,* II. Johannesburg: Ravan Press, 1982.

Wade, M. 'Gordimer's Rainbow'. Rev. of *The Novels of Nadine Gordimer: History from the Inside* by S. Clingman, and *A Sport of Nature* by N. Gordimer. *Southern African Review of Books,* July 1987, pp.13-14.

_____ *White on Black in South Africa.* London: Macmillan, 1993.

Wagner, K.M. '"History from the Inside"? Text and Subtext in some Gordimer Novels'. *Crisis and Conflict, Essays on Southern African Literature.* Proc. of the XIth Annual Conference on Commonwealth Literature and Language Studies in German Speaking Countries, Aachen-Liege, 16-19 June 1988.

_____ *Rereading Nadine Gordimer. Text and Subtext in the Novels.* South Africa: Maskew Miller Longman, Witwatersrand University Press in conjunction with Indiana Press, 1994.

Weinstock, D.J. 'The Boer War in the Novel in English, 1884-1966: A Critical Bibliography.' Unpublished Doctoral Thesis. University Of California, Los Angeles, 1968. Facsimile Reproduced by microfilm.

Weisbord, R.G. and Stein. A. *Bittersweet Encounter: The Afro-American and the American Jew*. Westport, Connecticut: Negro Universities Press, 1970.

Werblowsky, R.J.Z. 'Judaism'. In Bleeker, C.J. and Windgren, G. (eds.), *Historia Religiorum: Handbook for the History of Religions*, II, Leiden: E.J. Brill, 1971, pp.1-48.

Wessels, J.H. 'From Olive Schreiner to Nadine Gordimer. A Study of the Development of the South African Short Story in English'. Unpublished Master's Dissertation. University of Cape Town, 1988.

Wheatcroft, G. *The Randlords*. London: Weidenfeld and Nicolson, 1985.

Wilhelm, C.A. 'A Critical Study of Olive Schreiner's Fiction in a Biographical and Historical Context'. Unpublished Doctoral Thesis. University of Natal, 1985.

Williams, G.F. *The Diamond Mines of South Africa: Some Account of Their Rise and Development*. New York: Macmillan, 1902.

Winegarten, R. 'The Novels of Dan Jacobson'. *Midstream* 12(5), May 1966, pp.69-73.

Wisse, R.R. *The Schlemiel as Modern Hero*. 1971; rpt. Chicago and London: The University of Chicago Press, 1980.

Wistrich, R.S. *Anti-Semitism. The Longest Hatred*. London: Thames Methuen, 1991.

———— 'The Anti-Zionist Masquerade'. *Midstream* 29(7), August/September 1983, pp.8-18.

———— *The Myth of Zionist Racism*. London: World Union of Jewish Studies Publications, 1976.

———— (ed.), *Anti-Zionism and Antisemitism in the Contemporary World*. London: MacMillan, 1990.

'Worlds Apart'. [Report of AWB Rally]. *Sunday Times*, 15 March 1992, p.33.

Zand, N. 'Another Twist in the Great Jewish Plot that Never Was'. Rev. of *Protocoles des Sages de Sion*. ed. by P-A Taguieff, n.p., Berg International, 2 vols. in *Le Monde*; rpt. *The Guardian Weekly*, 8-14 May 1992, p.15.

'Zionism and Racism – The Slander'. Supplement to the *Zionist Record*, 30 March 1984, pp.1-4.

'Zionism Move Signals End of Third World Defiance'. *The Weekly Mail*, 27 September to 3 October 1991, p.11.

INDEX